INTRODUCING
SEMIOTIC

ADVANCES IN SEMIOTICS
General Editor, Thomas A. Sebeok

INTRODUCING
SEMIOTIC

Its History and Doctrine

by

JOHN DEELY

with a Foreword by

Thomas A. Sebeok

INDIANA UNIVERSITY PRESS

BLOOMINGTON

Manufactured in the United States of America

Library of Congress Cataloging in Publication Data

Deely, John
Introducing semiotic.

Bibliography: p. 205
Includes indexes.
1. Semiotics. I. Title.
P99.D4   149'.946   82-47782
ISBN 0-253-33080-7   AACR2
ISBN 0-253-20287-6 (pbk.)

According to the saying of Heraclitus
(*Diels 1922: I, ·p. 100, Fragment 115*),
''to the soul belongs the lógos that increases itself,''

this book is dedicated to

William Passarella
its sufficient and necessary condition

Paul Bouissac
its proximate cause

Professor Larry Crist
translator par excellence,
exemplar of practical semiosis

and to the memory of

Heinz Schmitz
(''Ernst-R. Korn'')
of the Little Brothers
† *26 January 1982* †

John Edward Sullivan
Ordinis Praedicatorum
15 September 1922—26 March 1981
student of Augustine,
who simply died too soon

ACKNOWLEDGMENTS

It was my intention in the writing of this book to make all acknowledgments by way of the dedication and appropriate comments distributed through the text and notes, particularly as my debts in the work have been extensive. Having pursued this design to the end, I yet find there is a remainder of debt that I have not been able to cover in this way, so I am adding here after all some separated lines of acknowledgment.

In writing the Section on Language for Part II, I profited in particular from remarks and suggestions of Dr. Dan Rogers and Dr. Ted Cruz, the latter a native Tagalog speaker and a living passage into the richness of our Latin heritage. In re-thinking the whole matter of language and experience, the work of Donald Thomas in the Brookline schools has always afforded me a kind of generalized inspiration that has been of the utmost value.

A cover design expressly integrating the nature and history of the work covered is thanks to the refined artistic sensibilities and pre-eminently semiotic consciousness of Brooke Williams, who also lent her hand to matters of style and proofreading. The most indispensable single proofreader was my student Felicia Kruse, who also undertook the greater part of the indexing of the volume, and no small part of the bibliographical labor. A third proofreader, particularly helpful with Greek passages, was Dr. Jeffrey Buller, an excellent classicist and valued colleague. It is customary for an author to discharge those who assist from all responsibility for errors in a volume, but in this case, conceptual matter apart, I am happy to leave all responsibility for errors in final proof to these three excellent workers.

Finally, I must thank Mr. Bud MacFarlane and Ms. Marcie Bowman of Composition Specialists in Dubuque, Iowa, for their many hours of patient professional assistance in the design and layout of the book.

CONTENTS

LIST OF DIAGRAMS

Foreword

"What is truth? said jesting Pilate; and would not stay for an answer."

"The idea of a general science of signs is . . . rooted in fallacy," said inscrutably Scruton; yet could not penetrate to the bedrock that undergirds the pair of contemporary treatises that fell under his hand.

It is this infrastructure of fundamental semiotic principles that Deely's extended — yet masterfully compacted and solidified — survey aims to introduce and interpret in the first part of this book. He argues for and, I think, authenticates the essential confluence of logic and semiotic, and convincingly shows how one invents and keeps reformulating the other in many imaginative if reticular ways.

Although we tend to associate this assimilation primarily with Peirce, Deely reveals the idea in the very earliest doctrinal blueprints of our Greco-Roman precursors and sketches out the location of major forks in the ensuing road. His scholarship gives evidence that the ancient paths converge and culminate in one unified disposition of the doctrine of signs in the fourth decade of the

17th century, in the work of the Iberian philosopher, Poinsot. His *Tractatus de Signis*, which may well be, in Deely's words, the "first systematic semiotic treatise in all the detail of its subtle and far-reaching exposition," had hitherto been known only to a privileged few, such as Jacques Maritain and José G. Herculano de Carvalho, through whose respective lectures and essays I had also come across his spoor. But Deely is the first to trace over the entire history of logic a mainstream of semiotic discourse, and to show how Poinsot's thought, soon to appear in a great modern bilingual edition, belongs decisively to that mainstream as the "missing link" between the ancients and the moderns in the history of semiotic, a pivot as well as a divide between two huge intellective landscapes the ecology of neither of which could be fully appreciated prior to this major publishing event.

After Poinsot, Deely rapidly carries us back to the far more familiar highroad that leads, with some deviations and a few reasonable detours (notably in the area of induction), directly from Locke to Peirce.

What about semiotic inquiry in the 20th century? It is to this that Deely addresses the second part of this book, suggesting fundamental realignments in accustomed approaches to basic questions of human experience. Here he proposes some novel considerations—notice, for example, the reversed order of what one would expect in the titles for the sections for this part—which may well prove seminal for developments yet to come.

Taking the situation as a whole, it appears to me that there are two trails in view. One track leads outward into the general culture, widening to become the grand boulevard of semiotic influence, with incursions into all the humanities and social sciences, law and medicine, the multiform arts, the life science in general, the participatory universe of quantum theory, and, of course, as Deely is especially concerned to indicate, deeply penetrating into the very fabric of both modern and traditional philosophy. (In this territory, surely, lies the transcendent answer to Quine's deceptively artless question: 'What Is It All About?') The other is the inward-turning, all but subterranean byway traveled by a handful of specialist practitioners of the *doctrina signorum* for its own sake. The objective of a sound education should be to instigate travel along both routes — that of the Signs of the Universe, and that of the Universe of Signs — the quaesitum for which Deely's contribution will be found indispensable.

Thomas A. Sebeok
National Humanities Center and Indiana University

Preface

This book had its origins in an evening lecture entitled "The Relation of Logic to Semiotics," given as part of the first annual Summer Institute for Semiotic and Structural Studies, held at Victoria College of the University of Toronto in June of 1980. (General reviews of this Institute can be found in Herzfeld 1981 and Deely 1981a.) Response to the lecture was such that it was subsequently published as an article in the journal of the International Association for Semiotic Studies, *Semiotica* 36 — 1/2: 193-265; and in discussion of the text with colleagues the suggestion was made that this essay provides a synoptic view of semiotic development establishing a general framework or conceptual horizon for the movement that, for the first time, would enable skeptics or newcomers to semiotics to see just how integral and foundational to Western culture the semiotic point of view really is according to its inherent possibilities.

This foundational standpoint, with the doctrine it implies (which are the subjects, respectively, of Parts I and II of this introductory book), must be seen as the source and inspiration behind the emergence in our own century of the large and, in one very important sense, practically limitless *field* of "semiotics," that is, the development of attempts to isolate and pursue the implications of specifically signifying *aspects and elements* of phenomena, natural or socio-cultural, in the work of Preziosi, Kim Smith, Eco, and a hundred others, phenomena that are studied in their own right (as objects) by the range of traditional specialized pursuits (music, architecture, ethology, etc.), now becoming sensitized to the semiotic *dimension* that permeates all things once they enter into experience. In the process, the traditional disciplines themselves are reconceptualized and gradually transformed, in the direction of a sharper awareness of foundations and presuppositions. The inherently philosophical and interdisciplinary ramifications of the development of a unified doctrine of signs — the practically unlimited range of implications and applications — is in my view probably the single most important feature of the semiotics movement, the surest guarantee of its continued growth and eventual acceptance within the formal curricula of the schools. From this point of view — that of its inherently interdisciplinary structure or "nature" — semiotics is "the only game in town."

Up until now, "interdisciplinary programs" so essential to compensating for the myopic tendencies of specialization in modern times have always required *ad hoc* contrivances for their development. As a consequence, such programs have never attained more than a tenuous, personalities-dependent status vis-à-vis the specialties. Within semiotic perspective, this situation changes radically for the better. No longer is an interdisciplinary outlook something contrived or tenuous. On the contrary, it is something built-in to semiotics, simply by virtue of the universal role of signs as the vehicle of communication within and between specialties, as everywhere else, wherever there is cognition, mutual or unilateral. Semiotic as the root discipline, with its semiotic branches, some scientific, some humanistic, will not only restore unity to the traditions of thought, including philosophy, but coherence to the life of the universities. The use of a general theory or, as I prefer to say — for the reasons stated elsewhere (Sebeok 1976: ix ff.; Deely 1978b, 1983, and Appendix to the present work) — doctrine of signs was thus finely stated by Professor Max Fisch, in his Presidential Address to the third annual meeting of the Semiotic Society of America held at Indiana University (Bloomington campus) in October of 1979:

> It will give us a map so complex and so detailed as to place any one field of highly specialized research in relation to any other, tell us quickly how to get from one such field to another, and distinguish fields not yet explored from those long cultivated. It will give us semiotic encyclopedias and dictionaries. It will supply the materials for introductions to semiotics. It will improve the expository skills of specialists whose reports and expositions are at present unreadable by anybody who does not have their specialties. It will thereby greatly improve communication between specialists in non-adjacent semiotic fields, as well as between semioticians and non-semioticians, or between semioticians and people who do not yet recognize themselves as such. It will enable us to place the results of researches now in progress; it will supply perspectives in terms of which to view and evaluate their results; but, at least for a long time to come, the general theory of signs will itself require continual revisions in the light of new findings.

The claims, like the possibilities, are considerable: semiotics, on the foundation of semiotic doctrine, is bound to rewrite the entire history of culture and philosophy. We are at the beginning of a new era: whereas the rise of modern science brought about the conditions requiring a new kind of specialization that gradually has led to a sort of atomization of research and fragmentation of intellectual community recognized by all as counterproductive in its extreme, semiotic can establish new conditions of a common framework and cross-disciplinary channels of communication that will restore to the humanities the interdisciplinary possibilities that have withered so alarmingly when scientific specialization in its advanced stages knew no check of alternative. "Semiotics," Pelc has summarized (1979: 51), "simply offers to representatives of various disciplines an opportunity for leaving the tight compartments of highly specialized disciplines."

It is time to acquaint a larger audience, especially those young students full of enthusiasm and promise who have yet to hear of semiotic, with the prospect, as I will say below, "of an integrated perspective on semiotic development grounded in the unity of philosophical culture which has been obscured for some three centuries now, but which semiotics make possible to realize again."

Such is the purpose of this little book as an introduction to the semiotic point of view for all those who love the life of the mind and the advance of intellectual culture in the schools.

John Deely
Stonecliffe Hall
March 7, 1982

INTRODUCING
SEMIOTIC

OBJECTIVES

The first part of this book is an initial attempt to establish an outline of the history of logic expressly from the standpoint of a doctrine of signs as defined by John Locke under the heading of semiotic. No effort has been made in this part to explore the standpoint so defined (that is left for the second part). What has been attempted rather is to indicate in a summary fashion and from the point of view of a philosopher a general sketch of the place and circumstances in Western culture where semiotic consciousness was first thematically achieved, to the extent at least that we are able to determine this in the light of the history of logic and philosophy as the "experts" present it to us, supplemented of course by an actual reading, first-hand, of the texts on which the outline relies — not all of which, by any means, have been weighed evenly if at all in the researches so far of the expert historians.

This fact already indicates the extent to which semiotic historiography will be achieved only by upsetting and revising, often in radical ways, the conventional outlines and histories of thought which have become standard fare in the universities of today. The writing of this

1

history eventually must inevitably take the form also of a
structuring anew of the entire history of ideas and of philosophy, in order to bring to the fore and make explicit the
semiotic components latent by the nature of the case (all
thought being through signs) in each of the previous
thinkers who have wrestled since ancient times with foundational questions of knowledge, experience, and interpretation generally.

The pages that follow seek to exemplify this task,
without any pretension at providing the fullness of detail
and documentation needed for its completion. Thus
whatever value this presentation may have lies more in its
heuristic than in its didactic aspect, according to the
saying of Aristotle in his *Ethics* (1098a20-25), that time is
a good partner in the work of advancing the articulation
of what has once been well outlined, but in the absence
of such an outline, progress in the arts and sciences tends
toward a standstill. That is what I have been concerned
to establish — the possibility of an integrated perspective
on semiotic development grounded in the unity of philosophical culture which has been obscured for some three
centuries now, but which semiotics makes possible to realize again.

Hence there remain gaps in the outline, to be sure:
it is subject to many retouchings and additions. But it illustrates the method, I think, by which semiotics is bound
to establish itself in general outlines and foundations. In
the section to follow, I will call this method an "archeology of concepts," as the metaphor best calculated to
convey what is necessary. I would like to add that the use
of such a method — the uncovering of the layers by which
concepts ultimately taken for granted in some specific
population acquired their illuminative power for human
culture (it is this process which constitutes the historicity,
the *Seinsgeschichtliches Wesen,* of man) — gives particular
grounds for optimism in the eventual fruitfulness of its
results, for (Kneale and Kneale 1962: 224) "in literary

history, as contrasted with [physical] archeology, the forays of enthusiasts do not destroy the evidence. On the contrary, they may provide the stimulus to research by which their own errors can be corrected.''

The second part of this book can no longer claim to be historical (though it tries not to be ignorant of history). Insofar as it differs from Part I, it does so under the inspiration of a remark made by Paul Bouissac at the sixth annual meeting of the Semiotic Society of America on the 2nd of October, 1981, in his presentation, ''Figurative vs. Objective Semiosis.'' All previous semiotic ''theories,'' he observed, be they Greimasian, Saussurean, Peircean, Poinsotian, have come to the study of signs late in the day, on the basis of a thoroughly worked out system of concepts, a ''pre-existing philosophical paradigm.'' To this prejacent paradigm, then, their subsequent notions of signification were referred and required to conform. The coming of age of semiotic as a perspective in its own right requires exactly the reverse. It can have no paradigm of philosophy given in advance. Beginning with the sign, that is, from the function of signs in our experience taken in their own right (semiosis), it is the task of semiotic to create a new paradigm — its own — and to review, criticize, and correct so far as possible all previous accounts of experience in the terms of *that* paradigm.

These remarks, filled at the time with the passion and life of the speaker, were spontaneous there and poorly paraphrased here. Yet they struck me then and seem to me now with undiminished force exactly *justes,* exactly to capture in a flash of insight the task against whose demands the movement that has grown up around us must finally be measured. To answer Herbert's question (1981), what contributes toward meeting these demands in the work going on today is the revolutionary part of semiotics, what does not so contribute belongs to merely passing fad and fashion.

Like Part I, therefore, Part II of this book is heuristic

rather than didactic. It seeks not to outline but to adumbrate the reorientation of thought made possible by the semiotic point of view not (indeed) in all areas, but at least in the area of the foundations of knowledge and experience, and at the interface of modern with (in lieu of the better term yet to be coined) post-modern times. Semiotics is capable of mediating a change of age as profound and total as was the separating off of modern times from the Latin era. Then, the cutting edge of transition was modern science, experimental and mathematical, coming of age. Today it is the interpretive activity of the mind becoming conscious of its full range, ground, and instruments, that is, semiotics.

No *Summa Semiotica,* therefore — a task that must wait at least twenty years beyond the *Encyclopedic Dictionary of Semiotics* in preparation under the editorship of Sebeok, Pelc, Posner, Shukman, *et alia* (that is, till at least the opening decade of the next century) — but only *semina semiotica*: the reader of Part II will find little in the way of familiar distinctions and well-established terminology. What she and he will find lies only, so to speak, at the near end of the rainbow, a map of the New World drawn as it were by a cartographer of the 16th century, far from final, but having the merit of incorporating in however rough a fashion lands that no previous maps were able to include.

In short, an introduction to semiotic — not in the sense of a comprehensive survey of the literature, but in a more contemplative and fundamental sense, by taking the reader directly to the point of land marked out in advance, whence it is possible to see what might be.

Part I

HISTORICAL CONTEXT

"Now it is hard for a logician trained in the contemporary variety of logic to think himself into another. In other words, it is hard for him to find a criterion of comparison. He is constantly tempted to find what is valuable only what fits into the categories of his own logic. Impressed by our technique, which is not by itself properly logic, having only superficial knowledge of past forms, judging from a particular standpoint, we too often risk misunderstanding and under-rating other forms . . . The modern mathematical logician certainly has a strong support in his calculus, but all too frequently that same calculus leads him to dispense with thought just where it may be most required."

—BOCHENSKI 1970: 17—

1

Point of Departure
and Method

If there were one thing on which all with an interest in semiotics would agree — and there probably is not — it would be that a history of semiotic has yet to be written (cf. Baer 1980; Bouissac 1979, 1976; Eschbach 1978; Pelc 1977; Romeo 1976; Sebeok 1975a, 1974; etc.). This is hardly surprising, in view of the fact that we must first understand with some clarity what semiotic is, before we can hope to write its history; and what semiotic is concretely has only begun to be realized on a social scale in the most recent of times (cf. Romeo 1977a, b).

Historically, and by accidents of national intellectual traditions, followers of Ferdinand de Saussure (1857-1913) in particular and scholars with backgrounds in the language sciences generally early constituted a kind of sociological majority within semiotics. Within this nucleus and beyond, there has been gradual awakening of consciousness to the extensive writings of Peirce as the true contemporary founder of a systematic foundational doctrine of signs (see in particular Fisch, Ketner, and Kloesel 1979) and, even more importantly, to the historical layers of semiological analysis that preceded explicit adoption of the viewpoint given its proper name by

Locke in 1690, but already defined exactly in the open-
ings of Augustine's first two books *On Christian Doctrine*
(c. 397-426), explored systematically with an eye to the
whole of our ancient past in the *Treatise on Signs* of John
Poinsot (1632), and palpably present in the origins of
Greek medicine as a "reading" of the human body in
terms of sickness and health. Indeed, taking onu- as
representing "a seminal concept" or "ἀρχή *in nuce*"
(Romeo 1976: 79, 88), precisely in order to avoid becoming entangled in (*ibid.*: 73) "a maze of obscure interpre-
tations involving the diverse acceptations in ancient history given to anything deriving from σημ-, such as
σημεῖον, σημαίνω, etc.," it must be said that "long
before Protagoras [5th cent. B.C.] for the sake of
philosophy, and long before Hippocrates [c. 460-377
B.C.] for the sake of medicine, the term involving a . . .
free morpheme . . . that contains σημ- is attested in
Heraclitus [6th-5th cent. B.C.]."[1]

This historiographical awakening has engendered
within the movement a renewed sense of expansion and
of the value and necessary function of intellectual tradition, in precisely that sense of continuity between past
and present concerns of the human spirit which has been
thought dispensable by most intellectuals enamored of
positive science since the days of Hobbes and Descartes.

An inevitable result of this awakening — this
historiographical *prise de conscience* of semioticians — has
been the experienced need for an "archeology of concepts" (in the felicitous expression of Eco[2]) related to the
sign and semiosis, if we are to understand the true dimensions and possibilities made accessible by the semiotic
point of view seeming, as it does, to call for a general re-
writing of the history of philosophy and culture from ancient times to the present. In this atmosphere, the potential contribution of philosophy to semiotic consciousness
— or rather, as Cohen indicates (1979: 28), the con-
spicuous absence for the most part of contributions to

the foundations of semiotic consciousness from the philosophers of our day (owing in large part, I think [Deely 1975a, 1975b: 253-271], to the very conception and type of logic that has achieved dominance in very recent philosophy, as will be seen by the end of the pages to follow) — has created a kind of vacuum within the movement of precisely the sort nature abhors, and one which semioticians too are eager to see filled, for the sake of a balancing out of the proportions of the overall movement as each eye is able to grasp it.

Umberto Eco's series of lectures at the first International Summer Institute for Semiotic and Structural Studies in particular (Toronto, June 1980) served to bring into focus the foundational issues and the privileged position the philosophical disciplines should occupy in contributing to such clarification. It was the opening lectures of this series (June 2-6), presenting the concept of sign as it developed over the period from ancient Greece up to the time of Augustine, that suggested to me the method that made possible the first part of this book. It consists in elaborating an archeology of concepts pertaining to a stated theme or central notion, thus making of history itself an inductive principle of explanation for our present understanding.

But whereas Professor Eco chose as his theme the concept of sign, I have substituted rather the theme of logic itself, the interpretive activity proper to understanding, as Poinsot remarked (1632: 642a15-18), provided entirely by signs with its instruments. I was led to attempt this substitution because it seemed, paradoxically, more promising of an immediate result exhibiting in a coherent and synoptic way the development of semiotic consciousness, first by reason of the ancient origins of logic in the West as *an explicit theme*[3] (in contrast to the sign, which, though perforce used everywhere, by very reason of its ubiquity and demurring character seems to have escaped specific thematization in the formal sense), and, from

this, by reason of the *continuous role* that logic has thematically played in the development of Western philosophy
and science.

On the contemporary scene, logic occupies a pride of
place in North American philosophy. Not only are some
of the philosophers most revered in the English speaking
world today — figures like Quine, Frege, Russell — distinguished logicians, but, as Jakobson's recent "Glance
over the Development of Semiotic" (1979) well shows,
from the very beginnings of the modern period semiotic
consciousness and logical studies have constantly intertwined. More than intertwined: in the researches of the
foremost background figure of contemporary semiotics,
C. S. Peirce, logic occupies a central role. Professor Max
Fisch (1977: 36) considers Peirce's focus in this regard
"his single most characteristic trait," in that

> Peirce from the beginning conceived of logic as coming in its
> entirety within the scope of the general theory of signs; that all
> his work in logic had been done within that framework; that,
> for a time in his fifties he distinguished a narrow and a broad
> sense of logic, in the latter of which it was coextensive with the
> general theory of signs; that eventually he abandoned the nar-
> row sense; and that the comprehensive treatise on which he was
> working in the last decade of his life was to be entitled *A System
> of Logic, considered as Semiotic.*

So, it would seem natural and almost inevitable that
logic should provide a fertile common ground for a rap-
prochement between the semiotics movement and the
traditional discipline of philosophy.

Following the proven canons of academic practice
which require us to narrow our topic to a focus sufficiently precise to be treated accurately, then, I am going to
consider the Western tradition solely from the point of
view of Logic, and, to be even more precise, I am going
to restrict my consideration to the period from the work
of Aristotle to the present. While this precise focus may
not seem exactly "narrow" in the sense usually applied

to an academic thesis, we will see that it is an adequate specification for the purposes of the method we wish to follow as it applies to the problem, or hypothesis, we have set ourselves to explore.

True, a conceptual archeology thus focussed inevitably falls short of the actual origins of semiotic "theorizing" (in the Greek fashion),[4] not only because in the largest sense the history of semiotics is, as Romeo puts it (1976: 88) "also a history of mankind," and because, again as Romeo points out (*ibid.*: 79 n. 13) semiotics is a *sine qua non* for grammar and logic alike; but because even *logic itself* in the formal sense is established by Aristotle from within the larger concerns of dialectic and methodology examined within the Academy where he studied under Plato. The "semiotic web" which provides the matrix even for our narrowly specified point of departure in the present study, therefore, showing its roots in pre-Socratic thought along with chronological and doctrinal connections on the other side down to Chrysippus, is well represented in the following table from Bochenski (1970: 26):[5]

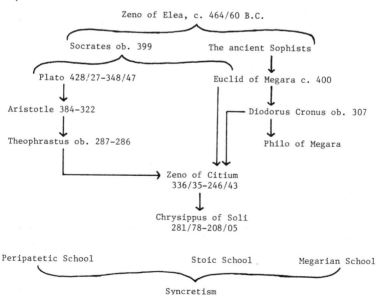

Within this matrix, then, the work of Aristotle enables us to establish a focus[6] for the application of our method which, while it does not carry as far backwards in time as the history of semiotics is obliged ultimately to go, makes up for this shortfall by at least providing us with the means of establishing a coherent perspective on semiotic development that is more comprehensive than anything that has been possible to now. And by sketching in the gaps between the Stoics and Augustine, between Augustine and John Locke, and between Locke and Peirce in our own day, we have gained, if not everything, at least a great deal. Inasmuch as, in accordance with historical evidence, "a complete history of the problems of logic must have formal logic at its centre," while this problematic in turn "was, so far as we know, in constant dependence in one way or another on that of Aristotle's *Organon*" (Bochenski 1970: 3, 2), the method of conceptual archeology applied to the case of logic — "those problems which have developed from that problematic" (see note 6, p. 147 below) — finds therein an Ariadne's thread* tying together more than has heretofore been possible of the heterogeneous materials of history under the unified perspective of the doctrine of signs.

---

*In the following of this thread across time, we will meet with the expression "Peri Hermeneias" many times, and in almost as many forms. Rather than superimpose upon these encounters an artificial uniformity, I have chosen to honor the contingency surrounding the development of this central semiotic notion, which is nicely prismed by this diversity.

Exploratory: The Ancient World (Greek and Latin)

Logic, like so much of our intellectual history, has its origins in ancient Greece, and specifically, in the qualified sense explained in the previous section, it has its origins in the works of Aristotle. The history of these writings is a somewhat haphazard tale. Suffice for our purpose to say that, after the principal edition of Andronicus of Rhodes ("published" roughly between 43 and 20 B.C.), the logical works were combined in Byzantine times under the general title of *Organon* (ὄργανον) or *Instrument*, "a name first given them [Coffey 1938: I, 40] by Diogenes of Laërte," a third century A.D. compiler of materials on figures in the history of philosophy. The subject matter of the works comprising the *Organon* is basically terms or objects of apprehension (in the *Categories*), propositions (in *On Interpretation*), and argumentation (in: the *Prior Analytics*, which deals with the forms common to any processes of reasoning; the *Posterior Analytics*, which deals with the relation of the forms of reasoning to particular subject matters for purposes of proving something about that material; the *Topics*, which deals with probable — what Aristotle calls "dialectical" as opposed to "demonstrative'' — proofs; and the *Sophistic Refutations*, which deals with the unmasking of specious arguments). So you can see that the conception of Logic in this original adumbration is rather comprehensive in relation to our cognitive processes, and became even more so in later medieval Islam, to be sure (see note on Reference entry ''Aristotle'').

But the point to note for present purposes is that Aristotle, who was the first to discover or invent (depending on the point of view you want to take) the subject of Logic, did not include logic within his own classification of the sciences. He regarded logic rather as the common or general instrument for the development of science; and knowledge itself, comprised of the sciences wherein logic would be employed, he organized as follows:

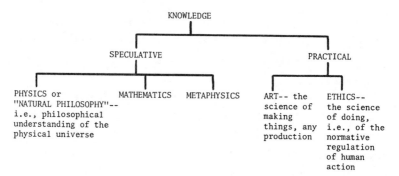

For the development of these sciences or forms of knowledge, logic would be the instrument that would principally be employed, particularly the analytics.

After Aristotle, there was the rather different development of Stoic logic, almost all of which has been lost; so that, for our purposes, there is not a great deal to be said about this development, especially as, up to very recent times, in the post-classical civilizations of Europe the works of Aristotle in logic really provide the main backdrop against which logical development took place.[1]

But there was one division of knowledge, apparently from the Stoics,[2] which continued to influence in a subsid-

iary way the thought of the middle ages. St. Thomas
Aquinas, for example, falls back on this Stoic division in
setting the framework for his commentary (c. 1269) on
the ethics of Aristotle, where he remarks (Book I, lect. 1,
nn. 1-3) that knowledge is of order, but order can be of
four different kinds, thus:

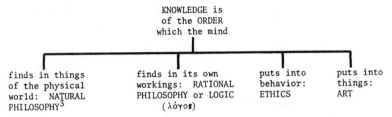

```
                    KNOWLEDGE is
                    of the ORDER
                    which the mind

  finds in things      finds in its own    puts into      puts into
  of the physical      workings: RATIONAL  behavior:      things:
  world: NATURAL       PHILOSOPHY or LOGIC  ETHICS         ART
  PHILOSOPHY³          (λόγος)
```

We have then from ancient Greece two rather different grand schemes of knowledge, the first from Aristotle, which was the primary one that was taken up and
used in the middle ages; but also, in the background, as
it were, a second scheme providing an interestingly different distribution of knowledge which seems to have
been basically Stoic in origin, and which expressly includes logic within the scheme of the sciences.[4] We will
have occasion later on to remark some relations — sim-
ilarities and differences — between this Stoic division of
knowledge and the organization for the sciences that
Locke proposes in the seventeenth century in his *Essay
Concerning Human Understanding*.

Besides the logical writings of Aristotle himself, the
really important development in Logic for Western
culture historically speaking (I mean, in terms of the
development of Logic as a part of the general philosophical culture, not in terms of the specific development of
specialized parts within logic as a specialized discipline)
does not then come from the Stoics but rather from
Porphyry, the student of Plotinus who authored c. 271
A.D. the little book that was to influence the entire age
of Latin philosophy subsequent to the fall of Rome (i.e.,
the European schools from Boethius to the very end of

renaissance times), namely, the *Isagoge*, which literally translates as "Introduction," but more accurately as "The Five Words," because what the *Isagoge* is about is the ways in which we apply our concepts to things when we seek to define what any one of them is[5] — a theory of definition, if you like. The five words that are involved in such efforts are genus, species, difference, property, and accident, according to the following rationale.[6]

In saying what any thing is, we describe it either in terms of what it is essentially, or in terms of characteristics it has over and above its essential constitution. If our statement captures the essence of the thing, it may do so wholly or only in part. If wholly, then we have *species*; but if only in part, we may have either that part which, though essential, yet pertains to the essence of other kinds of things as well, which is *genus*; or that part which is unique to and constitutive of the thing as distinct within its genus, which is *difference*. On the other hand, if our statement captures not the essence of the thing of which we speak but rather characteristics or attributes over and above what is strictly essential to it, these characteristics may be either necessarily consequent upon what is essential, in which case we have *property*, or merely contingently advenient upon the essential constitution, in which case we have *accident* (not to be confused with the category of "accident' in the sense of whatever is not a "substance" in the scheme of Aristotelian physics). Since this division of the ways of possibly speaking about things is exhaustive and exclusive from the standpoint of analysis, it is clear that any classification of types of definition which attempt to express what something is, intrinsically, can be referred to and explained in terms of it.

Porphyry wrote his *Isagoge*, which we have thus summarized very roughly, as an introduction to the study of the categories of Aristotle, and eventually it came to be studied everywhere in the Latin world as an excellent general introduction to the study of logic as a whole.

Porphyry wrote in Greek, but within approximately two hundred years, with the fall of Rome, and for the millenium after that, the knowledge of any tongue other than Latin became effectively lost to the development of European civilization. The figure who interfaces Greek logical tradition with what would develop in the West was Boethius (c. 480-524), the not-quite contemporary of St. Augustine (354-430), a figure of no importance to the development of the logical tradition as such in the Latin age, but one who is always listed along with Boethius as beginning the *mediae aetates*, and one who moreover, as far as my own researches have gone, emerges from the point of view of semiotic itself as the first figure absolutely to enunciate a pure semiotic standpoint, to wit, in his *De doctrina christiana* (c. 397-426).

Augustine opens Book I of this work with the distinction between signs and things, saying he will devote Book I to the consideration of things, and Book II to the consideration of signs. But, when he comes to the second Book, a very curious thing happens. He begins by enunciating what we would call a semiotic point of view — the treatment of things purely in terms of their signifying function. He then introduces a whole series of distinctions covering practically the entire range of semiotic phenomena — natural vs. conventional signs, signs as they function in animal cognition vs. their function in human cognition, words and groans, flags — but he distinguishes all these phenomena only in order to exclude them as not being germane to his more limited immediate purpose. Thus he begins with distinctions that establish the semiotic point of view and sweep over the horizon of prelinguistic, linguistic, and postlinguistic semiotic phenomena, but only for the sake of narrowly identifying the specific case of conventional signs instituted by God, namely, the words of Scripture and the Sacraments of the Church. Augustine's definition of the sign in this context (Book II, ch. 1, par. 1: "signum est res, quod praeter speciem quam ingerit sensibus, aliud ex se faciens in cogitationem venire'' — ''a sign is a thing which, over and above the impression it makes on the senses, causes something else to come into thought as a consequence''), particularly after its inclusion in the 4th book of Peter Lombard's *Sentences* (c. 1150), becomes the focus of what is in effect the ''high semiotics'' of the Latin age, namely, sacramental theology as it develops after Augustine continuously right down to the present day and to a great extent even across the post-Reformation denominational lines of competing Christian sects. For that specifically religious phase of historical theoretical semiotic development, as for many others, Augustine stands astride the split of renaissance Christianity into Catholic and Protestant as a kind of governing figure over the thinking of both sides.

Important as he is therefore for the general history of semiotic one day to be written, however, in terms of our immediate archeological quest, Augustine hasn't much to say on logic in its traditional development, so I pass over him without further comment, in order to discuss the more central role of Boethius.

Boethius set himself the project of translating into Latin and synthesizing through commentaries and other treatises the whole range of the works of Plato and Aristotle, in order to make them accessible to the decreasingly Greek and increasingly Latin world of learning, such as it was in the last days of the Roman empire. He got well along in this task, writing elaborate commentaries, including two on Porphyry's work, one a *Dialogue* on an earlier Latin translation (ante 509), the other (509-10) a *Commentaria* proper; and specifically completing translation of the *Organon*, before he was garrotted for treason under Theodoric the Ostrogoth, thus bringing to an abrupt end his project of Latin translations and treatises. The tragedy of this (apart from the more personal, we might say subjective tragedy for Boethius himself) was that no mainstream thinkers of the Latin West appear to have had much public access to the original veins (or *linguistic* community) of Greek thought, i.e., from Plotinus backwards through the Stoa, of course the Epicureans, and into the original schools of Megara and Athens, of which Aristotle still seems to have been the predecessor by some seventy or so odd years, from the standpoint of a *formal* logic.

But the situation was worse than so far appears. Not only would no *new* Latin translations, either of existing or of heretofore untranslated manuscripts, come into existence; but even most of those pertaining to the integral problematic of *the Instrument* or *Organon*, i.e., the Boethian translations themselves beyond the *perihermenias* text, were totally ignored and forgotten!

We know this, both from the certainty that Boethius did in fact render the whole of the *Organon*, as well as develop syllogistic treatises in his own right (see entry for Boethius in the References); and from the certainty that when the revival of interest in the more integral problematic of the Greek traditions began to show itself in the form of new translations of the heretofore unstudied "organonic" works of Aristotle — from the Analytics on, i.e., the entire third level (*ratiocinatio*) of the λόγος problematic in specifically human speech — a *versio antiquior* of (1) the *Prior Analytics*, (2) *Posterior Analytics*, (3) *Topics*, and (4) *Sophistics* began to be circulated under Boethius' name, "probablement à bon droit," as Cappuyns puts it (1937: 362).

We know then that Boethius' actual manuscript translations not only existed for the *Organon*, but were still accessible as late as 1150. These directly authentic manuscripts are now thought possibly lost entirely, but certainly not to be the later translations which are figured as "of Boethius" in Migne, P.L. 64 (p.1844). To us, as to the "dark ages" preceding the 11th and 12th centuries, only the first two organonic works, the *Logica vetus* of the Middle Ages, are accessible. Not all the writings "generously attributed to him by tradition" (Cappuyns, 362) are in fact his writings.

He was certainly the introducer of Aristotle to the Latin West, but what a fragmented and prismed introduction![7] As Cappuyns summarized the situation as of 1937 (col. 376):

> The exact role of Boethius in the transmission of the works of Aristotle is difficult to determine as of yet, and, even in the manuscript materials which exist with his name attached to them, the decisive separation between the authentic and the spurious attributions cannot be made today. To achieve any results in this matter which can be taken as verified, we must wait until the *Corpus philosophorum Medii Aevi* has published versions of all the relevant Aristotelian texts, and upon the development of more refined techniques of comparative philologies to supplement the customary external criteria which are insufficient in the case of the *versiones Boethii*. That means that the conclusions already formulated by A. Jourdain (1843) must be revised radically.

Tentatively, then, and in line with such historical reservations of an empirical type, we can say that, sociologically speaking, the community of early with later Latin logical thought was sustained in terms of Greek logic's problematic by the rather thin corpus comprising the translations of the *Isagoge* with the commentaries and the translated *Categories*, together with translations of *Peryermenias* (*On Interpretation*). These were the works that formed the body of study of "the old logic" when the new world of learning, the revival out of which our modern universities would come, began to jell around the twelfth century. In the excitement of that new awakening, the contribution of Boethius, small by comparison with the Greek heritage, but small also by comparison with horizons Boethius sketched for a century with no eyes for them in the translations he actually accomplished of the *Organon*, seemed so dazzling in its scope and daring (for all its lack) that the first half of the twelfth century has been called by custom in history "the Boethian Age," i.e., the last age restricted, in its thematic development of the *Organon*, to texts anterior to both the *Analytics*. After the mid-twelfth century influx of further translations of the Greek authors drew into focus the whole of the *Organon* (the *Prior* and *Posterior Analytics*, the *Topics*, and the *Sophistical Refutations*), authors began to speak of the new translations as the "ars seu logica nova" or new logic, in contrast to the "ars seu logica vetus" of the Boethian age and earlier.

Here should be mentioned in passing a fact of great importance for the eventual history of semiotics, namely, that in translating the *Categories* of Aristotle, and more particularly through his *Commentary* thereon (510), Boethius set the terms for the controversy over the reality and nature of *relations*, *ens relativum*, which would culminate in theology in the rational account of the Trinity achieved by the medieval scholastics, but in philosophy in the apparently first systematic treatise on signifying (Poinsot 1632). Here, perhaps also for the first time, the definition of signs laid down by Augustine is firmly repudiated as inadequate and the foundation is laid for fulfilling the project for logic first outlined outside the Greek or Latin world by John Locke in 1690, namely, the project of subsuming the internal means of cognition ("ideas") and the external means of communication ("words," gestures, etc.)[8] under the single perspective of signifying in a foundational *doctrina signorum* (see Section 5 note 9, below).

The central role of Boethius in our present investigation thus may be summarized at this point under two heads. The logical tradition from ancient Greece is kept alive by his work through the early centuries of the Latin age, and the discussion of relative being, of which signs are but a special case, gets off the ground in the Latin West as a result of that same work.

What happens as the twelfth century advances is that the entire literary corpus of Aristotle, including the

Organon, gets translated into Latin, and the writings of the *Organon* begin to be studied as a whole. This "new logic" ("ars" or "logica nova") — at the opening of the thirteenth century — is, so far as its pure foundation in the texts of Aristotle goes,[9] no longer the analysis of simple terms and of the results of judgments combining terms into propositions (the attachment of predicates to subjects) which was the focus, respectively, of the *Categories* and *Peri Hermenias*, so-called ("On Interpretation"); but is now the combining of propositions into arguments, which is the concern, as we have seen, of the two *Analytics*, the *Topics*, and the *Sophistic Refutations*.

Here we must note a third point of influence of Boethius on the schools of the high middle ages and the renaissance, namely, his representation at the beginning of his treatise *On the Trinity* (c. 520) of the division or scheme of the sciences which we have already seen in Aristotle. This little work on the Trinity, everywhere read and commented upon in the medieval schools, thus became a main vehicle for the shaping in an Aristotelian mold of the outlook on knowledge of the mainstream Latin philosophizing of both the middle ages and the renaissance. Thus Aristotle's original division, filtered to be sure through the Platonic and Neoplatonic influences that filled the mind of Boethius, but nonetheless unmistakable in their ancient origin, became the main division used in the theoretical discussion of the thirteenth, fourteenth, and fifteenth centuries, and even later. According to this way of looking at knowledge, it will be remembered, "logic is not included under speculative philosophy as a principal part but as furnishing speculative thought with its instruments" (Aquinas, c. 1255-1259: Q. 5, art. 1 ad 2).

3

Exploratory: The Indigenous Latin Development

In order to advance our investigation, we have to take leave at this point of the influence of Boethius on the Latin ages in order to see them also in the light of developments novel or indigenous to that post-classical period of, as it were, homogeneously Latin philosophizing. Let us begin with a division of the objects of knowledge that is both characteristic of and more indigenous to the middle ages, and highly instructive for our purposes, namely, the primary division that they made of being — *ens*, that which is or can be — as the first object (*primum cognitum*) of human awareness, into *ens reale* and *ens rationis*.

From the point of view of the analysis of the order of primitive concepts as originating in sensory experience, the medieval scholastics had a generally accepted saying that "primum in cognitione cadit ens" — being is the first thing that the human mind grasps. For them, *ens* was the term designating the start of human experience: from the initial grasp of being the whole of our experience will be articulated. And the first division of being, that is, the first contrast given in our experience of the world, is the contrast within *ens* between real being, by which they

meant what exists independently of the mind, *ens reale*, or
mind-independent being; and *non ens*, more commonly
termed *ens rationis* by reason of the framework of their
preoccupations, by which they meant what exists consequently and dependently upon the mind's own workings.[1]

Right away notice the hook-up between this notion
of *ens rationis* and the Stoic notion mentioned above of
philosophia rationalis: mind-dependent being, the order
which the mind through its cognitive workings introduces
into things, which *has no existence apart* from the mind's
cognition.

Non ens, "non-being," is an initially puzzling designation, no doubt; but *ens rationis*, the more common designation for what is being distinguished, appears retro-
spectively, from outside the medieval framework of preoccupations, at least, as a positive misnomer, one which
has in fact created no end of misapprehensions among the
students of medieval thought in our own day. Literally,
and in the standard modern readings, *ens rationis* "obviously" means in English *being of reason*. And yet, according to the Aristotelian psychology or life-science developed by the Latin scholastics (discussions in Deely 1971a,
1972a, 1974, 1975a, 1978a, 1980b, 1983: III.C. and D.),
animals also, more precisely, the higher animals, those
species endowed with the powers of internal sense and
therefore capable of perception, form "beings of reason"
in the course of structuring through experience their
awareness of the environment, although in this theory
such animals of course have no reason — *ratio* — in the
sense of *intellectus*, or understanding! Not to see this point
is to miss one of the potentially most important contributions of medieval scholasticism for the eventual development of the doctrine of signs, as John Poinsot (1632:
301a1-306b45, i.e., in the First Preamble to the 1983
edition) was so skillfully and with consummate subtlety to
show in that later period which can be viewed with equal

justice as the twilight of the Latin age or as the dawn of modern times. Instead of perpetuating the misunderstandings latent in the translation, "being of reason," let us simply translate *ens rationis* as *mind-dependent being*.

Hence *ens rationis* itself can be divided into what we might call (forgetting for a moment that we have just repudiated the standard rendering, for the sake of emphasizing through paradox the point of our repudiation) *perceptual beings of reason*, to wit, *entia rationis* formed by higher animals as well as by men, a subject in which the medievals typically took almost no interest; and *conceptual* or *intellectual beings of reason*, of which the Latin schoolmen recognized the possibility of distinguishing several different kinds or sub-species, but the only kind in which they were really interested was something that they called *second intentions*. What they meant by a "second intention" is fairly straightforward. Whenever you know something, insofar as you know it, it becomes an object of thought or awareness. In so becoming, that object acquires as such, i.e., as existing for awareness, certain characteristics — e.g., you are able to *predicate* things of it: predicability thus would be a second intention. Something can only be the subject of a proposition insofar as someone is thinking about it. So, second intentions generically are the characteristics that things acquire as they exist in intellectual awareness. Characteristics that things have independently of awareness, "outside" of the mind, as it were, or "in nature," they called *first intentions*: but the further characteristics these same things acquire as they come to exist within the mind are second intentions. And specifically, these second intentions include the ideas or concepts corresponding to the five words of Porphyry — genus, species, difference, property, accident. Moreover, these second intentions, among the many kinds of mind-dependent being which could be distinguished, were the kind the scholastics were principally focussed upon because they thought that this was the subject matter of logic — the order that the mind in its own workings introduces into things in order to know reality were the second intentions.[2] The order of what was dependent on the mind in its specifically intellectual dimension was distinguished from the order of what is independent of the mind in order that the mental constructs might be rightly organized — that is, critically controlled — so as to reveal the structure of reality, thus:

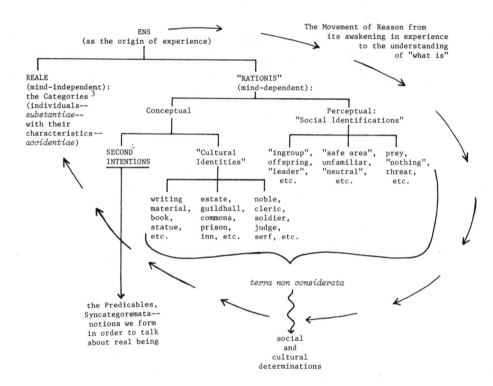

The five words of Porphyry which were used from the earliest days of the Latin era as the introduction to the study of the categories in the *Isagoge* were called *predicables*. But the division of real being — *ens reale*: the mind-independent realm of nature encountered in our sensory experience — is what Aristotle's book of *Categories* (*predicaments*) is all about.[4]

So, you can see why, in Porphyry's pedagogical scheme, if the categories (substance with its various modifications or "accidents") are the divisions expressive of being as it is able to exist independently of our thinking about it, and if being in this sense — *ens reale* — is what we are interested in understanding, then the study of the predicables would be an introduction (i.e., an advisable preliminary) to the study of the structure and classification of reality in critically controlled objectifications (see Section 2 note 5). And that is precisely the purpose that logic served within the mainstream philosophical systems of the Latin middle ages and renaissance times — a general instrument for acquiring knowledge of reality. Hence their almost exclusive concern in that dimension, the type of mind-dependent being that they were really interested in, was that aspect of mental construction which could be critically controlled for the purpose of identifying and segregating within the confusion of experience (*ens ut primum cognitum*) those aspects or elements which belong fundamentally to the order of what is independently of us — the constructs the mind would make in order to know the real.

This gave a precise focus to the problematic of logic as it came to the Latin West, to our civilization, in its integral Aristotelian form. Logic they defined as the art enabling us to proceed with ease, order, and correctness in the act of reasoning itself: "and thus it is seen to be the art of arts, because it directs us in the activity of reasoning, whence all the arts proceed."[5]

A further attempt to organize and clarify the integral problematic of logic embodied in the *Organon* is to be seen in the Latins' application to that problematic of the distinction between "form" and "matter." Already in the thirteenth century we find this terminology being used for the "logica nova," in the opposition of *formal* to *material logic*, which can be represented in somewhat simplified form thus:

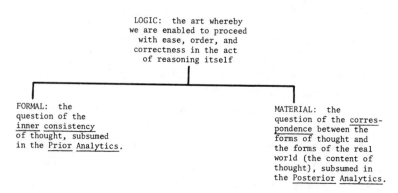

LOGIC: the art whereby
we are enabled to proceed
with ease, order, and
correctness in the act
of reasoning itself

FORMAL: the
question of the
inner consistency
of thought, subsumed
in the Prior Analytics.

MATERIAL: the
question of the corres-
pondence between the
forms of thought and
the forms of the real
world (the content of
thought), subsumed in
the Posterior Analytics.

The new way of speaking therefore is pretty straight-forward. "Formal logic" is concerned with the consistency of thought regardless of its content — pure consistency as such of thought: form. Inner consistency. And this corresponds, in the logical works of Aristotle, especially to the books of the *Prior Analytics*, though also of course to the treatment of propositions in the *Peri hermenias*, which is ordered to the discussions of the *Prior Analytics*. Indeed, that the *Prior Analytics* subsumes the central problematic of formal logic conceived as the concern with internally consistent structure remains true down to the present day (Bochenski 1970).

On the other side, the *Posterior Analytics* of Aristotle can justly be regarded as the first treatise on scientific methodology in the West, for this was the logic of proof, concerned not merely with the consistency of thought within itself, but with the *application* of consistent thought to the content of experience in order to show why the world is the way it is. In general, then, "material logic" is concerned with the correspondence between the forms of thought and the forms of the natural world.

Fallacies in reasoning can be similarly divided. There are *formal fallacies*, namely, those which can be detected by purely mechanical means, so to speak, because they violate the canons of inner consistency. Such are the celebrated (if misnomered) "truth tables" of logic in our own time, etc.:

p	q	p · q
T	T	T
T	F	F
F	T	F
F	F	F

Material fallacies, on the other hand, spring rather, in contemporary terminology, from mismatchings in the semantic field or space of a given linguistic community, e.g.:

> The delegates to the Democratic Convention come from all fifty states.
> Harry is a delegate to the Democratic Convention.
> Therefore Harry comes from all fifty states.

Yet — and this is a very important point — having introduced the distinction between "formal" and "material" logic, the medieval schoolmen and their successors in the renaissance mainstream did not extend the distinction in this hard and fast way to the consideration of the fallacies or indeed to many other details of logical theory. On the contrary, the "formal" logic itself as it was developed in the universities treated both kinds of fallacies in the context of the general introductory logic or prior analytics, and for a very good reason, namely, the fact that the sign system in terms of which they wanted to explore logical relations was what we now call a "natural" language — English in our case, Latin in theirs.[6] Stipulated symbols as such were used, to be sure, in the exposition and development of formal logic, but in a purely secondary and subordinate way. The main thing the Latins were interested in was seeing how the workings of the mind relate to the understanding of the "real" world of experience, as we have seen; and the principal medium for that is a natural language. Artificial symbols were used only as convenient devices for explaining the workings of the system of signs comprising the actual

language of the community. "Scholastic logic," in summary, is "a thorough-going attempt to grasp formal laws
expressed in natural language (Latin) with plentifully dif-
ferentiated syntactical rules and semantic functions"
(Bochenski 1970: 13).

"Formal logic" thus in the medieval and later
renaissance worlds of Latin learning came to have a particular meaning, directly linked, after 1150, to the technical problematic of Aristotle's *Prior Analytics*, but also
linked directly and more fundamentally to the general
problematic of the primary access to intelligibility afforded the mind by the resources of its native linguistic
community. This twofold attraction for logical research
— one purely technical (which the Latins, under Arabic
influence, came to call *logica docens*), the other purely instrumental (which the Latins, again under the Arab influence, called *logica utens*) — gave rise in the Latin world
to a singular development, cardinal in importance for
semiotic historiography. Besides the early medieval Aristotelian heritage of the *logica seu ars vetus* and the distinctively high medieval acquisition of the integral Aristotelian logic called the *ars seu logica nova*, influenced by
the *logica nova* but rooted in the rich, para-Aristotelian
Boethian and Stoic heritage of a propositional logic and
nascent syllogistic (de Rijk 1962), the introductory course
in logic as it jelled in the Latin universities of the renaissance came to possess, beginning from the earliest period
of the universities' foundings in the 12th century, a
uniquely rich, independent, and common flavor throughout Europe (the *Latin* world) precipitated typically by the
unique and precious treatise (c. 1245) of Petrus Hispanus
titled the *Summulae Logicales*. The influence of this work
was twofold.

On the one hand, Peter's little work is filled with
mnemonic devices and verses (not all of them original
with Peter) by which the different types of propositions,
the figures and moods (i.e., valid forms) of the syllogism,

and the rules determining those forms can be readily mastered by beginning students. So ingenious was Peter of Spain's format in this regard that his basic formulae have survived even the transition begun around the 17th century from Latin to the modern national languages, and are still in use today with beginning students in logic. One can only imagine how much more effective these mnemonics must have been to those earlier students whose native tongue was that Latin from which Petrus Hispanus crafted and organized his verses. In this respect, Peter's work has never been surpassed, which in part explains its nominal and wide influence in the Latin world: "This work came to be accepted as the standard textbook of logic through all the later Middle Ages and was still in use as late as the beginning of the seventeenth century" (Kneale and Kneale 1962: 234; but note Ashworth's caveat, 1974: 2: "the picture is altered considerably when one looks at dates and places of publication"[7]).

On the other hand, the independent development of Peter's treatise, taking account of the *logica nova*, but integrating it objectively according to the demands of the subject matter with other and prior notions, instead of following the newly developing fashion of commentary on the Aristotelian texts which was fast becoming the staple of the curriculum of arts in the new universities, set a pattern which, particularly within the Iberian university world (Coimbra, Salamanca, Alcalá), came to be synonymous with formal logic itself (*"analytica priora"*). Within this world, "summulae" was often used (e.g., Soto 1529; Bañez 1618; Poinsot 1631) as a synonym for "formal" or "introductory logic," and strict Aristotelians were known to complain of the independent course summulist logic had taken![8]

Thus, in the later Latin period (post-1200), three compenetrating but distinct logical arenas or zones are discernible, the Aristotelian *logica vetus et nova*, and the

summulist *logica modernorum*, also commonly referred to,
especially after the *Summa Logicae* of William of Ockham
(*inter* 1317-1328) as *terminist* logic, because the logical
forms common to all reasoning were introduced in light
of the properties of terms, particularly of the contrast between the properties terms have as simple elements of discourse (*significatio*) and the further properties they acquire
through their employment in syntactical arrangements
(*suppositio, copulatio, appellatio,* etc.). Of these three, then
(the *logica vetus, nova,* and *moderna*), the *logica moderna* or
modernorum became the textbook tradition of logic for the
renaissance period and beyond, relating to the integral
problematic of Aristotle's *Organon* roughly on the following pattern:

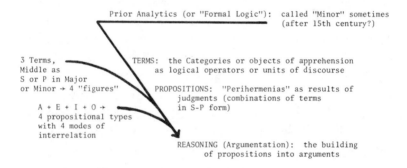

Formal logic was seen as beginning with the study of
simple terms, commonly identified with single words —
e.g., "man," "horse," "tree," "or," "and," "of." Primary among these simple terms were those pertaining to
Aristotle's categories of possible real existence, viewed
now as logical units of discourse. The combining of terms
into propositions gave a second level, that of judgment,
corresponding to Aristotle's *Peri Hermenias*. Finally, there
was the third level of study, the level to which terms and
propositions are ordered, namely, the level of reasoning
or argument. Here, propositions are combined, just as at
the previous level terms were combined, and as at the
initial level sounds and concepts were combined to form

terms. Any statement of common speech, they held, could in theory be reduced to a series of A, E, I, or O (universal affirmative or negative, particular affirmative or negative) propositions. Those propositions have certain necessary relations among themselves (contradiction, contrariety, subcontrariety, subalternation) expressed in the "square of opposition" — a fairly simple number, that is, of possible logical relations. Finally, the four types of propositions, each admitting of four types of interrelation, give sixteen possible combinations of propositions; and these, multiplied by the four "figures" or possible arrangements of the three terms (major, minor, middle) comprising an argument (middle term as subject of the major and predicate of the minor, middle term as predicate in both major and minor, middle term as subject in both major and minor, middle term as predicate of major and subject of minor), give sixty-four possible combinations of terms and propositions in reasoning. But of these sixty-four combinations, only nineteen prove to be valid when the rules of reasoning are applied — the so-called "moods" of the syllogism. Only these nineteen combinations are valid, that is, internally consistent in the context of natural language. Such, basically, and skating over, needless to say, the thin ice of many controversies,[9] was formal, terminist, or "summulae" logic as it came to be developed in the Latin universities.

The *Posterior Analytics* was subsumed along with other philosophical matters that logic in the formal sense requires in order to become a tool for the study of real being. This complex of problems early came to be called *material* in contrast to formal logic, later also *major* as opposed to minor (formal or "summulae") logic. Here the materials of the categories and the peri hermenias are covered not in terms solely of their function in discourse ("scientia sermocinalis") but rather now from the standpoint of their as it were metaphysical content or aspect, i.e., their relation to real being. So the content of *logica major* or *material logic* came to be regarded as a transition between dialectical studies (*logica minor seu formalis seu summulae*) and philosophical studies proper. It was the study of the hook-up between the forms of thought and the forms constitutive of the world of physical being. By the 17th century, for example, in the Iberian universities, where the continuity of Latin tradition with the high middle ages remained strongest, "material logic" would be comprised of a discussion of the metaphysical side of the problems raised by Porphyry (the problem of universals, the nominalist controversy), so that the *Isagoge* came to be treated as a tract within material logic; a discussion of the applicability of the categories to the world independent of discourse; a discussion of judgment (*peri hermenias*) in terms of, as we would say, its epistemological content or value; and finally, in many ways most importantly of all, the discussion of "posterior analytics," scientific proof and demonstration.

The following diagram of the integral course in logic taught in the Faculty of Arts of the major University of Alcalá in Spain of the 1630's and 1640's may be regarded as typifying the mainstream Latin development as it took place after the full-scale translations of Aristotle were introduced subsequent to the mid-12th century:

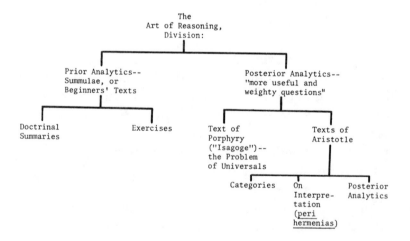

(In the early medieval universities, these courses in material and formal logic were distinguished in order of importance by the requirement that the formal course needed to be taken only once, but lectures on the posterior analytics had to be sat through twice — which was their way of emphasizing the greater difficulty and importance of the questions. Today, their *logica major* is no longer recognized generally as logic at all!)

With the form of reasoning and its relation to proofs about what is well in hand, the student would proceed to the study of the natural world in a course of lectures comprising what came to be called everywhere in the Latin renaissance down to the time of Descartes and after "natural philosophy" — *philosophia naturalis*.

The integration of logical with philosophical studies in the curriculum of the Faculty of Arts of the Latin universities was thus complete, as can be usefully illustrated by the following sequence of diagrams based on Poinsot, 1631-1635, of the plan of the course of studies in the curriculum of arts at the University of Alcalá (c. 1630-1650), which gives one a breathtaking view of the scope and rational world-view achieved philosophically by the Latin age in the very period of gestation of the more typically "modern" thought as it would erupt in Descartes and after: *(See charts following pages).*

This sequence of tables unfolding the philosophical dimension of the Latin worldview achieved in the tradition of natural philosophy that developed continuously over the span separating the twelfth from the seventeenth century has a certain semiotic value in its own right. Coming just before the ramification of knowledge that would definitively separate science in the modern specialized sense from the more common and generalized concerns that can only be analyzed in the perspectives proper to philosophical understanding (much as rational analysis separated off from mythical thinking in ancient Greece, and philosophical thinking came into contrast

Diagram 9

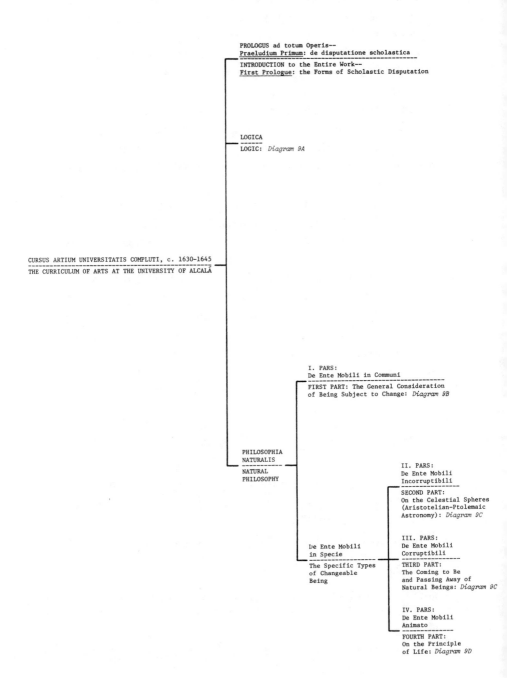

PROLOGUS ad totum Operis--
Praeludium Primum: de disputatione scholastica
INTRODUCTION to the Entire Work--
First Prologue: the Forms of Scholastic Disputation

LOGICA
LOGIC: *Diagram 9A*

CURSUS ARTIUM UNIVERSITATIS COMPLUTI, c. 1630-1645
THE CURRICULUM OF ARTS AT THE UNIVERSITY OF ALCALÁ

I. PARS:
De Ente Mobili in Communi
FIRST PART: The General Consideration
of Being Subject to Change: *Diagram 9B*

PHILOSOPHIA
NATURALIS
NATURAL
PHILOSOPHY

II. PARS:
De Ente Mobili
Incorruptibili
SECOND PART:
On the Celestial Spheres
(Aristotelian-Ptolemaic
Astronomy): *Diagram 9C*

De Ente Mobili
in Specie
The Specific Types
of Changeable
Being

III. PARS:
De Ente Mobili
Corruptibili
THIRD PART:
The Coming to Be
and Passing Away of
Natural Beings: *Diagram 9C*

IV. PARS:
De Ente Mobili
Animato
FOURTH PART:
On the Principle
of Life: *Diagram 9D*

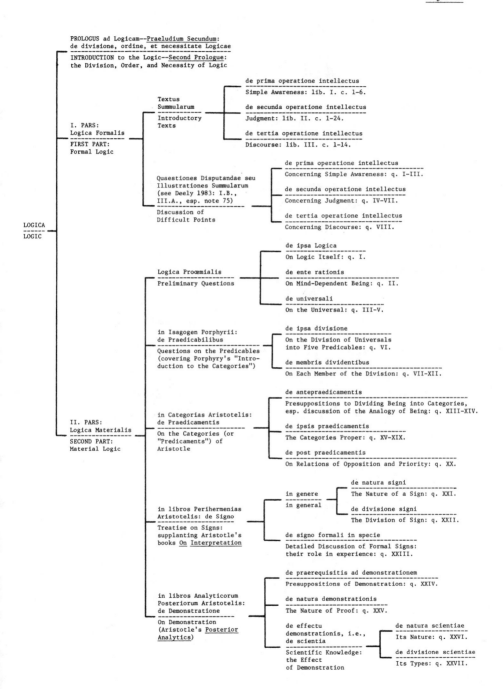

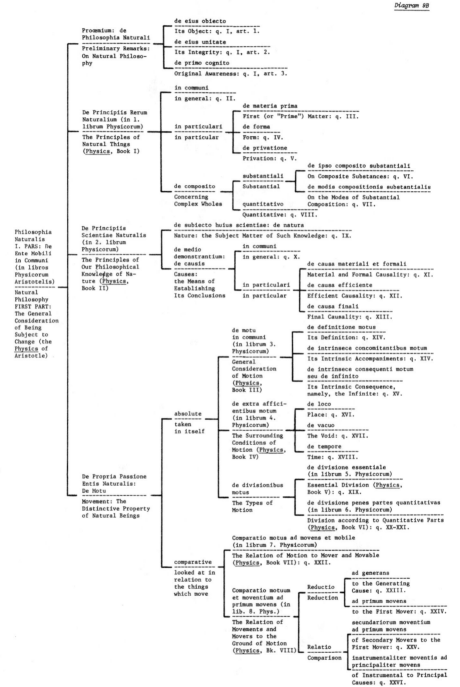

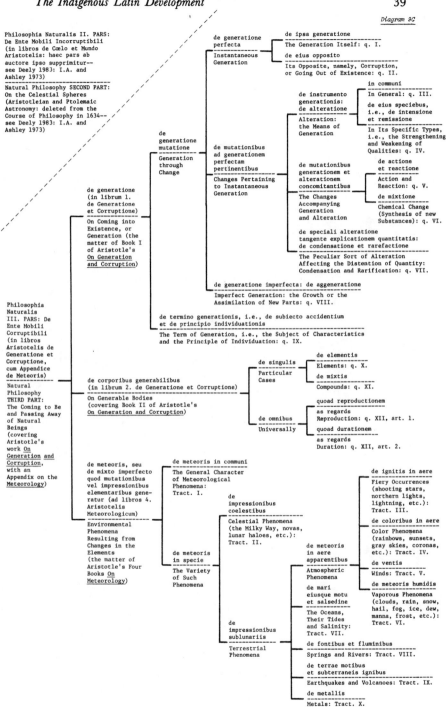

Diagram 9C

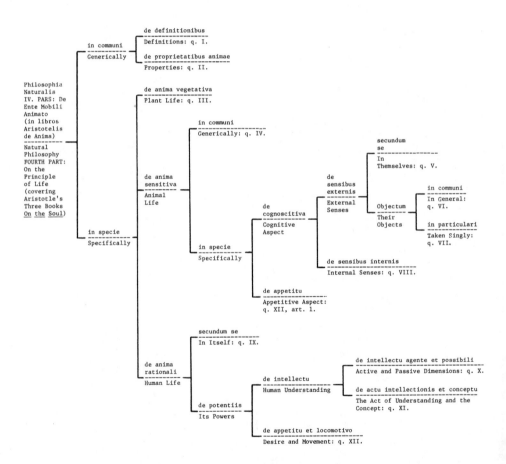

with the reasoned analysis of theology in the high middle ages), this curriculum provides a useful foil for reflecting on the possible unifications of rational concerns that might take place under the inherently interdisciplinary umbrella which semiotics provides. At the risk of getting ahead of ourselves, it might be worthwhile to pause at this juncture just long enough to contemplate for a moment such a possibility in this historically prismed way:

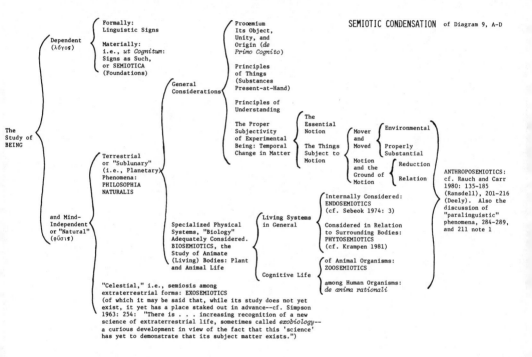

4

Exploratory: Cognition Theory among the Latins

So much for the general development.

Now, specifically with regard to the discussion of signs, already by the time of William of Ockham (d. 1350), the notion of treating ideas as signs within the mind contrasting with spoken words as nature contrasts with convention was becoming an established way of speaking among the logicians. Fragments of such a perspective can also be found in the Latins before Ockham, as indeed in Aristotle himself (cf. *Peri Hermenias*, 16a3-8[1]). But, as Professor Hawkins in our time well remarked (in a radically unsemiotic attempt at philosophizing in his own right, 1945: 14-15; cf. 1946: 134-135), this was not at the time of transition between medieval and renaissance times a characteristic way of speaking, whose presuppositions and consequences had been well explored. On the contrary, we encounter such references in the 13th and 14th centuries in truncated contexts that make them seem inevitable, but underdeveloped.

The study of ideas (for which their main less technical word, along with several others, was "concept"), was assigned in their culture not to logic but to the life sci-

ences, as we call them, and particularly to the *de anima* or
"psychology," which was for them a science co-extensive
with the investigation of living things. "Psychology," for
the Latins, insofar as it concerned itself with the formation and function of concepts, meant zoosemiotics just as
much as it did anthroposemiotics — a point that tends to
get lost after Descartes. Here, in the psychology, the cul-
mination of the whole curriculum of philosophy was
reached in the study of the problems of cognition and
concept-formation, as can be seen from our tabular sequence at the end of the preceding section.

In their psycho-biology, ideas (concepts) were studied as the forms of knowing — literally, the structures of
the contents of awareness — common to human and non-
human animals in many respects, unique to men in other
respects, namely, in the domain of reason proper or intellectual understanding (including logic). At some risk of
oversimplification, it can be said that in the analysis of
the medieval and renaissance philosophical mainstream,
ideas are seen as the specific and irreducibly cognitive
response of the organism to stimuli impinging upon it
from the physical environment. As a response to the environment, ideas structure the world as it appears or will
appear to the individual organism, first of all in terms of
circumstances to be sought and circumstances to be
avoided — the basic opposition of friendly and hostile.
What ideas then were for them was first of all what the
organism expressed to itself as important (helpful or
harmful, pleasant or unpleasant, to be sought or avoided)
in its encounters with the "real" being of the physical
world.

Viewed precisely as such, that is, as objective self-
expressions of cognitive life, the Latins called concepts by
a name they took over from the Greek, one which, as
Maritain has noted (1959: 115), "has no equivalent in
our modern languages," namely, *species* (pronounced
"spay-chee-ehs") *expressae* — "expressed species," a

term (*species*) that can also be translated as *form*, a form expressed by the mind in response to an environmental stimulus, thus:

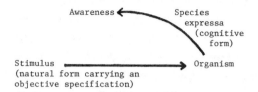

Psychology, thus — Aristotelian psychology, really a psycho-biology — added to the natural forms of Aristotelian physics a notion of specifically and irreducibly cognitive forms,[2] the "spay-chee-ehs" (*species*), or, as they also came generally to be called among the later Latins, apparently under the influence of the commentaries of Averroes (d. 1198) on the *De Anima*, *intentional* forms.

The "forms" by which things exist in nature independently of awareness would be natural forms; but the forms that these same things have in our thought and experience of them would be cognitive or intentional forms, i.e., *species expressae*. I have introduced here this understanding of *species expressa*, because it was in the Latin vocabulary perhaps the most generic technical term for what Locke and the moderns after him called simply ideas:

> *An Essay Concerning Human Understanding* (Locke), 1690, introductory paragraph 8, *What 'Idea' stands for*: Thus much I thought necessary to say concerning the occasion of this Inquiry into human Understanding. But, before I proceed on to what I have thought on this subject, I must here in the entrance beg pardon of my reader for the frequent use of the word *idea*, which he will find in the following treatise. It being that term which, I think, serves best to stand for whatsoever is the *object* of the understanding when a man thinks, I have used it to express whatever is meant by *phantasm, notion, species,* or *whatever it is which the mind can be employed about in thinking*; and I could not avoid frequently using it.

That generic use of "idea" for what the imagination, memory, or reason indifferently produce in order to know corresponds in Latin philosophy to the notion of "species expressa." Several other terms have to be added in nuancing the generic notion, reflecting the complexity of the Latin Aristotelian analysis of cognition. From a certain point of view, particularly as they occurred at the level of perceptual awareness, the *species expressae* were also called *images* (*imago*); as providing the raw material of intellection they called *phantasms* (*phantasma*); as establishing an immediate awareness of objects they were called "notices" (*notitia*); as constituting a realm apart from the real they were called *representations* (*repraesentatio*) and *icons* (*idolum*); as precise effects proportioned objectively to the natural forms of environmental stimuli they were called *similitudes* (*similitudo*); and so on.

But the extension to these forms — the cognitive or intentional forms — of the notion of *sign*, although found here and there throughout the Latin writings, is only (as it were) by way of a second thought, and by analogy to the signs of oral communication, especially speech (words), and to the signs of nature, as clouds signifying rain.

The possibility of a semiotic analysis of concepts, that is to say, the possibility of an analysis of the being proper to concepts considered precisely as signs, was only beginning to be sensed and probed here and there, it seems, in the time of transition within Latin culture between medieval and renaissance times, but without gaining any clarity as to its consequences and implications not only for logic itself, but also for the life sciences and psychology by which the Latins generally developed a theory of knowledge rather from a point of view that we would characterize in retrospect as ontological, or even metaphysical, rather than epistemological. The question of a general treatise on signs seems never to have been raised at this period, nor would it be, as we shall see, until the end of the Latin age.

5

Exploratory: The Drift toward Semiotic Consciousness

The historical unit of focus for further research into the original coalescence of a thematically semiotic consciousness, I would suggest, should be the period between 1350 and 1650. I choose these dates not arbitrarily, but because they represent the death of the last seriously studied figure of mainstream Latin development, practically speaking, namely, William of Ockham, and the death of the first seriously studied post-Latin mainstream thinker, namely, Descartes. Such is the sorry state of research into the history of philosophy in the contemporary period that this interlude is *terra incognita*, astonishingly enough, the "least known period in the history of Western philosophy" (Randall 1962: vii-viii) — a situation quite detrimental for the development of semiotics, as very recent studies (e.g., Herculano de Carvalho, 1969, 1970; Romeo 1979) have begun to make clear. The common prejudice, established in the century after Descartes and prevailing down to the present day, has been stated with perfect clarity by Charles Sanders Peirce (1871: 14):

> With Ockham, who died in 1347, scholasticism may be said to have culminated. After him the scholastic philosophy showed

a tendency to separate itself from the religious element which alone could dignify it, and sunk first into extreme formalism and fancifulness, and then into the merited contempt of all men.

Professor Savan has observed in discussing this remark that Peirce made it at a very young age, and that a man so young, breathing the air of the age, should perhaps not be held too strictly to account for so gross and fallacious a generalization. With this I am inclined to agree, particularly when one considers how extraordinarily at variance Peirce's thought stands in its totality[1] with the complacent contemporaneity with which philosophers today, as in Peirce's time, continuing the Cartesian heritage as though the intervening centuries had revealed nothing of its limitations, shamelessly indulge what Levy-Bruhl once described (1899: ix) as "a taste for abstract and too simple solutions, a conviction that it is sufficient to argue soundly upon evident principles in order to discover the truth, even in the most complex problems of social life — in short, a lack of historical spirit," an almost total naiveté regarding the historicity of man.[2] Nonetheless, in that early statement, Peirce truly represents the prevailing prejudice at the turn of the century which endures, although it has most recently begun to be qualified and the period which it has consigned to oblivion may soon (let us hope) be invaded by intellectual explorers who will bring its true character and riches into the light of day. In this regard, Gilson (1952: 657), speaking of course of Latin philosophy after Ockham, well remarked: "We enter here upon a doctrinal territory ill understood, extremely complex and of which we know at least this much going in, namely, that the term 'nominalism'," a term long used to characterize the totality of post-Ockhamite scholasticism, "does not in any wise suffice to define it." Kristeller, whose work has gone further in this area than that of any other toward undermining the ignorant prejudices that have shrouded the early

Latin phase of modern thought in myths and caricatures, suggests summarily how the present situation came about. "Historians of thought," he remarks (1961a: 34), "have been sympathetic to the opponents of Aristotelianism in the Renaissance, whereas most of the defenders of medieval philosophy have limited their efforts to its earlier phases before the end of the thirteenth century, and have sacrificed the late scholastics to the critique of their contemporary and modern adversaries."

The situation that confronts us here may be described as follows (Kristeller 1961b: 114-116 *passim*).

> . . . Renaissance Aristotelianism continued the medieval scholastic tradition without any visible break. It preserved a firm hold on the university chairs of logic, natural philosophy, and metaphysics, whereas even the humanist professors of moral philosophy continued to base their lectures on Aristotle. The literary activity of these Aristotelian philosophers . . . is difficult of access and arduous to read, but rich in philosophical problems and doctrine. It represents the bulk and kernel of the philosophical thought of the period, but it has been badly neglected by modern historians . . . . Consequently, most modern scholars have condemned the Aristotelian philosophers of the Renaissance without a hearing . . . . If we want to judge the merits and limitations of Renaissance Aristotelianism we will have to proceed to a new direct investigation of the source materials, instead of repeating antiquated judgments

— such as the one enunciated by Mr. Peirce in 1871. We should note here, as the above passage from Kristeller already suggests, how little useful for our purposes is the division which standard historiography makes into "early" ("Frühscholastik" — 1050-1200), "high" (Hochscholastik" — 1200-1300), and "late" ("Spätscholastik" — after 1300) scholasticism. This division, especially as between "high" and "late" Latin philosophy, and particularly if we look to the lines of development linking the Paris of Thomas Aquinas with the Iberian schools at Coimbra, Salamanca, Alcalá, and elsewhere, is arbitrary to a fault, chronological in the thin-

nest sense. The truth is that there is no name or place in
the currently conventionalized ''history of philosophy''
for the epoch of *philosophia naturalis* that begins with the
12th century translations of Aristotle and culminates in
the curricula of the 17th century Spanish schools.

The translation of the works of Aristotle in the 12th
century coincided within about seventy years with the
founding of the European universities, as they continue to
this day. A look at the contents of the entire works of
Aristotle reveals that they comprise in their own way
practically the whole range of academic studies down to
this day. What the contents of the works of Aristotle became in those early times, therefore, was, not surprising-
ly, the basis for the university curriculum of the West
throughout the later Latin age. By comparison, the developments of humanism (literary humanism, not the
secular and philosophical humanism meant by the term
today) and of Platonism in the renaissance were something beside or sustained within this mainstream. After
Descartes, where today a graduate student's continuous
historical knowledge of philosophy typically ends (when it
even goes back that far), ''everyone knows'' that those
earlier Latin Aristotelians were victims of idle specula-
tion, having nothing worthwhile to say to later ages. So
why study them? Almost any professor of philosophy in
the mainstream departments of universities in the
English-speaking world can tell you that, without even
having to look at the books of the period.

On the other side, even when the great revival of
medieval studies took place, largely, in the ''English-
speaking world,'' owing to the great and recently de-
ceased Gilson, the new interest in Latin philosophy only
carried its workers up to the time of Ockham, usually to
limn in him the clear beginnings of a ''decadence'' that
would only advance in the remaining Latin ages (a view
indeed not wholly wrong as far as education in the
English universities was concerned!), but sometimes to

champion him rather as the last outpost of Latin greatness in philosophy, as in the work of Boehner.[3] Thus, from both sides — whether one deals with the historians of the middle ages moving toward the present, or with the contemporary philosophers so far as they see themselves as heir to an historical tradition — a point is reached, Ockham in the former case, Descartes in the latter, where there is simply a gap, populated it is true by a few odd figures like Nicolas of Cusa, Marsilio Ficino, Pomponazzi; but basically the period in question is a big black hole. Yet precisely in that "black hole," there is good reason to suspect, lies the richest and most fertile ground for understanding the epigenic unfolding in our own times of semiotics. I would suggest that this is precisely the principal gestation period for the development historically of the semiotic point of view.

First of all, not only from the point of view of philosophy proper, as we have seen, but particularly from the point of view of semiotic, this period (1350-1650) does not at all develop along those lines of vision that are familiar in the standard histories, which tend to concentrate on the renaissance in Europe and the Italian peninsula, and on figures that are identified either with the humanist movement, or with Platonic movements that were indigenous to the renaissance with its newly awakened sensitivity to and interest in linguistic diversity which, as much as anything, sets the renaissance apart from the earlier "middle ages."

The recovery of Greek and awakening awareness of the feedback effect of language on underlying structures of thought and experience are events of first importance to the gestation of semiotics. Initially, apart from ecclesiastical concerns with "orthodoxy," scholars were delighted at the great find made available by the early translations of Aristotle. But as time went on, particularly as scholars fleeing Constantinople made Greek more and more accessible to the Latin West, further translations of

the same works were made, with the semantic fields distributed often in troublingly alternative ways on key
points "settled" in earlier commentaries. Two or three
hundred years of such endeavor, needless to say, created
a situation of some considerable complexity.

From the point of view of semiotic, the crucial lines
of development over the period in question seem to lie in
the university traditions of Iberia, Spain and Portugal.
These university traditions, as we have said, are continuous substantially with the doctrinal achievements of the
high middle ages, particularly in the three great centers
already mentioned, namely, Coimbra, the principal university of Portugal, Salamanca, the principal center in
Spain, and Alcalá, rival to Salamanca for a time in the
late 16th and early 17th centuries. In these and related
schools, dispute over signs and signification was rampant
— "a matter of daily dispute in the schools," as one
author of the period put it (Poinsot 1632: 680a38-39 —
"quotidianis disputationibus agitare solent").

Within the summulist logical tradition, therefore, at
least within the Iberian university world, there is a considerable development of controversies over signification
during the period we have circumscribed. The possibility
of a unified science or doctrine or "theory," of abstracting, as it were, a *common object* in the experience of signification, was, by the end of the 16th century, a matter on
which sides were being taken, often against, as in the case
of the celebrated Suarez (1605: disp. 1, par. 6).

How central semiotic notions were becoming in the
thought of this period can be indicated best, perhaps, by
the case of Petrus Fonsecus (1528-1599), a Portuguese
philosopher who became the principal professor at
Coimbra and the organizing force of the group of thinkers
there whose work came to be known collectively as the
Cursus Conimbricensis. Of particular interest for our study
was the publication in 1564 of his *Institutionum dialecticarum
libri octo*, essentially a summulist logic text, which was

read far and wide in the Latin world, having gone through some fifty-three editions by the year 1624 (Romeo 1979: 190).

In Pedro's work, already we find a special terminology, adding to the traditional ontological-epistemological analysis of knowledge not just another set of terms for dealing with the, as we have seen, already complex notion of "ideas" (*conceptus*), but a set of terms specifically designed to assimilate the entire prejacent analysis as developed from the point of view of ontology to the quite different point of view of signification, or, as we could say, *semiosis*. Signs were divided, in this new way of speaking and thinking, into "formal" and "instrumental," the former being the "forms" (*species expressae*) or ideas within the mind whereby experience is structured, the latter being words and, more generally, any sense-perceptible item or object of experience which functions as a sign, i.e., to bring something other than itself into awareness. In Pedro's own words (1564: lib. I, cap. VIII):

> Formal signs are similitudes or certain forms (*species*) of things signified inscribed within the cognitive powers, by means of which the things signified are perceived. Of this sort is the similitude which the spectacle of a mountain impresses upon the eyes, or the image which an absent friend leaves in another's memory, or again the picture one forms of something which he has never seen. These signs are called "formal," because they form and as it were structure the knowing power.
>
> Instrumental signs are those which, having become objects for knowing powers, lead to the cognition of something else. Of this sort is the track of an animal left in the ground, smoke, a statue, and the like. For a track is a sign of the animal which made it: smoke the sign of an unseen fire: a statue finally is a sign of Caesar or someone else. These signs are called "instrumental," either because through them as instruments we signify to others our ideas; or because just as an artist must move his instrument in order to shape his material with it, so must powers able to know first perceive these signs in order to know anything through them.
>
> Hence may be gathered the most striking difference be-

tween instrumental and formal signs: since indeed formal signs
do not have to be perceived by us in order for us to come to
an awareness of the thing signified by the perception they structure; but unless instrumental signs are perceived, they lead no
one to an awareness of anything.[4]

It seems probable that this division, apparently
indigenous to our neglected period, was drawn specifically in light of a growing uneasiness with the long-
accepted definition from Augustine's *De doctrina christiana*
(c. 397-426: Book II, c. 1), which was taken over, as we
remarked in citing it in Section 3 above, in the *Sentences*
of Peter Lombard (c. 1150) and thereafter by all of the
Latin writers on sacramental theology. According to the
terms of this definition, being sense-perceptible is essential to the proper being of a sign. By Fonseca's time, as
already in Ockham's forthright designation of ideas in the
mind as *signa naturalia*, it was becoming evident that the
concepts of the mind, being as we have seen the very
structures which form our experience of nature, indeed
function as sense-perceptible signs function insofar as
these latter function *as* signs, yet without being for all that
in anywise accessible to sense perception as such. Moreover, not only concepts were designated by the Latins as
signa naturalia, but all those phenomena of human experience which seem to have a connection with what they
signify antecedent to and independent of social interaction. For these and other reasons, the need began to be
felt for a new way of thinking about signs, and the new
division of signs into formal and instrumental appears to
have been the most seminal coinage within the period to
accommodate this need, as can be seen in the lecture
course given by Professor Bosserel at the University of
Graz, Austria, in 1615 (MS 133 of the University), on the
logical doctrines of Fonseca (*Synopses in quibus doctrina
dialectica R.^{i} P.^{i} Petri Fonseca ad ordinem Aristotelicam revocatur*), at the point where Bosserel synthesizes Fonseca's
discussion of signs in the *Institutiones* of 1564:

To signify means to represent something to a being able to know, as, for example, to the sense, the imagination, the understanding. Signs are divided into two groups. The first comprises formal and instrumental signs. The formal ones are similitudes, like images of things signified that exist in cognitive powers, through which the things signified are apprehended, as, for example, the resemblance of a friend. In order that these signs may be known, it is not necessary to see the eyes through which one sees the signs. Instrumental signs are those which are represented to cognitive powers as soon as they are recognized by them, and also when they lead to the recognition of other things, as the footprint of an animal, smoke, or wrinkles in the forehead.

The second group contains natural and conventional signs. Natural signs are those which signify the same thing to everybody, such as moans and laughs. Conventional signs are those which signify through as it were a socially structured human intention, such as words and letters, as well as those which have entered the usage of all people, such as ivy and cypress.[5]

Note that natural signs can also be formal, but not all of them. For a concept and a moan are both natural signs, yet a moan is not formal, but instrumental.[6]

Whether the division of signs based on their function in experience relative to the cognizing organism, with the revision of the classical Augustinian definition that the new division implies (by restricting it to the one class of instrumental signs only), was original with Fonseca or suggested to him by earlier writers, I cannot say at present. The parenthetical remark, "liceat enim ita loqui," immediately following Fonseca's own introduction of the division into his text (1564: lib. I, cap. VIII), taken together with the reservations he gives about this way of speaking ("priora illa" — scil., *signa formalia* — "nec admodum usitate nominantur signa, nec satis proprie dicuntur repraesentare: haec vero posteriora" — scil., *signa instrumentalia* — "maxime,"), and his attempt finally to soften the criticism of St. Augustine's proposed definition that the new perspective implies ("Unde D. Augustinus quasi complexus omnia, quae populari

sermone signa dicerentur, hoc modo signum definivit:
Signum est, quod et seipsum sensui, et praeter se aliquid
animo ostendit''), would seem to suggest strongly that the
division is not Fonseca's own, but that he is rather react-
ing to and attempting to assimilate to his own more con-
servative thought (remember his criticism of the summulist tradition for departing too far from the reading of
Aristotle, in Section 3 note 8 above) elements that have
already been introduced into the summulist tradition by
others before him.

Of immediate importance, however, is not the question of authorship, but the fact of a new, specialized
terminology insofar as it attests to a new, unmistakable
direction — the direction of semiotic — in which the late
Latin renaissance mainstream in its most vigorous current was unmistakably moving.

In line with this development, we find in Fonseca
also an explicit attempt to identify the precise role of representation in signification (1564: lib. I, cap. VIII):

> To signify is nothing else than to represent something to a
> cognizing power. But since everything that represents some-
> thing is a sign of the thing which it represents, it happens that
> whatever signifies something is its sign.[7]

And as this text shows, for Fonseca, the relation of representation to signification is one of identity, one wherein
the two are equated.

But thirdly, we find in Fonseca, as a consequence of
his reservations concerning the notion of formal ''signs''
noted above — namely, that ''they are not called signs in
full accordance with the customary usage'' (''nec
admodum usitate nominantur signa''), that is, the usage
established by Augustine; ''nor are they said to represent
with sufficient propriety'' (''nec satis proprie dicuntur
repraesentare'') — we find in Fonseca (and this goes
against the line of development otherwise indicated thus
far), a specific denial that there is really a common notion

that unites these two kinds of signs. This in effect is a denial of a unified object at the base of semiotic analysis, and hence of the possibility of a general account, theory, or doctrine of signs. In other words, we find in Fonseca a man pressured by the development of thought and terminology in the summulist tradition to envisage the specific possibility of a semiotic, but he resists the prospect and in the end denies it. The possibility, he says in effect, is not a real one, in this anticipating the view of the major Latin professor who would almost alone influence the specifically modern thinkers of the 17th century such as Descartes and Leibniz, who in turn would set the direction of mainstream philosophical development in the national language traditions. I refer of course to the magistral Francis Suarez, already mentioned above (1605: disp. 1, par. 6; cf. Poinsot 1632: 658b30-659a39), who has found in our own time an unknowing disciple and unwitting echo in Roger Scruton's denial (1980: 14) that clouds signify rain in any sense univocal with the way that words signify.

Fourthly therefore we find in Fonseca, contrary to the obvious sense of his own words, and again *contrary* to the semiotic development he otherwise furthers in spite of himself, an effort to promote continued acceptance of St. Augustine's definition of the sign as a correct general definition, that is, one valid for all cases — the definition, it will be remembered, from the *De doctrina christiana* cited in Section 2 above: "A sign is something which, on being perceived, brings something other than itself into awareness." This definition obviously applies to instrumental signs — sense-perceptible realities which function subsequently as signs; so, if it is truly a general definition of signs, then indeed the possibility of treating ideas in semiotic perspective is precluded.

But, finally, to return to a positive point, we also find at this period, clearly illustrated in Fonseca's work, proof of a developing sophistication in the understanding of the

distinction between natural and conventional signs, as involving in fact more than two terms. This is a point of
considerable theoretical importance, as I have tried to
show elsewhere (1978a; cf. Rollin 1976). Here, I want
only to note its active presence in the summulist currents
of the Latin renaissance (Fonseca 1564: lib. I, cap. IX):

> Conventional signs are those which signify by deliberate inten-
> tion and as if by a kind of compact. Such signs are of two types.
> For some signify as the result of stipulations, such as the words
> by which men converse, or the letters by which absent parties
> communicate; others, however, signify as the result of customs
> and traditions of use, in the way that items displayed in a shop
> signify what is for sale. And of those signs which signify by
> stipulation, there is again a twofold signification, proper and
> improper . . . . Indeed practically all words have an improper
> signification as a result of adaptation and change in use,
> through metaphor, catachresis, metalepsis, or metonymy.[8]

What is clear then at this point — roughly two-thirds
of the way through our "lost period" in the history of
philosophy and semiotic — is that there is a growing complexity of considerable interest and not without its anti-
nomies in the understanding of signs. The definition of
sign is becoming unsettled, the division of signs is ramifying and intersecting in unexpected ways that demand
further analysis and, in particular, have consequences for
the very attempt at definition.

The first thinker that we encounter who both debates
the possibility of a unified doctrine or "general theory"
of signs and affirms it unequivocally, setting himself to
work out precisely such a doctrine in a unified treatise, is
a Spanish philosopher (Deely 1983: II.A. and note 31)
whose mother's name was Garcez (Portuguese) and whose
father's name was Poinsot (Burgundian). He published an
introductory logic text under the rubric of *Summulae* in
1631, the year before Locke's birth. He preceded his *textus
summularum* with a very interesting announcement of his
own forthcoming *Treatise on Signs*, to be published in the

following year as part of the course in material logic; and with an equally interesting complaint. The introductory logic texts that have been written in recent generations have become excessively complicated, he asserts, through the intrusion into the introduction of the problems attendant upon the notion of sign, which involves many matters from metaphysics and psychology which are customarily treated at length only toward the end of the curriculum (see the tables at the end of Section 4 above) — the whole problem of knowledge and ideas. As a result beginners have experienced needless and excessive difficulty in getting clear about the more simple business (being exclusively glottocentric) of formal logic as traditionally conceived (in contrast with signs as such, which are co-extensive with the whole of cognitive life, perceptual as well as conceptual, pre- and post-linguistic).

Therefore, he says, what he has done, in order to simplify the *summulae* texts and at the same time clarify the larger logical and philosophical tradition in this area, is to reduce to their proper unity all the basic issues which have been raised concerning signs, and insert the discussion of these issues into its proper place in the tradition of logic and philosophy, by substituting a general treatise on signs (*tractatus de signis*) for the heretofore customary commentary on the *De Interpretatione* (*Peri Hermenias*) of Aristotle. The reason for this substitution, he explains (1632: "Super libros perihermenias," 642a1-644b15), is that in the logical tradition up till now, e.g., in the commentary of St. Thomas (c. 1269-1274) on the *Peri Hermenias* or in its completion by Cajetan (1496), or in the writings of the other Latins on the subject all the way down to the 17th century, *interpretation*, following Aristotle, has been treated solely in terms of intellectual or *logical* interpretation. But logical interpretation itself is only one mode or form of interpretation; interpretation as such is rather co-extensive with the cognitive life of organisms; and logic achieves its specific forms of interpretation (not only in dependence upon enculturated perceptual and sensory habits — such as the ability to recognize the words and syntax of a given language, but) entirely through the use of signs. And therefore, lest the foundations of the exposition of logical form go unexamined, it is necessary to substitute for the narrow logical discussion of interpretation customary in the second part of logic (i.e., in the problematic of ''material'' logic) rather a general treatise on signs, which is what the name ''perihermenias'' properly would mean.

In 1632, the year of Locke's birth, Poinsot's *Treatise* proper is published. Needless to say, an examination in all the subtle abstract detail (matched in my opinion only by Heidegger's *Sein und Zeit* in our own time, which produces a similar exhaustion in the reader) and far-reaching exposition of this (so far as we presently know) first systematic semiotic treatise is out of the question here. Since, however, Poinsot, being himself a graduate of Coimbra (1605), was thoroughly familiar with da Fonseca's work, it will perhaps suffice for present purposes to single out against the background of that work three points of basic theoretical importance, and to leave to a note at the end of this section discussion of the manner in which the points are to be ultimately integrated into a comprehensive doctrine.

First of all, the critique of the definition of the sign handed down by all the Latin generations from Augustine, implicit in the introduction of the division of signs into formal and instrumental, as we have seen, but hedged by Fonseca, is on the contrary made explicit and championed by Poinsot (1631: 10a6-12; 1632: 646a14-28; resumed in Deely 1978a: 5-7). The ground of this critique, as of the existence of a unified subject matter for semiotic, is the insight that what is essential in our experience to the being and functioning of a sign is not that it be something perceived but that it bring something other than itself into the awareness of an organism, which is exactly how ideas function within the mind — to bring something other than themselves into awareness. When one thinks of a horse, for example, it's the horse you are thinking of, a determinate object, not the subjective mental state, the idea in your mind, that objective presence presupposes. The consequence of this is that formal and instrumental signs, precisely as signs, are indeed univocal in their way of being, and are therefore equally truly signs: the crucial point of doctrine that Poinsot establishes from a number of angles (e.g., 1632: Book I, Questions 1 and 2; Question 5 at 684b10-42) before tackling it *ex professo* in the opening Question of Book II, "Whether the Division of Signs into Formal and Instrumental Is Univocal and Exhaustive."

Secondly, Poinsot expressly denies the equation (explicit in Fonseca and implicit in most writers on signs down to the present day) between *representation* and *signification* (1631: 9b30-41; 1632: 646a29-b15, 649a11-b36). Representation and signification differ in this: an object can represent another than itself, and thus be a sign, but an object can also represent itself; whereas it's a contradiction for a sign to be a sign of itself: a sign is a sign only if it is a sign of something at least modally other.

Poinsot explains this in terms of the account of relation traditional in Latin thought from the time of Boethius. According to this tradition, relation involves three basic elements: what they called the foundation, or *ground*, in our terms — some characteristic of an individual; the relation itself, which is over and above the individual — supra- and inter-subjective, we would say; and that *to which* the thing is related through its foundation, which they called the term or *terminus* of the relation. In terms of signs, what Poinsot is saying is that the sign — signification — consists in the relation, the second of the three elements. Representation at best is the *foundation* for the relations of signification. So, apparently for the first time, Poinsot establishes a systematic distinction between signification and representation, where the role of representation is isolated and identified within signification. All signs, thus, involve representation, but not all representations are signs (*pace* Fonseca).

As an aside, in order to glimpse in passing the theoretical importance of this point, recall how Locke begins his *Essay Concerning Human Understanding* with the notion of ideas as directly apprehended representations of objects. At the conclusion of his *Essay*, when calling for a semiotic analysis of ideas, he suggests that such an analysis will perhaps result in a different sort of logic and critic than we have been acquainted with hitherto. What Poinsot shows in the course of his treatise is that when indeed ideas are analyzed as signs, it is impossible for them to be the direct objects of our awareness in the sense that Locke lays down at the beginning of his *Essay* (Introduction, par. 8). Viewed in this light, Poinsot's semiotic appears historically as an alternative epistemology to the solipsistic course that modern thought actually takes in the national language traditions (see discussions in note 9 to this Section, pp. 168-179, esp. 175 ff., below).

Thirdly, our author in some sense sees that an essential feature of semiotic analysis (*"doctrina signorum,"* in his terms) is that it is a new beginning for the whole enterprise of philosophy. For one thing it entails a new analysis of experience that subsumes what were previously the last conclusions of the system within its experiential starting point (Deely 1983: I.B.). For another, the analysis of sign — semiotic — provides a point of view that is superior to, that literally transcends, the traditional division of being into what is independent of the mind (*ens reale*) and what is dependent upon it (*ens rationis*), because in the sign, as in experience, both orders of being are found (Poinsot 1632: 646b25-33). When clouds, through our experience, come to function as signs of rain, we have a natural sign; but of course, in some culture, clouds might also function as signs of a particular relationship to the gods, which is to us obviously not a question of something natural. Social and natural being come together in the sign.

Compare this last point to Locke's notion of semiotic, as put forward in 1690. In concluding his *Essay*, Locke proposes his new division of knowledge, which we may schematize thus:

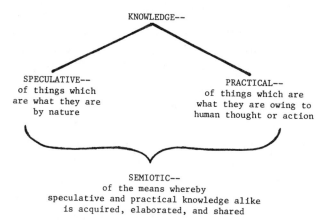

KNOWLEDGE--

SPECULATIVE--
of things which
are what they are
by nature

PRACTICAL--
of things which are
what they are owing to
human thought or action

SEMIOTIC--
of the means whereby
speculative and practical knowledge alike
is acquired, elaborated, and shared

This proposed division is reminiscent in different ways both of Aristotle's division of the sciences and of the old Stoic division introduced in Section 2 above, but with a very important difference which I failed to notice before in another treatment of this matter (Deely 1978b: 152-154). Notice that in the Stoic division, as also in that of Aristotle, the various types of objects specifying the various types of knowledge are distinguished, and they are kept distinct. Locke divides knowledge at first exactly the way Aristotle does — essentially he divides it into *speculative* (the knowledge of things which are what they are, independently of us, which Locke calls *physics*, betraying not only a Greek influence but, much more proximately, the influence of the Latin renaissance) and *practical* (that is, the knowledge of things which depend for their coming into existence upon human thought and action). So far he is merely repeating Aristotle. But now, when he brings in his semiotic, what we are confronted with is a proposal for studying in a systematic and unified fashion the ways and means whereby speculative and practical knowledge alike are acquired, developed, and communicated. This establishes a threefold division of the sciences, all right, but it is more unlike than it is like the division either of the Stoics or of Aristotle; because with Locke's third branch we are given a *distinction which unites*: it distinguishes the different orders only in order to show how they are brought together in the sign — and this is exactly the point of view superior to the division of being into *ens reale* (the principal object of speculative thought in the Aristotelian tradition) and *ens rationis* (certain forms of which are the object of practical thought) that we already encountered as the entrance to Poinsot's *doctrina signorum*.[9] The object of semiotic is neither *ens reale* nor *ens rationis* preclusively, but both in the ways they get mixed up with and compenetrate one another in experience.

What is being drawn here, by Poinsot, by Locke, by — more fundamentally — semiotic, is a new line: in the old tradition (cf. Russman 1981), the basic concern is with what is what it is independently of man, and secondarily with the things that are brought about by and depend upon man. With semiotic, the basic concern is with both equally. For the first time, the standpoint is achieved which of itself opens — to borrow an apt formulary from a contemporary philosopher (Maritain 1966: 32) — "onto the avenues of non-being windows as large as those open onto the avenues of being"; and the basic realization behind this achievement is that "what is" is circumscribed not by a fixed but by a shifting line whose shifts are determined precisely by the interaction between the two orders of being through the function of signs, through semiosis. The study of that shifting reality, that shifting line, is semiotic. Clouds as signs of rain is the classical case of the natural sign as something which is what it is independent of man. Now of course there are people trying to seed the clouds to produce rain, bringing what was formerly wholly outside human control partially within that control — hardly a possibility the medievals envisaged. More centrally, "heroes" for a given culture shape the development of that culture through myth and folklore in ways that cannot be reduced to causal lines stemming from actual achievements in the order of physical events, just as stories false in their origin can become true shapers of a course of social events, thus acquiring a reality which must be dealt with in its own right and even in the "institutionalized forms" and customs of cultural life, so that "the paths of non-being" become "as difficult as those of being."

The older divisions separated the various orders of knowledge, the "sciences." This division shows how they are united in human experience. We may schematize the relation of knowledge to experience on this basis thus:

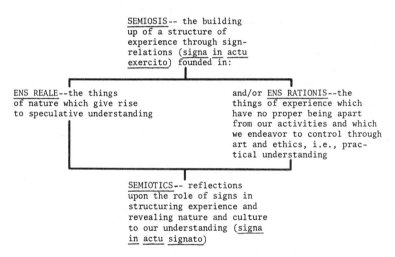

SEMIOSIS-- the building up of a structure of experience through sign-relations (signa in actu exercito) founded in:

ENS REALE--the things of nature which give rise to speculative understanding

and/or ENS RATIONIS--the things of experience which have no proper being apart from our activities and which we endeavor to control through art and ethics, i.e., practical understanding

SEMIOTICS-- reflections upon the role of signs in structuring experience and revealing nature and culture to our understanding (signa in actu signato)

It is with Poinsot, we may say, that the long tradition of Logic and *Philosophia*, winding back over the centuries to ancient Greece and beyond, finally achieves semiotic *in actu exercito*, while with Locke it is achieved *in actu signato*, that is, the *doctrina signorum* first systematized by Poinsot receives from Locke what was destined to become its "logically proper name." From the 17th century onwards, the relation of logic to semiotics is something achieved both in fact and in name, though the achievement will not be recognized for another three hundred years.

Exploratory: Modern Times to the Present

Keeping within our chosen perspective of logical development, what happens between Locke and our own day?

From the point of view of semiotic, just as Poinsot's *Tractatus de signis*, so also Locke's proposal for a new approach to the sciences, falls still-born from the press. If one looks at the posthumous editions of Poinsot's *Ars Logica*, one finds that the editors unmistakably and systematically misunderstand or make nothing of the standpoint of his semiotic, concerning themselves only with reducing it so far as possible to the prejacent perspectives of logical and ontological philosophical analyses, as witnessed 'in Gredt in our own time (discussion in Deely 1983: EA note 94). If one looks in the national language traditions for traces of Locke's influence, indeed one finds it everywhere, but nowhere on the point of semiotic as "another sort of logic and critic than we have been hitherto acquainted with." Indeed, the chapter proposing semiotic is commonly omitted from the many abridged editions of Locke's celebrated work that appear in succeeding centuries. The silence is broken, it would seem, only by Leibniz's superficial criticisms in his *Nouveaux Essais sur l'entendement humain* (composed 1704; published 1765), which Fraser appends in the notes to his classical 1894 edition of Locke's text (p. 463), and for the evaluation of which the best preparation might well be a careful reading of the Aristotelian tract so influential in the 13th and 14th centuries, *De Sophisticis Elenchis*, on the unmasking of spurious arguments. Until of course Peirce's reading of Locke's proposal (cf. Sebeok 1974: 5-10), soon after which the silence is thoroughly shattered![1]

From the point of view of logic too, whether "formal" or "material," as from the point of view of semiotic itself, we encounter from the 17th century an extended period of barrenness, curiously styled "classical" logic,[2] and which is characterized by a diffuse interest centered "much more on rhetorical, psychological, and epistemological problems than on logical ones" (Bochenski 1970: 254) — and, in general, by a drift away from awareness of foundations. As a consequence, if we omit, as (we have seen) has long been the custom of researches in these areas, consideration of the contributions of the Latin Iberian mainstream, it can be said that "from the 400 years between the middle of the fifteenth and the middle of the nineteenth century we have," as the Kneales (1962: 298) put it, "scores of textbooks but very few works that contain anything at once new and good." Bochenski (1970: 9) speaks just as harshly of "the utterly barren period" stretching from Descartes to the mid-nineteenth century, when the new development of formal logic begins. Typical of and early in this decadent phase was the famous *La Logique ou l'Art de Penser*, the so-called *Port Royal Logic*, of Arnauld and Nicole (1662).

Barren as this period seems to have been respecting the problematic of formal logic, if we recall the more integral problematic adumbrated by the entire organon, it should be noted that this period at least stands out in the work of thinkers who sought to flesh out in the context of experimental science our understanding of *induction*. This general process whereby the mind forms from its commerce with sensible nature *ideas* about how that nature works had of course been recognized and set in contrast to the syllogism (deductive reasoning) from the earliest times, and indeed by Aristotle.[3] That there is such a process is evident from the fact that we are not born with a predetermined set of notions about the world, but develop our concepts first from experience.[4] As a late modern author summarized (Maritain 1923: 272), ''there must indeed be two distinct kinds of inference, one of which will lead or introduce us to the knowledge of universal things starting from singular facts of experience, and the other which will lead us from previously formed universal propositions to other propositions on the same universal plane,'' that is to say, one process by which we first reach our ideas,[5] and another by which we are able to elaborate those ideas once acquired.

It is also true that the Greek and Latin periods of logic developed primarily in terms of the understanding of deductive reasoning, so that inductive reasoning, though known, was underdeveloped in these traditions, and indeed, with a few exceptions (notably Albertus Magnus, e.g., 1250-1264: II, tract. 7, ch. 4; 1264-1270: I, tract. 3, ch. 4), neglected. Thus the way was prepared in early modern times for an emphasis on inductive reasoning to appear as something almost entirely new, ''ignorantly or perversely rejected by our forefathers in favour of the deductive reasoning, which they associated with the name of Aristotle, and now held to be in comparison an idle thing,'' as Joseph described the situation (1916: 394).[6]

This was precisely the situation Bacon sought to cultivate and exploit with his *New Organon* (1620) and *De Dignitate et Augmentis Scientiarum* (1623), not altogether fairly from the standpoint of an integral familiarity with the ''old'' *Organon* of Aristotle, it is certain (Joseph 1916:

391-392; Maritain 1923: 282-283), but with a virtually complete success from the standpoint of sociology of knowledge. In the process, as we will shortly see, the interrelation of certain essential structures of the mind's working were lost from view, structures which had none-theless been clearly labelled and recognized, even if not thoroughly utilized or analyzed, in the older Latin tradi-tions. In the modern period, following in the line of Bacon (and not helped in this particular by the influential ''lack of subtlety on Hume's part'' concerning the nature of necessities outside of thought, as Wallace remarks [1980: 127]), induction, conceived simply as the ascent from particular facts to general conceptions, laws, or principles, came to be the subject of studies going far beyond anything to be found in the earlier periods, but with the curious result that, instead of bringing about a progressive clarification of our understanding of the mat-ter, induction became ''one of the most confusing terms in Logic'' (Joseph 1916: 395). The mid-19th century brought in many respects the climax of this modern development, in the works particularly of Herschel (1831), Whewell (1837, 1840), Lotze (1843, translated into English 1884), and Mill (1843). Of Mill's *System of Logic* Joseph writes (1916: 395):

> To that more than to any other work is to be traced the prevalence of the opinion, that inductive reasoning, or Induc-tive Logic as the theory of it, is a discovery of the moderns — an opinion which certainly contains less truth than falsehood. The name induction may be said with him to have stood for more than a particular form of inference; it was the battle-cry of a philosophical school, the school, as it is called, of experi-ence. But as a result of this, and of its previous history, it has become one of the most confusing terms in Logic.

Knowing apparently nothing of Peirce, Joseph sum-marized the results of the post-Baconian studies of induc-tion thus (p. 397):

> We incline to think of Deduction and Induction as processes

moving between the same points, but in opposite directions; Deduction, we think, argues from general principles to particular facts, Induction from particular facts to general principles. Even if this were true, such a statement tells us nothing of the difference in the nature of the reasoning between the two cases; and in point of fact, though there are arguments of those two kinds, the distinction is by no means the most important that can be drawn, does not coincide with the distinction between the arguments traditionally assigned to Deductive and Inductive Logic respectively, and leaves out some of the operations of reasoning that best deserve to be called scientific.

In terms of the clarifications in principle that such a situation cries out for, it would seem that the most fertile development for semiotics in this area of logic comes with the re-discovery by C. S. Peirce around 1866 that the notion of induction is heterogeneous, comprising not one but two distinct species of movement: the movement of the mind whereby we form an hypothesis on the basis of sensory experience, which Peirce called *abduction* (sometimes "hypothesis," also "retroduction"), and the movement back whereby we confirm or infirm our hypothesis with reference to the sensory, for which movement Peirce retained the name *induction*. Fisch (1980: 11) writes as follows:

> The extreme diversification of Peirce's work had a focus and a purpose. The focus was in logic, conceived at first as a branch of a branch of semiotics, but eventually as nearly coextensive with it, though with a distribution of emphasis different from those of semioticians who are not logicians. The purpose was to distinguish the possible kinds of semioses or sign-functions, and, among them, to make the most thorough study he could of arguments in particular, and above all of their functions in mathematics and in the sciences. His major single discovery was that what he at first called *hypothesis* and later *abduction* or *retroduction* is a distinct kind of argument, different both from deduction and from induction, and indispensable both in mathematics and in the sciences. This discovery came at least as early as 1866 . . . .

I call this a re-discovery, because it seems to be a

fruitful elaboration of the distinction commonly taught in
the summulist tradition under the heading of induction,
between *ascensus* ("abduction") and *descensus* ("induction"). For example, Poinsot, 1631:

> *Liber Tertius Summularum*, cap. 2: . . . St. Thomas [c. 1269-
> 1272a: Book I, lect. 30] posits but two ways of acquiring scien-
> tific knowledge, to wit, demonstration [deduction] and induc-
> tion. Demonstration indeed is a syllogism, which proceeds
> through universals; whereas induction proceeds in terms of
> singulars, by the fact that all of our knowledge originates from
> the particulars perceived by sense.
>
> Induction accordingly is defined as "a movement from
> sufficiently enumerated particulars to a universal"; as if you
> were to say: "This fire heats, and that one, and that one, etc.
> Therefore all fire heats." And since opposites have a common
> rationale, under this definition of induction, which is in terms
> of ascent, its opposite is understood, namely, descent, that is to
> say, the movement from universals to singulars. And induc-
> tion, as regards *ascent*, is ordered to the discovery and proof of
> universal truths as they are universals, that is, insofar as they
> correspond with the particulars contained under them. For it
> cannot be shown that anything is the case universally except
> from the fact that its particular instances are such. *Descent* from
> a universal to particulars, on the other hand, is principally
> ordered to showing the falsity of a universal as such. For the
> falsity of a universal is best established by showing that some-
> thing that falls under it is not the case. At the same time, sup-
> posing the truth of a universal established and discovered
> through ascent [abduction], descent [induction] also serves to
> show the correspondence of the universal to those singulars
> contained under it.
>
> *Liber Tertius Summularum*, cap. 3: "On the Manner and
> Means of Resolving Terms by Ascent and Descent."

In this way of understanding the matter, a simplistic
"contrast of opposite directions in the reasoning process
between the same two points" (cf. Eco 1976: 131-133) is
replaced rather by the phenomenological contrast between thought in its interaction with the realm of material
things outside itself, on the one hand, which interaction
moreover is of a twofold character, and thought consid-

ered in its internal development according to the relations which are proper to its own realm.[7] Thus we have the three irreducibly distinct movements recognized in common by Peirce and some among the older Latin authors grounded in the integral treatment of the *Organon*:

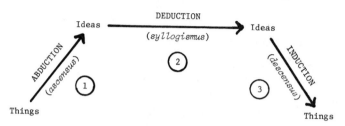

The reversal of terminology here — reserving the traditional term "induction" for the phase of the process least commonly but properly associated with it in tradition, while substituting the new term "abduction" in place of the erroneously univocal common use of the term "induction" for the ascent wherein the mind unifies experiences through the formation of representative notions — has considerable pedagogical merit. In conceptualizing the matter thus, Peirce characteristically transcends his modern contemporaries in the direction of a different and more profound understanding of the foundations and origin of thought in experience, that is to say, in the direction of semiotic. But, equally characteristically, coming late in the modern development, it is not with him a question of any simple *return* to a prior understanding. With Peirce what is always at stake is a creative development of the basic problems. From this point of view, he considers (1902: in CP 2.98), "the division of all inference into Abduction, Deduction, and Induction may almost be said to be the Key of Logic," explaining (*ibid.*: 2.96):

> An Abduction is Originary in respect to being the only kind of argument which starts a new idea. A Transuasive Argument, or *Induction*, is an argument which sets out from a hypothesis, resulting from a previous Abduction, and from virtual predic-

tions, drawn by Deduction, of the results of possible experiments, and having performed the experiments, concludes that the hypothesis is true in the measure in which those predictions are verified, this conclusion, however, being held subject to probable modification to suit future experiments.

The creative development of basic problems in philosophy, however, always has the result in principle of making possible a better integration of the *whole* history of thought. Thus, we are far removed here from the superficial contemporary contrast (e.g., Copi 1982: 389; Halverson 1976: 31) between arguments whose conclusions are necessarily true (deductive arguments) and arguments whose conclusions are only probably true (inductive arguments). The old notion of material logic may have gone out of fashion for good reasons, but that hardly justifies us in making light of or glossing over the fact that an argument can be deductive in form and hence necessary in its conclusion while being at the same time only probable in its truth by reason of uncertainties bearing on the matter or content of the premises. It is glib superficiality to contrast deductive to inductive arguments as arguments with necessary conclusions to arguments with probable conclusions, since conclusions can be necessary in point of form and still remain only probable in point of matter. What is required rather is an answer to Joseph's question of the difference in the *nature of the reasoning* in the two cases,[8] and when this is given (e.g., Maritain 1923: 206-213, 258-287, one of the few modern authors, and perhaps the only one of genius, to be steeped — if anything, overly so — in a philosophical awareness of the Latin past), it becomes clear that the *reason for probability* in the conclusion of *any* argument is always *the same*, namely, a material deficiency.[9] It is not probability and necessity that fundamentally contrast induction and deduction, therefore (*pace* Cohen and Nagel 1934: 278-279[10]), but rather the very nature of the mind's movement as proceeding in terms of the connection between propositions or concepts as such (deduction) or in terms of the connection between propositions or concepts as representing sensible data under a determinate form of unity (induction, whether ascending or descending).

In the line of formal logic itself, the middle of the 19th century also brought a more or less sudden awakening with the pioneer work of George Boole, *The Mathematical Analysis of Logic*, published in 1847, the same year as De Morgan's *Formal Logic*. From that time to the present, in several different directions (Jevons 1864; Schröder 1877, 1891-1895; Frege 1879; Peano 1889; Hilbert 1905; Whitehead-Russell 1910-1913; Carnap 1934; and many others), of "formal logic" we might say that if the Aristotelians of the Latin period developed a formal logic, then the development over this period (in which Frege plays a privileged role — some, e.g., Quine 1952, Dummet 1967, Sluga 1980, etc., would say rather the *founding* role — through the introduction of the quantifier-variable notation for expressing generality) must be called formal with a vengeance!

Leibniz (1646-1716) envisioned the possibility of a logical language so perfect that merely by mechanical manipulation it would be capable of traversing all the possibilities of human knowledge (see entry for Leibniz in References). He dreamed indeed of a kind of religious order that, by this logistic method, would resolve the theological disputes which had plunged Europe of his day into unending sectarian warfare![11]

Russell's theory of descriptions in our own day (1905, 1910, 1919), or Carnap's work on a logical language (1934), is not so different. What happens in logic to inspire such dreams in periods otherwise so diverse?

I think basically two things, one fundamentally erroneous, the other ingenious and of considerable technical merit, but both of which have the effect of divorcing logic from concerns of common life or substantive use in philosophy, and reducing it to a sub-species of semiotics far removed from the foundations of a doctrine of signs.

The first and chimerical notion is that mathematics is essentially continuous with logic, such that the one is a part of the other. In the most extreme form owing especially to Frege, the contention was that all mathematical terms can be defined by logical terms, and all mathematical theorems can be deduced from logical axioms. Russell and Whitehead set themselves to demonstrate this thesis in their *Principia Mathematica* and failed. Indeed, that the thesis in question is not only difficult to establish, but false and therefore impossible to establish, came to be the accepted view.

The other notion, which has merit on its own terms if pursued for what it is, is that the understanding of purely logical relations might in some respects be advanced if the semiotic web of natural language were abandoned, and in its place were substituted an artificial symbolic system totally controlled by stipulations. The pure forms of inner consistency within such a system of axioms and stipulated markers can then be explored with a thoroughness and rigor that proves impossible in the complex historical system of actual language. Moreover, within such a construct, the use of methods of calculation becomes possible to such a degree that this latest phase of formal logic is commonly called "mathematical," a designation which has not advanced clarity in the understanding of what is fundamentally involved in the study of inner consistency when an artificial symbolic system is substituted for one that is capable of performing the actual task of sustaining a socio-cultural system in its manifold relations to the extra-linguistic realities which surround and penetrate human life. Nonetheless, what is revolutionary about contemporary logic is not the aspect of calculus; on the contrary, the aspect of calculus is itself entirely dependent upon, becomes possible only in function of, the fundamental innovation that, as Bochenski puts it (1970: 412), in contrast to all the previous forms of logical development, the so-called "symbolic" or "mathematical" logic:

> proceeds *constructively*, i.e., by investigating logical laws in an artificial language that it has devised. Such artificial languages exhibit very simple syntactical and semantic relations, as compared with natural languages, with the result that formal logic has undergone a change very like that effected by Galileo in the domain of physics. Instead of the immediate, but complex facts, the simpler underlying connections can now be investigated.

All the earlier varieties of logic, notably the Latin summulist traditions in Iberia and elsewhere between 1350 and 1650, this same author notes (p. 266):

> make use of an *abstractive* method; the logical theorems are gained by abstraction from ordinary language. Mathematical logicians proceed in just the opposite way, *first constructing* purely formal systems, and later looking for an interpretation in every-day speech.

The constant and deliberate increase in formalism, i.e., use of a calculus as the general principle of logical method in the late modern period, especially after Frege, becomes possible precisely and only because, as in mathematics, "the *shape* and not the *sense* of the symbols" (Bochenski 1970: 266) is the matter of the rules of operation. Where a natural language is concerned, resort to formalism is possible only within the limits imposed by the *sense* of what is being formalized: hence the importance of the discussion of *suppositio* among the scholastic logicians, which cannot be directly compared with the use of quantifiers in symbolic logic, let alone be dispensed with in favor of them, as some contemporary logicians think (e.g., Kneale and Kneale 1962: 511; Geach 1968: esp. chs. 3-5). The reason for this is straightforward, as can be gleaned from the following remark of Copi 1982: 380, substituting the expression "natural language" where he uses the expression "English":

> One cannot translate from a natural language into our logical
> notation by following any formal or mechanical rules. In every
> case one must understand the meaning of the sentence in the
> natural language, and then symbolize that meaning in terms of
> propositional functions and quantifiers.

But it is precisely the understanding of sentences in a natural language that the doctrine of *suppositio* is designed to
express.[12] Hence it deals with a concern that is presupposed
as settled whenever quantification is employed.[13] Since
they do different jobs, the one cannot be replaced by the
other. Hence also the fact that while formalism has
already been employed and highly developed "in scholasticism especially," it could never there receive "such
thorough-going application" as to become the general
principle of method it becomes in 'mathematical' logic
(cf. Bochenski 1970: 266, 412).

   In the early stages of this development, as by a rem-
nant today (e.g., Geach 1968, 1972), it was commonly
held that there was an opposition and competition between the "old" "Aristotelian" logic and the "new,"
"true" logic. Of course, the mere fact that no scientific
history of formal logic existed at the time, and that a few
centuries had intervened between the "new" logic and
any tradition that could seriously and substantively be
called Aristotelian, did not at first interfere with anyone's
enthusiasm, least of all Bertrand Russell's. "No wonder
then," comments Bochenski (1970: 9), "that with the rise
of mathematical logic theorems belonging to the elementary wealth of past epochs were saddled with the names
of De Morgan, Peirce, and others."[14]

   As sanity and sobriety began to prevail, thanks to the
more profound inquirers in the new area such as Peirce,
Lukasiewicz, and most recently Bochenski, it became
possible to see that even the logic of the *Principia* can more
profitably be viewed as an outgrowth and a development
and in one very precise sense the perfection of the formal
problematic of the *Analytica Priora*,[15] because now the

entire philosophical-epistemological baggage of "material logic" has been, through the simple expedient of purely artificial language, effectively jettisoned in favor of a study of the inner consistency of symbolic forms purely and entirely for its own sake, divorced from any check of further concerns. In this sense there is a continuity, it is possible to argue, between mathematical logic and the problematic of the prior analytics, if that problematic is first isolated within the *Organon* and then pursued entirely for its own sake — no longer for the purpose of an *ars seu logica utens*, but solely for the purpose of developing a "science" in its own right, the science of necessary relations so far as they can be traced to the control and stipulations of men. Viewed in this light, "mathematical" logic does indeed appear as an outgrowth, development, and perfection of the constant tradition of formal logic, so that, as Bochenski says (1970: 413), "there can be no doubt that in this period formal logic once more attained one of its peaks of development," or that "by using the formalized languages of symbolic logic as a means of representation," as Menne remarks (1962: VIII), "classical and traditional theory can be made more precise logistically and its consequences more easily examined" — although (Bochenski 1970: 22) at "appreciable risk of misunderstanding," not only because such is present "in every case of translation," but particularly because it is a question of translation into "a terminology with so narrowly defined a sense as that of mathematical logic."

From the point of view of semiotic, however, "perihermenias" in that full sense of the interpretive activity coextensive with cognitive life,[16] mathematical logic appears only as a most restricted form of interpretation, far more restricted even than the too narrow tradition of Aristotelian commentary on the *De Interpretatione* criticized so effectively by Poinsot (see pp. 59-60 above) for leaving the *foundations* of logical form unexamined.

To appreciate this, recall the division of instrumen-

tal signs into ''ex instituto'' (stipulated) and ''ex consuetudine'' (customary). Applied specifically to the signs of
language, linguistic forms, it is possible to show that both
these aspects are constantly at play in ordinary language
and in fact that it is precisely this interplay that defines
the term ''natural'' as it functions in the expression ''natural language'' (cf. Deely 1978a). The habit structures of
a population, the experiences of a people; the fact that
when I communicate with you using words of a common
language, those words yet have resonances in your mind
that they don't have in mine, and conversely; the fact that
there are riches of connections in the linguistic traditions
of the English language or of the Nahuatl tongue or of the
Eskimo tongues, sign relationships that are carried there
embodying a collective history of the peoples and specific
populations: when you substitute the element of *ex instituto*
so far as possible for all elements of custom, when you cut
off what is arbitrary from all that has become naturalized
in a language, all that is exactly what drops out — history, experience, the past of a people. These are the very
elements that, by their presence and incremental growth,
gradually pressured thinkers of the renaissance in the summulist tradition who strove constantly to take account of
them — instead of devising ways to anesthetize and am-
putate them — in the direction of an ever richer understanding of signification culminating eventually, in a privileged instance, with a grasp of the foundations of logical
interpretation in semiosis, with all that that implies for
the theories of knowledge and truth (Deely 1974: 856-857).

  With the dominant contemporary logic, the pres-
sures on the movement of thought tend in precisely the
opposite direction. In the context of natural language, the
understanding of logical interpretation tends to broaden
beyond the confines of what can be stipulatively controlled. Ultimately, following out this tendency leads
from within logic itself to a foundational doctrine of signs,
both philosophically and historically. In the context of

an artificially stipulated symbolic system, the understanding of logical interpretation tends rather to narrow itself
precisely to the elements of control, and become a pure
technique, a calculus of consequences more and more
empty of natural substance. In the extreme, this tendency
leads logic itself into a hollow or empty formalism, more
and more technically perfect, as relations of reason build
upon one another constructs ever more intricate and
subtle, but by the same token further and further removed from foundations in reality — what the older logicians used to call "distinctions of reason reasoning" (cf.
Poinsot 1632: 294a1-300b48).

The philosophers of our universities today who have
attached themselves to such a method and see in its exercise the very progress of philosophy, therefore, not sur-
prisingly find themselves without a great deal to say of
general interest for semioticians. Theirs is a technique
which belongs to the field of semiotics, not to the area of
semiotic foundations (Deely 1976: 171-173; 1977; 1978a;
and esp. 1983: I.C.); a technique which is not even by
itself properly logic (Bochenski 1970: 17), and which has
an *ad hoc* rather than properly systematic value (which can
nevertheless be considerable) for the exposition of any
given problem or set of problems in philosophy or anywhere else (Deely 1975a, 1975b: 254-271). Thus:

> For particular logicians, or a particular form [of logic], the use
> of an artificial symbolism is not only possible, but to be desired.
> But then every case requires a *special* symbolism. What we can-
> not do is to create a unique symbolism suitable for all the ideas
> that have been developed in the different varieties of logic
> (Bochenski 1970: 22),

particularly when it is a question of investigating the very
foundations and prior possibility of logical form!

You can see then that the maturation of semiotic im-
poses the conditions of a revolution on contemporary
philosophers. It will, for the first time, exhibit unmistakably the proper and central place of historical experi-

ence in philosophical reflection; secondarily, as a consequence of this if nothing else, it will force an overall re-
evaluation and redistribution of the materials of intellectual history; and it will end the diverting of students away
from questions that properly form the substance of philosophical education.

Of course it may be that, as Heidegger believed
(1947: 119), the logistic and "scientific" philosophers are
so far gone down their by-way that future thought in these
areas will no longer be called philosophy.

Be that as it may, semiotic and semiotics are here to
stay.

SECTION

7

Summation

The relation of logic to semiotics, therefore, is complex, both in itself and historically, depending upon how logic is conceived. In its most proper conception as formal logic, it falls under anthroposemiotics at the linguistic level of exchange. So viewed, it can be further specified according as it is regarded as an interpretive activity, such as it was for the Greeks and Latins, or as a constructive activity first of all, such as it has largely become in contemporary academe. As an interpretive activity, however, it can also be expanded as the self-reflective use of signs in the way suggested by Peirce, Locke, and Poinsot. Pursued in this way, logic becomes the doctrine of signs, coextensive with semiotic itself and synonymous with it. But in this sense it also absorbs the whole of epistemology and traditional philosophy of nature, at least in foundational respects.[1] It is in this sense that the history of logic provides a privileged access to the understanding of semiotic, and a striking proof of Gilson's thesis (1937) that knowledge of history is for the philosopher what laboratory experiment is for the scientist, namely, essential for reliable progress in his or her speculations. The same of course holds for the semiotician, if possible with even greater force.

For semiotic, in becoming thematized consciously, and especially in *ramifying* as it penetrates and reshapes the "traditional" disciplines — art, ethology, architecture, etc.[2] — reveals itself as no work of a single person, but as constituted from the efforts of human thought from the remotest of times, embracing the labors of generations often contrary in fashions and modes of structuring perception and expression, yet gradually being brought together. The method employed in establishing the foundational doctrine should reflect this reality, which demands an open-ended culling of the pertinent intellectual traditions that have developed in whatever linguistic community or age, each application by one leaving to others the further application of results by their own lights and abilities, establishing for future workers landmarks and beacons marking over the ages where and how principal contributions were first adumbrated or secured.

Part II

DOCTRINAL PROSPECTIVES

"One can conceive therefore a science which studies the life of signs at the heart of social life; . . . we shall call it semiology *(from the Greek sēmeîon, 'sign'). It would teach us what signs consist of and what laws govern them. Since it does not yet exist, one cannot say what form it will take; but it has a right to existence, its place is marked out in advance. Linguistics is only a part of this general Study. The laws that semiology will discover will be applicable to linguistics, which will thus find itself assigned to a well-defined area within the totality of human phenomena."*

—SAUSSURE 1916: 33—

1

Language

"*Semiotic inquiry cannot, and should not, be reduced to a mathematics, nor can it be easily made to conform to the quasi-rigor of linguistics. . . . semiotics is as much a perspective for critical inquiry as it is a methodology. In this sense semiotics does indeed serve as a framework for examining our universe and the way we understand it. By approaching our investigations from a common point of departure, by examining our world from a shared perspective, we should find that we are after all much closer to one another than we had thought.*"

—Peters 1978: 159—

Much has been made since the turn of the century of a distinction between "natural" and "artificial" languages, the former being equated usually with something called "ordinary" language, the latter with interpreted (already specified as to their reality-reference) formal systems put forward as improvements upon and substitutes for the varieties of ordinary discourse, either *toto coelo* or in specific contexts alone. In advancing the distinction thus, the whole emphasis and interest has been on the "artificial" side of the proferred dichotomy, as representing an "improvement upon" and "remedy for" the alleged "defects" of "ordinary" or "natural" language, notably, context-dependence, ambiguities, equivocations, and endless sub-species of inexplicitness.

Discussions of philosophers of recent years have largely focussed on making a case "for" or "against" the use of artificial languages (cf. Caton 1967), while the clarification of the foundational distinction itself has never been undertaken.

The root of the problem lies in the notion itself of "natural language," which is used throughout these discussions as a mere *terminus a quo relictus* or jumping off point, after the manner of an unanalyzed but intuitively transparent constant — as if it were enough to say (Caton 1967: 168) that by natural language we mean "English, French, and so on" (or "Tagalog, Guarani, and so on"), thence proceeding directly to discussion of the merits and drawbacks of proposed "artificial," i.e., completely controlled, symbolic systems. One way to underscore the problem with the approach which has dominated philosophical discussions of language at least since 1905 (the year of publication of Russell's theory of descriptions under the title "On Denoting"), but already called for expressly by Frege in 1892 (if not earlier: preliminary discussion in Deely 1975b), is to point out the inadequacy of the identification of a mythical "ordinary" language which is distinct from technical vocabularies and wholly artificial systems alike, and is supposedly one with the (in fact) much broader notion of "natural" language.

To best appreciate what is at stake here, it is helpful to turn away from recent and current philosophical discussions, to look, for example, at the more semiotically fruitful researches of linguistics, particularly of Roman Jakobson (c. 1928-present), which have shown how *mutability*, in a *very specific* way, is an organizing principle of natural language (Waugh 1976: 20):

> Change is both a synchronic and diachronic fact. A given synchronic state, then, will always have the remains of past changes and the beginnings of future changes built into its

structure. And, in fact, it is the built-in potential for change without collapsing which differentiates language from other [especially mechanical] systems. The time axis is part and parcel of the system.

This dynamic essence of natural language, which underlies its potential for creativity, is precisely what the recourse to artificial languages in philosophy excises. So-called "ordinary language," in contrast to technical vocabularies and artificial systems alike, is a synchronic abstraction from this same dynamic essence. For what is "ordinary" is decidedly relative to and completely determined by the popular culture and consciousness of specific groups within the human population, a given structure that is the product of past changes viewed apart from that past and apart too from the future changes it harbors within itself as only inadequately distinct from special vocabularies and experiences and constantly modified by them (cf. Marcus 1979: 35-36). In short, every "ordinary language" or whole thereof is a sociological subspecies abstracted within a natural language, which itself is the more extensive web constituting a linguistic community as a specific semiotic carrier of historically structured experiences, and constituting it in its totality of users both diachronically and synchronically.

Thus there are, from a semiotic point of view, at least two decisive features of natural language in particular that are left out of account by the recent partisans in philosophy of "ordinary" and artificial languages alike.

The first and most important is its *transcendence of stipulative controls* by those who make use of its communicative possibilities. A natural language links the individual user to an entire population of previous speakers and, imperfectly, to the particular ways in which they have experienced the world in terms of idiosyncratic as well as specific needs, interests, and concerns — i.e., as an objective network supraordinate to and differently divided from the merely physical environment in its mind-independent being. It carries an entire tradition of perceptions and orientations distinguishing a people, even at intersections of enculturated social life, modifying this tradition in the present and extending it into the future through the individuality of its users who are cybernetically, as it were, both constituted by and constitutive of the linguistic and cultural tradition they express, in a kind of circular feedback relationship. Artificial languages, by contrast, reduce such linguistic and cultural tradition down to the state or ''size'' of a purely current understanding, suppressing or making ''invisible'' the questions of how this understanding was achieved and what it fails to bring into account (its *filtered* and *perspectival* qualities), if they are deployed without critical attention to their proper ground. Thus, while a natural language is expansive, an artificial language is restrictive and tends to close down the understanding of its users upon those elements that can be perfectly controlled — a kind of triumph of safety over life.

The second feature of natural language glossed over by current speculations is its *linkage with non-linguistic and non-conceptual communicative channels*, both zoö- and phyto-semiotic, in establishing concretely the interaction possibilities linked to communication within and for a group. Thus, for example, when linguistic means are employed in the training of and communication with unquestionably non-linguistic life forms, this is possible only because and insofar as the linguistic means themselves extend to and are bound up with pre- and praeter-linguistic semiotic components, which have a virtual autonomy of function even within the properly linguistic system (Deely 1980b; Sebeok 1977, 1979a, 1981a, *et alibi*). This feature of natural language, generically dismissed as its ''open texture'' or ''context dependence,'' to be ''remedied'' and ''cured'' (i.e., eliminated) by recourse to artificial systems, is in fact of the very essence of natural language as the means whereby a population and community constitutes itself within the physical world semiotically as able to establish and function within its particular "lifeworld." It can be seen thus that the natural languages extend, "irrigate," and totalize in public consciousness the pre- and non-linguistic communicative channels essential to existence in the physical and social environments, and provide the immediate networks constantly presupposed and required by the more limited efforts to *take full control* of symbolic systems evidenced *ultimate et non ultimate* by technical vocabularies and artificial formalized systems.

Natural language is the fundamental semiotic phenomenon of human life, at once distinguishing it within the biological community and establishing the possibility and context for more limited, strictly controlled symbolic systems which serve to clarify and systematize (always presupposing a mosaic natural language context) particular theories and areas of cognitive concern. But such systems can be viewed as *supplanting* (actually or potentially) natural language whole and entire only on the basis of a profound ignoral — as I think it should be called — of the ways signifying animals achieve their higher states of cognitive organization in the first place through the spinning of webs rooted semiotically in lines of communication that go beyond language proper into the realms of phyto- and zoosemiotics.

In this regard, the linguists, too, inasmuch as they try to insist upon their object of study as a "fully autonomous system," are making the same mistake (in a far less exaggerated form, however) of "overstipulationism" that in our time has ruined the would-be "philosophy of language" in British and American circles, both "ordinary" and "logical" — the "English speaking world" of World War times to the present.[1] For the linguistic system ultimately depends in its functioning on channels of communication with what is not linguistic, just as the controlled artificialities of language are possible and have point only insofar as they have channels of contact with symbolic elements that are, by contrast, "natural." In all these ways, we may expect the notion of "natural language," as something yet to be adequately explored within semiotic (or any other) perspectives, to become increasingly a focus of research and analysis in coming decades as we seek to understand the mysterious communion and compenetration of nature with culture that transpires in anthroposemiosis. For language in this basic manifestation (Wilden 1981: 10) "is neither a copy of reality, nor a misrepresentation of reality; it is part of human reality." What has up to now merely been labelled in order to contrast it with supposedly more interesting and important but in fact impoverished and strictly derivative phenomena of cognitive concern will assume its rightful place as the center and focus of the richest, most heterogeneous form of semiosis on our planet, namely, anthroposemiosis.

2

Knowledge

"For the first stirring of the idea [of the understanding] as distinct from [ideas in the sense of perceptual and sensory] images, the intervention of a sensible sign is necessary. Normally in the development of a child it is necessary that the idea be 'enacted' by the senses and lived through before it is born as an idea; it is necessary that the relationship of signification should first be actively exercised in a gesture, a cry, in a sensory sign bound up with the desire that is to be expressed. Knowing this relationship of signification will come later, and this will be to have the idea [or understanding], even if it is merely implicit, of that which is signified. Animals and children make use of this signification; they do not perceive it. When the child begins to perceive it (then the child exploits it, toys with it, even in the absence of the real need to which it corresponds) — at that moment the idea has emerged."

—Maritain 1957: 88—

Most of what offers itself today as "philosophy of knowledge" would be more accurately designated a study of the conditions under which affirmations and negations are justified or verified. Yet knowledge in the sense of judgments (however important and valid, particularly in technical and scientific contexts, such as preoccupy modern society in its drive for domination over natural forms) is a derivative phenomenon, a specification or determination at one level of the more basic, perhaps the basic, phenomenon of semiosis, namely, *awareness*, or, as it is more traditionally called, "cognition." Cognition, knowing in this widest sense of the term, as including all processes of awareness by which experience is built up, is the term used to designate those aspects or elements of experience which are distinguished from the observable tendencies of entities to locate, move, or interact in whatever ways, both independently of cognition (natural appetite) and dependently upon it (elicited appetite: feeling, desire, will). As such, cognition not only can be considered from a semiotic point of view, but must be so considered if we are to arrive at an adequate understanding of what is proper to it, inasmuch as it is equivalent to a process of communication by signs, or semiosis.[1]

To see how cognition is equivalent to a process of communication by signs, or semiosis, it is necessary to consider how the function of signification is realized at the various levels of cognitive life.

The first or lowest level of cognitive life is considered to be sensation, the grade of cognition wherein an organism achieves initial *awareness* of features or aspects of its surrounding environment under the direct stimulus of those features upon its sensory receptors. These stimuli are transformed into *impressions* by the response of the sense organ, which is *cognitive* insofar as the organism responds to the stimuli not merely by undergoing some mutation at the point of contact, but by attaining an *alertness* over and above such physical mutation wherein the organism begins to orientate itself *mediately* relative to the stimulating environment through the impression (or "datum") according to its subjective appetites (needs and desires). Thus cognition is described as an *immanent* activity, i.e., as an activity superordinate to the transitive activity or physical interaction which directly produces mutation of alteration in the body stimulated or acted upon. The cognitive response, in other words, always involves a *triadic* character, as opposed to the dyadic nature of purely physical (transient or transitive) interaction, and it is this characteristic of *thirdness* that marks the beginnings of *semiosis*, the structuring of experience by means of signs that sets cognitive levels of organization (biosemiosis) apart from the so-called *endosemiotic* levels of "information exchange" that precede and prepare for the appearance of cognitive life properly so called.

The element of thirdness at the level of sense cognition requires very careful analysis if the proper workings of signs at this level are not to be misconstrued. This is all the more difficult, as the level of purely sensory awareness can only be attained by us *analytically* rather than *experientially* in any direct way, and though purely sensory consciousness most certainly seems to exist at the lower boundaries of animal life, and though sensation as a distinguishable aspect of awareness most certainly exists at the base and core of the perceptual awareness of the higher animals including ourselves, there is no way we have access to this level in an actually separated state. Laboratory attempts to isolate the condition of sensory awareness as such in humans, indeed, have to proceed in a negative way, isolating the input of the higher levels of cognitive organization by *sensory deprivation*.

Pre-semiotic attempts to analyze sensation philosophically have almost universally assumed with the modern philosophers (Descartes, Locke, Hume) concerned with these questions that the sense impressions or "data" are little images formed within the organism and are what constitutes the *direct object* of which the organism achieves awareness. A more careful analysis of the role of *representations* in semiosis, however, suggests that this all but universal assumption is entirely gratuitous, and should never have been made in the first place. Representative forms or *icons* in consciousness (ideas and images: see Deely 1980b) must be posited to account for the higher levels of cognitive organization, as we shall see, but the reasons for this positing, namely, to proportion the subjectivity of the knower to the level of objective organization apprehended in the surrounding environment and to account for the presence in cognition of objective elements not given as such in the immediate sensory environment, are in no way operative at the level of sensory response as such, since the external senses respond directly to objects (or rather, environmental features and elements) physically present here and now, and to these precisely and only as they directly act upon and physically stimulate the organs or channels of sensation (the "exteroceptors").

Thus the "data" or "impressions" of external sense, semiotically, should be regarded neither as intrinsic properties of physical things nor as mere modifications of the subjective faculties ("effects" wholly within the cognitive organism), but precisely as features or properties exhibiting how things are *in their action here and now* on an organism possessed of this determinate range of sensitivities, i.e., as "properties" neither of "things in themselves" nor of "knowers of their subjectivity," but of the situation of interaction as co-determined by the structure of the stimulating source on the one side and of the receiving organs and organism on the other side. This third alternative accounts for the experimentally demonstrated relativity of sensory qualities without making of them mere constructs of subjectivity — while preserving, that is to say, their status as here and now revelatory of "the way things are" but only so far as involves the experiencing organism. The initial contact between cognizing organism as such and environment, on this view, cannot be analyzed under the heading of "subjective" or "objective," since it is *indistinctly both* and prior to the applicability of any such dichotomy. In sensation, that is to say, in the origin of cognitive life, the cognition that arises within the organism is coordinated and continuous with the physical impingements of surroundings on the organism.

The world *appears* thus and thus (e.g., colored, textured, resonant thus and so) only to a subject, but it really *is* that way modally *given this totality of conditions*. A pre-modern formula of the Latin philosophers, taken over from Aristotle's Greek, captures the semiotic situation at this level far better than the unwarrantably subjectivist dreamings of the moderns concerning primitive cognition: "sensatio est actus sensibilis in sensu" ("sensation is precisely the action of the sensible upon the sense").

The element of thirdness comes in from the fact that, while each channel of external sense, each "exteroceptor," in and of itself is directly proportioned to reveal immediately (dyadically) some one aspect or feature of the immediate environment — e.g., color through the channel of sight, sound through the channel of hearing, flavor by the channel of taste, etc.) — called its *formal or proper object* (also *proper sensible*) in philosophical tradition, *simultaneously*, given *with and by* that unique or proper feature of the environing situation, *other* features of the situation (called *common sensibles* in philosophical tradition), such as shape, movement, position, are brought into the organism's awareness as well. Thus, the features of the interaction environment made known uniquely through any specific sensory channel bring along with themselves into awareness other features which are not uniquely attained by any one channel but overlap with and are attained in common by several channels — simultaneously with the unique features, although dependently upon them. Here therefore we have already the type of relationship constitutive of signification, at the very first moments of cognitive awakening. The initial sensory "data" are not "atomic" in character ("this blue here and now," "this noise here and now," etc.) but strictly semiotic; and the initial synthesis of sensations formed within cognition is neither arbitrary nor subjectively controlled, but *naturally determined* by semiotic means, as described above. Since a sign is anything functioning to bring something other than itself into an organism's awareness, and since colors, sounds, textures, etc., immediately bring along with themselves an awareness of plurality, positions, shapes, movements, and so on, one has only to regard sensation semiotically in order to realize that we are already given within it an outline of objective structure that is relative and changing, surely enough, but naturally determined nevertheless. "Sense data," in other words, already comprise an objective structure (not atomic elements logically discrete but habitually combined) that is the same, in the above sense of naturally determined, for all organisms. Species variation, consequently — that is, subjective differences of sensory range, orientation, and variety — are strictly background phenomena at the level of the sensory core; and that is why biological mechanisms of camouflage (such as protective coloration) and deception, though principally dependent on the "qualitative" appearances or "properties" of bodies, are so widespread and consistently useful in nature across species lines (Huxley 1942: 414). Species variation comes to the fore only in the interpretation of the "common" data and in the uses that they are put to in predation and social exchange.

This brings us to the second and higher level of cognitive life, what can be called, for want of a better term, *perception* in contrast to sensation. Impressions of sense, precisely as constituting a network or *web* of semiotic relations centered on the cognitive organism, are passed on through the channels of external sense to the higher levels of cognitive activity — synthesis, imagination, memory, evaluation and estimation (called *internal sense* in philosophical tradition) — as the basis for the organism's apprehending and responding to its surroundings at a higher level than merely as affecting it here and now, namely, at the level of things to be sought and things to be avoided, offspring and enemy, insider and outsider, and the like. Here we arrive at the level of properly objective organization of the physical environment which is to some extent idiosyncratic but overarchingly *species-specific* to each life form, so that the *physical environment* which, insofar as it exists independently of cognition is "the same" for worms and grasshoppers, gophers and spiders, humans and sharks, is *transformed* out of this abstract "sameness" by being *organized objectively*, i.e., as cognized, according to a pattern of relationships that express precisely the needs and desires and interests of the cognizing organism. *This* world, the *objective world*, incorporates the elements of the physical environment according to quite different patterns of interrelationship of its elements, unifying and dividing them diversely according to the interests of the organizing center. Each individual, more precisely, each *specific* individual, creates and spins its own objective world or *Umwelt* (von Uexküll 1926) out of the physical environment that is unified by its typical interests, needs, and desires, so that the divisions of nature in the realm of physical being are quite a different matter from the divisions cognition makes in the realm of objective being.

Here emerges clearly the contrast between perception and sensation, namely, that there supervenes upon the semiotic but naturally determined relations of sensory awareness an active formation and construction from the side of the organism whereby the elements of the physical environment become organized and presented to the organism in ways *other than* the ways they exist physically as stimulating here and now. It is this active construction elevating environmental components to a higher level where they can be evaluated apprehensively as prey or predator, offspring or alien, or where (in the human case) a black shape on the wall can be "seen" as a telephone, which requires the introduction into cognition of *icons* or *representative forms* serving (not at all to terminate cognition objectively but) to *found relations* whereby the superstructure of objectivity is erected on the foundations of sensations rooted in the physical world. These "ideas" or "images," then, are not *known as objects* but are emphatically *unknown*, being only the foundations and basis in subjectivity proportioning the organism's relation to the objective world. This world, as *Umwelt*, is strictly *suprasubjective* respecting the individual and *transsubjective* respecting the species, being precisely, as *Umwelt*, a *common world* for members of the species, invisible as such (being in its proper existence and unity but a network of relations, a *semiotic web*), but comprising perceptible elements and features of the physical environment differentially netted or ignored by the lace of objective relationships cast by the interests and needs (the "subjectivity" in the broadest sense) of the organisms centering the different webs, the various "objective worlds."

The basic function of ideas or representations thus is not to provide the terminus of cognition, but is rather strictly semiotic, establishing a proportion between what is given in sense versus what is perceived in experience, since "perception" includes elements that are just not given as such at the level of sensory information, and makes known with some indifference to presence or absence of the known in the immediate surroundings.

We have then in sensation just two elements, the cognitive activity and the cognized (which already involves thirdness), while in perception there is the additional element of a thirdness on the side of the very cognizing, in the icon produced to proportion the cognized to the cognition of it:

Activity:	Production:	Cognized:
Sensation		Physical Aspects of Environment Semiotically Structured
Perception	Icons ("Ideas or Images")	Present and Absent Objects Proportioned Semiotically to Subjectivity

In sensation, nothing is produced, and what is known is a really existing thing, not in itself but under some determinate aspect as here and now affecting the organism within its sensory range. At the next level, in perception, we have something produced, and an object cognized which may or may not be a thing but would normally include some aspects of things, so that object is the wider of the two notions here: only a small number of things, and those only under certain aspects, will actually be objectified in any given case; objects conversely, therefore, include elements of "thingness," i.e., of the cognition-independent world, the physical environment, but only as incorporated into the awareness of the organism according to a web spun of needs and desires. Thus the notion of signification must already be introduced in a quite general way to account for the manner of functioning of the representations produced by the cognitive powers superior to external sense.

The "objective world" therefore is a universe quite distinct from, quite other than, yet not without relation to, the physical world, as the earliest systematic semiotic (Poinsot 1632: 678b18-23) had already revealed:

> It can well be the case that something which is not a being is yet an object. For the differences of things in physical nature and being are one matter, differences in the rationale of an object and cognizable entity quite another.

Yet through sensation a permanent connection between the two is inseverably maintained. Since at that level there is no room for an intervening cognitive product, the cognition there does not take place on the basis of any constructed icon; the whole point of cognitive productivity is to establish proportion and supply presence to the object at levels which transcend the here and now. In sensation, the proportion and presence of object to organism are already given. There is nothing to supply.

Together, these two levels of cognitive activity enable the spinning of a *semiotic web*, that is to say, a structure of experience built up through sign relations. How this web functions can be briefly described.

Prior to the advent of cognitive organisms, relations are only physical, that is, obtaining among presently existing entities. Once cognition is introduced, the situation begins to alter drastically. Now the relation of A to B (e.g., of clouds to rain, of smoke to fire, of seed to mature plant, etc.) acquires the possibility of a new, further dimension: A can *represent* B to C, a cognitive organism. What was formerly *only* a physical relation can now become *also* a recognized (a known) relation that makes A, besides being the *cause* of B (or B, besides being the *effect* of A), its *sign*. Nor is this all. Because the relationship as such has its proper being "between" A and B (that is to say, intersubjectively), while it has its reality independent of cognition from the existence of A as, say, cause of B (or from B as effect of A, depending on which relation is considered), it can now exist as "between" A and B at the higher levels of cognition (in memory, say, or in imagination) even after A (or B) has gone out of existence. Essence and existence, in the case of relation, do not go together in a way that ties relation to a unique subjective ground.

This indifference of relation to its subjective cause or ground, indeed, is precisely what opens the way to semiosis: the same relation existing independently of cognition can also exist dependently upon cognition, and can continue to exist in cognition after its physical ground no longer exists. Moreover, relations existing first in cognition can subsequently be introduced into the physical order (e.g., an irrigation system) by bringing about the proper conditions within that order; and relations can be established in cognition that have no counterpart in the physical world, just as there are physical relations that have not yet or may not ever enter into the cognition of an organism.

Physical relations are the paradigm case of "natural'' relations, but cognitive relations too are forms of ''nature,'' and many such are exhibited in the genetically controlled behavior of animal species, particularly insect forms. The important thing for semiotics is simply that these two orders of relations are *functionally equivalent in perception* wherever it is a question of inter- or intra-specific interaction between individual organisms or between organisms and relevant features of the physical surroundings within an *Umwelt*. Comparatively ''real'' and ''unreal'' from the standpoint of what exists independently of cognitive activity as such, physical and cognition-dependent relations (*both* of which are equally objective, be it noted) are strictly on a par from the pragmatic standpoint of what works within experience to satisfy some interest.

This brings us to the third and, on our planet at least, highest level of cognitive organization and life, namely, the level of understanding as distinct from (but arising within) perception. Perception reveals objects as they are only relative to the interests (dispositions, needs, and desires) of the organism perceiving, whereas the further realization that these objects of experience don't entirely reduce to that experience of them — that there is a ''surplus'' in the *Umwelt*, more to objects than their relation to me, something there to be considered in its own right, something *existing* beyond the question of my experience of it and interest in it — is the unique achievement of human understanding. In other words, understanding adds to the perception of an objective world the revelation in these same objects of the further dimension of existence in their own right independent of relations to the knower.

In our direct experience of ''objects,'' the field of awareness is something unified (*Umwelt*), in the sense that the significant elements making it up, whether their signification is genetically determined, purely a product of social interaction, or also reflective of environmental connections that obtain apart from the cognitive process, function in common to reveal to the organism its own interests in the environment. Under this predominating *arche*, the above noted differences among signs and sign-systems are a matter of supreme indifference. What counts is their *functional equivalence* for purposes of enabling the satisfaction of interests. Yet, from an independent standpoint, there remains a profound difference between an element of experience considered in its own right and that same element considered purely objectively as a "thing" accounted for by a perceiver in terms of its own (the perceiver's own) needs and desires.

Precisely the possibility of such an independent consideration is what the understanding adds to the cognitive networks of perception and sense, although it can also forego that proper independence by placing itself at the service of perceptual interests as well. Yet within the interweave and mix in experience of cognition-dependent and cognition-independent relations comprising in its formality the objective world (in counterdistinction to the physical environment, which comprises only cognition-independent relations), only those organisms possessed of the capacity to understand in its distinction from the capacities to sense and perceive, are able on occasion to discriminate among objective elements and structures the "real" (cognition-independent) and "unreal" (cognition-dependent) components. Both are essential, as we have seen, to the constitution of the superstructure of experience, the *Umwelt*; but within experience, what is the contribution of the subject and what is the contribution of the environment to the objective structure of a given interaction situation does not so much as begin to manifest itself prior to the recognition that there is more to the objects experienced than the mere experience of them, a recognition that understanding introduces into the perceptual field as its unique and proper contribution to cognition.

Subsequent investigation of this "more" is what gives rise to natural science and philosophy, inasmuch as this comparative discrimination of cognition-independent elements in the objective structures of experience (and much later, beyond the experimentally given) is what underlies the possibility of a system of signs containing irreducibly stipulated components demonstrably understood as such by the controlled flexibility human beings display in discourse. "Language" indeed in the sense that it is species-specific to *homo sapiens*, is nothing else than the "unreal" component of semiosis[2] expressly segregated and seized upon in its unique signifying potential by the understanding in its distinction from perception and sense, which is thus revealed as a peculiar, unique, and species-specific capacity for thematizing and critically assessing under various circumstances the labile line beween reality and unreality, exhibited in the partially controllable indifference of discourse to what is and what is not the case.

With these remarks, however, we have reached the boundary of cognition theory as such, and begin to skirt on the further concerns of linguistics and the study of culture. Suffice to conclude this side of the boundary by noting that the added perspective understanding brings to perception dramatically transforms from within the merely perceptual *Umwelt,* by introducing the recurrent consciousness of explicit "otherness." Out of such consciousness science and philosophy can arise, as we have remarked; but much more primordially, out of this change in experience *ethics* (morals and mores) arise as a concern within human groups. Drawing on the Latin philosophical tradition which gave to estimation in animals a different name from the conceptually influenced estimations of mankind, despite their involvement through the level of perception of common abilities and cognitive processes, I would suggest that the human *Umwelt* — the intellectualized perceptual environment — should rather be called *Lebenswelt*, the lifeworld of common human concerns within which all specialized pursuits arise. On this usage, just as intellection presupposes perception and rests on sensation as on a "reality core," so the *Lebenswelt* contains virtually within itself the *Umwelt* of animal life and rests ultimately on the incorporation of the immediately surrounding physical environment into an objective network of cognition-dependent (socio-cultural) relations. It is the *Umwelt* which is the adequate object of *zoosemiotic* study, while the expansion into a *Lebenswelt* is the concern of *anthroposemiotics*.

3

Experience

"*Anthroposemiotics, that is, the totality of man's species-specific signaling systems, was the first domain concretely envisaged and delineated under the designation, semiotic. For most investigators, from 1960 to this day, both notions still remain synonymous. The second domain, zoosemiotics, which encompasses the study of animal communication in the broadest sense, was named and comprehensively outlined only in 1963. It would now seem more accurate to consider anthroposemiotics and zoosemiotics, separately and conjointly, as two principal divisions of semiotics, having in common certain essential features but differing especially as to the fundamental and pervasive role that language plays in the former in contradistinction to the latter.*"

—Sebeok 1974: 3—

The emergence of semiotics as the architectonic of communications study as such sheds new light on and calls for a reconceptualization of the very notion of experience and of the relation thereto of language as linguistics in the traditional scientific senses studies it. The reconceptualization called for, it seems to me, needs to take account particularly of the *content presupposed* for the possibility of using language to communicate in the first place, and of the "shaping effect," as Chomsky calls it (1979: 3), of language upon experience, such that a given language *in actu exercito* itself already constitutes a *form of experience* specifically mediative of the totality (*especially* in its primary "modeling" function: see Appendix II below) among those organisms able to deploy and perceive it formally (i.e., to recognize it *as* a sign) and not just materially as an expressive structure mediative in the sense of facilitative of social interaction.

Of course, already in "traditional" perspectives (cf. McLaughlin 1981), the difficulty of defining the term "language" or the term "experience" in a satisfactory way is a celebrated one, a difficulty perhaps as much as any single factor responsible for the currently faddish but philosophically (Deely 1971a, 1975a), methodologically (Umiker-Sebeok and Sebeok 1979, 1980; 1981a, b; Sebeok 1979b, 1981b), and scientifically (Chomsky 1979; Terrace 1981; etc.) unsophisticated claims of animal experimenters to have taught "language" to chimpanzees, etc.

But it is not my purpose here to join directly in the attack on the distortions needlessly introduced into our understanding of semiosis by naiveté and willful confusions. So, to put my cards on the table, as it were, I will confess simply that I agree with those who, like Maritain 1943: 196, 1957: 90, Sebeok 1978: 21, Umiker-Sebeok and Sebeok 1979-1981, and a baker's dozen of others, regard this current fad as "counterproductive and misleading," in order to proceed with minimum ado to a related but different objective, one that is purely constructive and positive and, I think, more fruitful for the long run. I want to propose and suggest in outline a framework or model of *experience itself*, taken as a whole, wherein the function and status of language in relation to behavior and social structure appears in its proper light. It does not seem too much to suggest in this line that even the impossibility so far of achieving a satisfactory definition of "what language is" may well be the result of the failure to appreciate the *proper functional status* of language in the context of individual experience and social behavior, or that the rise of semiotics provides an opportunity to reconceptualize our understanding of the matter in a framework that makes this proper functional status for the first time generally apparent and directly accessible. In other words, I want to go so far as to suggest that the "coming of age" of the doctrine of signs may warrant the repeal by the *Société de Linguistique de Paris* of the famous "deuxième article" of its *Statuts* adopted in 1866: "La Société n'admet aucune communication concernant . . . l'origine du langage . . . ," as being principally (in effect) an admission of the radical inadequacy of presemiotic approaches to the semiotic phenomenon *par excellence*, human discourse.

For example, Chomsky (1979: 34; cf. 1968 *et alibi*) seeks to account entirely within linguistics "for the traditional observation that human language is a system for the infinite use of finite means" (a phenomenon described within anthropology as "the cumulative transmission of culture," and before that within Greek philosophy by the expression, as the Latins rendered it, "anima [humana] est quodammodo omnia"). He nonetheless considers it quite plausible (*ibid.*: 37) "that the study of word meaning . . . concerns other cognitive systems which are connected in part to language" only "through some sort of 'labelling'," not to say linguistic designation or, to go back even farther in ways of describing, "extrinsic denomination." Maritain, by contrast (1957: 89-90), against his "private opinion" as he grants (*ab ipsa veritate coacta*, mayhap), suggests rather that the explanation for the infinite use of finite means by linguistic animals may be given along integrally semiotic rather than distinctively linguistic lines, such that any uncompromising division of content from linguistic form would be a later and decidedly derivative development:

> **The discovery of language, then, coincides with the discovery of signification**, and this would explain why, as a matter of fact, the invention of language and the birth of

ideas, the first release of the intellect's power, probably took place at the same time.

It is conceivable, I think, that a genuine language of *natural* sensory signs may have preceded language strictly so called (made up of conventional sensory signs), and that the latter may have developed out of the former. The 'miracle' would have happened at the moment when man, beyond the fact of using natural gestures to express hunger, anger, or fear, would also have grasped the notion that this gesture was possessed of the virtue of signifying. By the same stroke **a field of infinite possibilities would have opened** [because the contrast between *ens reale* and *ens rationis* in the order of relation *ut actu exercito* would have opened up: see Part I, Section 3 above]. Then, once the relation of signification was discovered, the process of arbitrarily selecting or inventing other gestures and of using them as *conventional* signs no doubt developed quite rapidly.

In such a perspective, integrally semiotic, as I have said, and therefore — witness Maritain's own discomfiture noted above — not (yet) traditional,

> **what defines language is** not precisely the use of words, or even of conventional signs; it is the use of any sign whatsoever *as involving the knowledge or awareness of the relation of signification,* and **therefore a potential infinity**; it is the use of signs *in so far as it manifests that the mind has grasped and brought out the relation of signification.* . . . **the invention of** those particular **conventional signs** which are words, the creation of a system of signs made up of 'phonemes' and 'morphemes' **was** in itself a second 'miracle,' a further discovery of human intelligence, no less characteristic of man, but **less essential** than, **and by nature not prior** to, the discovery of the relation of signification. (Bold face only added.)

The task I set myself and the reader in this section, then, is defined by the possibility of interpreting experience — from the ground up — along integrally semiotic lines, nothing less — with whatever is implied for the perspectives and disciplines currently labeled "traditional." And since each has and is in principle able to judge "experience" as his, her, or its *own*, each one must accept responsibility for the outcome — a kind of grand game of "you be the judge," and the conclusion to our enterprise.

Let us start from one of the first and broadest divisions of semiotics, the division into anthroposemiotics, or sign-systems as they function in a uniquely human context, and zoosemiotics, or sign-systems common to human and non-human animals. I think that language, properly conceived in its relation to and origins within perceptual and sensory experience, is the key to rightly understanding the rationale of this contrast.

To manifest my reason for thinking this, let me introduce two distinctions. First, I want to distinguish zoosemiotic sign systems against the linguistic system that is species-specific and unique to man. Then I want to set *both* of these systems in contrast with what I am going to call *post-linguistic* structures or systems,[1] by which I mean systems that come into existence on the basis of language and can only be understood in what is proper to them on that basis, but are not themselves linguistic; and once they have come into existence, they *re-descend*, so to say, into the purely perceptual to become assimilated in a behavioral way to the society of non-linguistic animals.

Thus, post-linguistic systems are normally simultaneous with language, and even, from the point of view of the individual language-learner, in certain ways *precede* "language"; but they always depend upon language for their *proper* existence, which transcends the modalities of simple perception and zoosemiotic signalling. Post-linguistic structures exist beside, alongside, aside from, language — yet based on and derivative from it. And they *react* upon language (they "shape it," as might be said), by influencing the semiotic exchanges that transpire through language (just as sensation does in pre-linguistic ways). We thereby find in linguistic behavior, as it were, a *twofold non-linguistic inlay* embedded in and influencing semiotic exchange, one from the pre-linguistic order of perception, and one from the *users themselves* of language, as they are products of and have been shaped — even in their eventual perceiving — by a world of *post-linguistic experience*.

Here, the expression, "post-linguistic," must not be separated from the notion of "experience." I mean to say that "experience" can be *either* pre-linguistic or *both* pre- *and* post-linguistic (though not post-linguistic without being also pre-linguistic), and that this is the proper contrast between zoosemiotics and anthroposemiotics taken in their fullest amplitude.

To see what is involved in these distinctions, let me develop the discussion around a sequence of diagrams or tables illustrating the double dichotomy between language and pre-linguistic structures of experience, on the one hand, and language and post-linguistic structures of experience, on the other hand.

Consider first of all pre-linguistic experience (from which comes the first non-verbal inlay in linguistic communication), in a purely zoosemiotic sense. For ease of imagination, I am going to focus only on the peculiarly anthropoid structure of experience as it began to emerge, say, roughly from the time of the Australopithecines; because, of course, to take into account insect and other animal forms far removed from the human (cf. Chapman 1971: esp. Section E, XXVI-XXXI), a great many conceptual modifications irrelevant to our present purpose would have to be introduced into the scheme. I think we would not be far wrong in envisioning an experience structure for anthropoids somewhat along the lines indicated in Table I on the opposite page.

The initial and sustained immediate level of cognitive contact between organism and extra-organismic world is through the so-called "external senses," whence we encounter colors, shapes, tastes, textures, odors. But connected with these, inseparably, and with no temporal gap, is a great deal else besides: to see colors *is* is see shapes, places, a plurality of things — so, the whole series of notions in Table I below the term "synthesizing" (which takes place within the organism experiencing) comprises the first data of experience out of which, even-

TABLE I

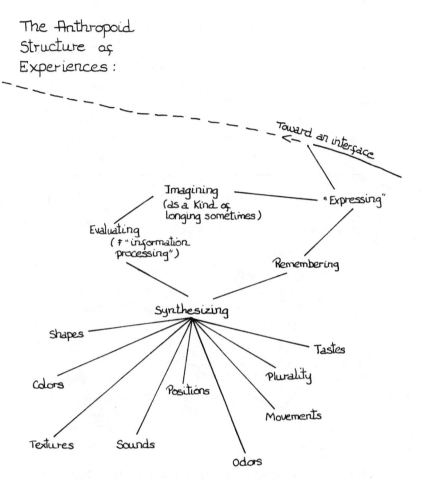

The Anthropoid
Structure of
Experiences :

Toward an interface

Imagining
(as a kind of
longing sometimes)

"Expressing"

Evaluating
(≠ "information
processing")

Remembering

Synthesizing

Shapes

Tastes

Colors

Plurality

Positions

Movements

Textures   Sounds

Odors

tually, language itself (the *interface*, let us say, between pre- and post-linguistic structures of experience) will arise.

The situation here bears looking at more closely (see Table II, following page).

In this Table, we have the same picture of anthropoid experience, but broken down more clearly into its structural components. Note particularly the relation between the whole of perception and its immediate sensory core. Precisely here semiotic analysis enables us to give,

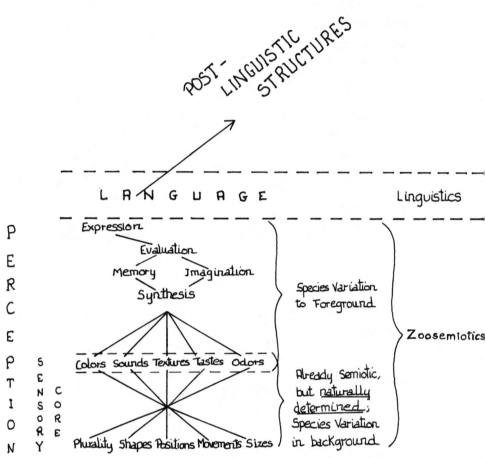

TABLE II

for the first time, a satisfactory resolution to the controversy over "sense data," as that controversy traces back in empiricist philosophies from present-day positivism to its beginnings in John Locke with his "simple ideas" of sense. The empiricist tradition has always had a problem figuring out why the mind structures sensory objects in the ways that it does. The origin of this difficulty was twofold. First, the direct objects of each external sense — colors, sounds, textures, tastes, and odors — were considered to be wholly effects within the mind itself, perhaps *caused* by external objects, but certainly not properties of those external things as such. This was in contrast to an older, less critical "realist" tradition which simply considered color to *be* in the grass, etc.

What eluded our early modern forebears, as their successors, was yet a third possibility for these initial data of sense: they could be regarded as neither intrinsic properties of physical things nor mere modifications of our subjective faculties, but precisely as properties exhibiting how things are in their action here and now on an organism possessed of this determinate range of sensitivities. This third alternative would account for the experimentally demonstrated relativity of sensory qualities without making of them mere constructs of subjectivity — while preserving, that is to say, their status as here and now revelatory of "the way things are" so far as involves the experiencing organism. The initial contact between cognizing organism and environment, on this view, is indistinctly subjective and objective. The world appears thus (e.g., colored) only to a subject, but it really *is* that way *given that totality of conditions*.

Equally serious was the characteristic modern failure to see that the initial sensory data are not "atomic" in character, but strictly semiotic. Thus, the initial synthesis of sensations made by the mind is not arbitrary or habit-controlled, as the early moderns, notably Hume, opined, but *naturally determined* by semiotic means. Since a sign is anything functioning to bring something other than itself into an organism's awareness, and since colors, sounds, textures, etc., immediately bring along with themselves an awareness of plurality, positions, shapes, movements, and so on, one has only to regard sensation semiotically in order to realize that we are already given within it an outline of objective structure that is relative and changing, true, but naturally determined nevertheless.[2] "Sense data," in other words, already comprise an objective structure (not atomic elements logically discrete but habitually combined) that is the same, in the above sense

of naturally determined, for all organisms. Species varia-
tions, consequently — that is, subjective differences of
sensory range and variety — are strictly background
phenomena at the level of the sensory core; and that is
why biological mechanisms of camouflage (such as protective coloration) and deception, though principally dependent on the "qualitative" appearances or "properties" of bodies, are so widespread and consistently useful
in nature across species lines.[3] Species variation comes to
the fore only in the interpretation of the "common" data
and in the uses that they are put to in predation and social
exchange.

Now, language, in the sense that linguistics studies
it, and as it constitutes a species-specific system, is something that emerges, so to speak, "on top" of this common
structure of anthropoid experience. To understand it in
relation to that experience sufficiently for present purposes, it is enough to indicate how the "natural" and the
"conventional" relate in the separating off of specifically
linguistic from purely behavioral sign systems in anthropoid interaction (detailed background in Deely 1978a).

Prior to the advent of cognitive organisms, as we saw
in the preceding section (pp. 102-103 above), relations
are only physical, that is, obtaining between presently
existing entities. Once cognition is introduced, the situation drastically changes. Now the same relation existing
independently of cognition can also come to exist dependently upon cognition, and can continue to exist in cognition after its physical ground no longer exists. Moreover, as we remarked above, relations existing first in
cognition can subsequently be introduced into the physical order by bringing about within that order the proper
conditions; and relations can be established in cognition
that can have no counterpart in the physical world, just
as there are physical relations that have not yet or will not
ever enter into the cognition of some organism. Comparatively "real" and "unreal" from the standpoint of what

exists independently of cognitive activity as such, physical and cognition-dependent relations are strictly on a par from the standpoint of what works within experience to achieve some determinate end.

Both types of relation are essential to the constitution of experience, as is clear from the above remarks; but within experience, it is not essential that the two be explicitly distinguished according to type, and indeed it is not always possible to separate out in experience what is the contribution of the subject and what is the contribution of the object to the experimental structure of a given interaction situation.

In philosophical tradition, one little-realized way of grounding the putative distinction between understanding and perception (''intellect'' and ''sense'') was precisely in terms of relation: perception reveals objects as they are only relative to the dispositions, needs, and desires of the organism perceiving, whereas understanding reveals in these same objects the further dimension of existence in their own right independent of relations to the knower.[4]

It is this way of interpreting the difference between ''sense'' and ''intellect,'' it seems to me, that is decisive for semiotics.[5] For within the interweave or mix in experience of cognition-dependent and cognition-independent relations, *only those organisms possessing the capacity to understand in its distinction from the capacities to sense and perceive, in the way just described, will ever be able even on occasion to discriminate between real and unreal elements in semiosis,* that is, in the process of communication through signs. Stipulation, as a distinctive semiotic process, presupposes exactly this ability; and it is *only* in relation to stipulative decisions and their consequences that language can be said to be ''conventional.'' But stipulations, when successful, pass into customs, and customs into nature. Thus, sign-systems arise out of nature in anthropoid experience, become partially ''conventionalized'' in the sphere of human understanding, and pass back again through customs into continuity with the natural world as it is experienced perceptually by human and non-human animals alike (Deely 1978a:7ff.).

"Language," in short, in the sense that is species-specific to *homo sapiens*, is nothing else than the "unreal" component of semiosis explicitly segregated and seized upon in its unique signifying potential by the understanding in its distinction from perception and sense. As a result of the intervention of language, those organisms capable of seizing upon the difference between the "real" and the "unreal" elements of experience soon find themselves in an entirely different world. In pre-linguistic experience, relations are not distinguished from the *objects related*. With language, it becomes possible to separate the two. The consequences of this simple feat are enormous, and without end — literally, for it is this that makes human experience an "open-ended" affair as a matter of principle (see Table III, opposite page).

In this diagram, which looks very complicated at first glance, notice, to begin with, the same basic structure of anthropoid experiences — the zoosemiotic structure that is common to man and the higher anthropoids — which we examined in Table II, retained in the lower half of the diagram. But in man, the processes eventuating that structure go up one step — but what a step! — higher. Passing through the layer of language, the social structures of anthropoid life "come out on the other side," so to speak, in the form of such things as military establishments, civil governments, religious traditions — things which are not linguistic, which are much more than the linguistic system, but which *couldn't come into being apart from language*. This step enables us systematically to differentiate between relations (as offices and social roles, for example) and the things here and now related (the individuals concretely playing those roles in any given case). So, although this diagram looks complicated, when it is

TABLE III

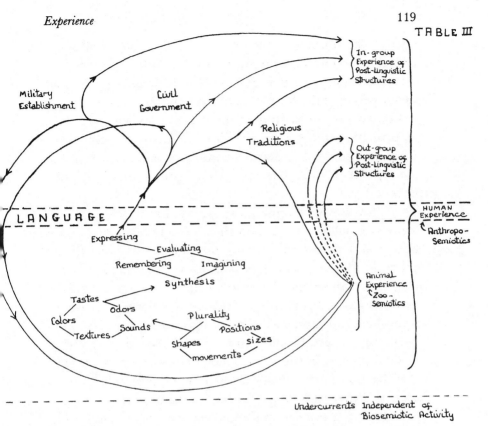

examined carefully, it is evident that the upper portion is
structured representatively by only three arrows (though
indefinitely more, of course, could be added), each of
which splits into two.

Follow, first, the left-most arrow. As it splits toward
the right, it leads toward a military establishment as experienced by linguistic animals belonging to the society of
which that establishment is an expression. That same
establishment, of course, has an impact within the experience of any non-linguistic animals having commerce
with the society, and elements of it will be perceived and
assimilated by semiotic processes, but now only insofar as
these elements of the military establishment have ''gone
below'' the linguistic layer. This is indicated by the left-
most split of the leftward arrow, which leads back toward
the sphere of simple perception and pre-linguistic experi-

ence. The domesticated dog, for example, will well perceive a relative social importance of individuals as they affect his own well-being; but without language, he will never perceive the four stars of the general, the bars of the lieutenant, or the stripes of the sergeant for what they are as properly *military* insignia. Post-linguistic structures, in what is proper to them, are forever hidden from the standpoint of pure perception and pre-linguistic experience.

Thus we have animal experience in the sense of zoö-semiotics below the broken lines of language, and, both above and below the lines, and indeed "centered" by them, human experience which, for the reasons given, includes, besides what the animals have, the post-linguistic institutions or structures which exist properly consequent upon language and owing to it. It is thus that human experience is much broader than that of even the highest of animal species in the total biological community without "understanding."[6] Post-linguistic structures exist *properly above* the linguistic interface; but they *also* exist *in some way other than what is proper to them assimilated and accounted for* in animal experience *below* the interface. Moreover, as they are encountered perceptually, we must further distinguish the sense in which they are encountered by non-linguistic anthropoids from the sense in which they are encountered by post-linguistically formed but alien organisms ("outgroups": the broken arrows to the right of the diagram leading back up through the interface).

In the taking account of things in experience by animals, one way of describing what results from post-linguistic structures would be as two levels of natural systems — a primary (or infralinguistic) level and a secondary (or supralinguistic) level, as in Table IV opposite.

If we adopt in imagination the point of view of an alien — an alien in the sense of someone from outside the given culture, or even from another planetary system — observing for the first time life in a given human society,

TABLE IV

The
"UNREALITIES"

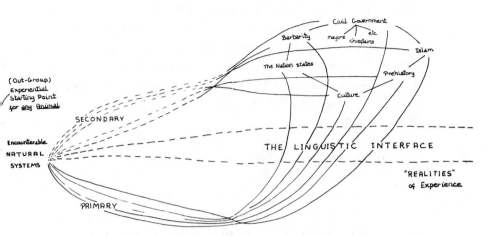

what would appear? A series of regularities, or "natural systems," which, upon examination, would appear in one sense primarily as objects or patterns of perception, but in another sense, as objects of understanding, that is, as derivative from the unique indifference of language to "reality" as perception alone reveals and grasps it. The so-called "primary" natural systems comprise real (physical, i.e., cognition-independent) relations of the human organisms to one another and to their *Umwelt*.

Further observation would reveal, however, within this primary network of perceptually accessible interactions, and *carried* by them (*conflated* with them in social life), a secondary network of (comparatively) unreal relations conveying the historical experience of the group as something transcendent — not to individual and social reality, but — to the perceptually accessible elements as such expressing the "primary" systems. The so-called "primary," or perceptually available systems, thus, "feed into" the linguistic interface in and through social interaction;[7] but what "comes out on the other side," so to speak, is not language, but society enculturated, society as a potential *cultural* system.

This would suggest that the complete reduction of culture to social system, as characteristic of British anthropology and of American anthropology since the time of Radcliffe-Brown, is an oversimplification. Earlier American anthropology, with its concept of culture system as "superorganic" and wholly transcendent to social system, went too far in assigning autonomy to the cultural vis-à-vis the social. But the opposite view, that culture is nothing but the uniquely complex forms of social organization proper to man, also goes too far, as a result of an inadequate understanding of semiosis as it occurs through specifically human language.

It is true that the unreal relational components of human experience only exist through the cognitive functioning of living individuals, and in this sense the cultural system does have actuality only in and from social interaction. But this "unreal" dimension of experience recognizable as such, and as providing "a substitute for experience which can be passed on [through language] *ad infinitum* in time and space" precisely because it is *cognitively separable* from this or that specific concrete individual or group of individuals with whose activity it is here and now — or was there and then — de facto identified, is in itself something distinct from even though immanent within social interaction and social system (cf. Wilden 1981: 3-4). It is then this unreal dimension which is the ground of the cumulative transmission of learning that makes human society as enculturated different in kind from the animal societies that cannot jump the links of individuals connecting the generations. This is one of the points of view, I would suggest, that reveals most sharply the revolutionary importance of semiotics for anthropology, and for clarifying the foundations of the human sciences generally.

Presupposed to such clarification is an accurate understanding of the structure of human experience (anthroposemiosis) and of the central, but not all-consuming, role of language therein. The lines of distinction suggested above seem to me indicative of the sort of infrastructure that must be recognized if we are to advance along this way.

APPENDICES

APPENDIX

I

On the Notion
"Doctrine of Signs"

The potential of special significance in Locke's choice of the term "doctrine" for introducing his notion of semiotic was something first taken note of by Thomas Sebeok (1976: ix and following). In the natural language environment of the 17th century, this term was a direct derivative of the Latin philosophical term *doctrina* which expressed with great clarity and richness the notion of a level or type of knowledge which, we can see in hindsight, is critically distinct from scientific knowledge or *science* ("scientia") in the modern sense that term has acquired since Locke's day, as also the term 'theory.' Attention to this difference can be of considerable help in clarifying the dimensions of semiotic development in our own day.

A "doctrine," in Latin or English, refers first of all to a "teaching" in the most general sense, i.e., to *what* some person or persons, even unknown, assert to be the case about something. Thus, *doctrina* may concern natural or social reality, or any web and admixture of the two. In the systematic context of Latin scholasticism, with a remarkable constancy spanning the later centuries of that epoch — as illustrated, for example, early in Aquinas

c. 1266: I q. 1, or late in Poinsot 1637: disp. 2 — *doctrina*
referred to a body of thought sensitive to its own implications and *striving* for consistency throughout, while
achieving explanations (however provisional) at a level
beyond what can be empirically circumscribed in un-
ambiguous ways. Thus, the notion of *doctrina* is one of the
avenues expressing the differing ways in which the sensory core of cognition is relied upon in dominant moods
of thought which are typically "scientific" as contrasted
with those that tend more to typically "philosophic"
analysis.

In the former case, crucial theoretical claims are considered established in a satisfactory way only when they
have been successfully correlated with an empirically accessible instantiation of consequence that is *as* thus accessible unambiguously circumscribed. An example of
this would be the requirement of Einstein's equations that
light passing in its propagation close by a star be bent in
its path to a degree proportioned to known physical
properties of the star; or the Michelson-Morley require-
ments for the presence of ether.

But inasmuch as empirical ambiguity surrounds in
principle the structure or structures demanded by some
concern of theoretical understanding, and this concern requires a natural language to achieve satisfactory explica-
tion of its concepts, we are in the realm of philosophical
reason and the field proper to the development of *doctrina*.
An example of this would be the requirement of Aristotle's natural philosophy that there be principles of being
neither existent in their own right nor accessible in perception (not isolable as variables), two in number, and
constitutive of individuality at its base as something subject to alteration and exercising an existence independently of our cognition; or the requirement of Kant's account
of reason that the objects of our experience be conformed
to our concepts insofar as they are phenomena, rather
than the other way around.

Semiotic, thus, as *doctrina*, is a department of knowledge belonging to the order of what is not as contrasted with what is susceptible of critical resolution at the empirical level. It is an objective discipline ruled by intrinsic demands indifferent to subjectivity in its individual but not in its social dimensions, and grounded in the signifying whereby the here and now acquires coherence of structure, and what may be absent or non-existent becomes a part of the texture of present experience — whereby, in a word, the transcendence of the given distinguishes cognitive life from the dyadic processes (or "brute force") of merely physical production. The semiotic tradition of Peirce after Locke in particular envisions the possibility of establishing and developing a philosophical *doctrina* in this sense, as distinguished from the much larger, and, in one very important sense, limitless *field* of "semiotics": that is, the development of attempts to identify specifically and think through the implications of signifying aspects and elements of phenomena, natural or sociocultural, that have been studied heretofore in their own right by the range of traditional specialized pursuits (music, architecture, ethology, etc.) now becoming sensitized to the semiotic dimension that permeates all of human experience.

This new field of semiotics in turn can be conceptualized prospectively as a discipline in its own right, "an ancient discipline, stemming from a pre-Socratic clinical tradition, which then led to the development of three fundamental semiotic traditions — the medical, the philosophical [so understood as to include religious thought and theology], and the linguistic — that have thoroughly intermingled at various periods in Western intellectual history, although there were times when they strove for autonomy" (Sebeok 1979d: 272). Thus the interdisciplinary perspective so long sought for in *ad hoc* ways belongs *de jure* to semiotics as something inherent, by virtue of the universal role of the sign as the vehicle of communica-

tion within and between specialties as everywhere else —
wherever there is cognition.

II

On the Distinction between Words and Ideas

The semiotic solutions to problems concerning the foundations of knowledge and experience advance the discussions so far beyond those to which we have become accustomed in modern philosophy that I had quite forgotten how temerarious it is nowadays to mention among philosophers the classical notion that words and ideas are in some basic sense distinct media, unless of course one mentions the notion for the purpose of dismissing it out of hand. Fortunately, in time for the final revision, I was awakened from my semiotic slumber by a sharp reprimand from George Kennard in his letter of 20 December 1981: "It is a decisively crippling feature of Locke's thought — and of most scholastic thought too, which is indistinguishable from it in this respect — that he posits the duality you refer to [between] 'ideas' and 'words'." I had quite forgotten the contemporary near-dogma that these mythical "ideas" behind words, like the epicycles of Ptolemy, are, to borrow a formulary from Geach (1968: 54), "idle wheels, useless reduplications of the linguistic structures."

Therefore, in order to obviate needless misunderstandings in advance (e.g., such as those of Alston 1964: 22-25), I will at once enter, upon first mentioning this distinction in relation to semiotic, an explanation of the sense in which I understand it, a sense that I think that anyone reflecting upon the distinction would be likewise inclined to accept. Regardless of what Locke may or may not have held about this distinction in his own time, therefore, it has the following minimum validity for semiotic.

I begin from a point remarked by A. J. Ayer (1947: 12), which it is very difficult, perhaps impossible, not to concede: "Certainly there is a difference," he writes, "between understanding what another person says and merely hearing the noises that he makes."

No more than this need be admitted in order to get onto the way of correctly discriminating between words and ideas. Let me re-state Ayer's observation in the form of a question: In the case of a mark, sound, or movement — be it a word or a sentence, and be it verbally or graphically manifested — actually used to mention an object, what is it that transforms the in itself physical mark, sound, or movement into a linguistic occurrence? My thesis is that in any case where discourse concerns an object, that is, in any case where heard or seen noises are understood linguistically, it is the difference between the mark, sound, or movement *as such* and *as conveying the linguistic signification* (or between the physical *as such* and *as making a linguistic reference),* that is the key to understanding the nature and function of discourse, and that is, therefore, *de jure,* the fundamental *datum explanandum* for any philosophy of discourse that wishes to be grounded in principle.

Let us state the factors involved in this problem in neutral terms, i.e., terms that should be acceptable to any philosopher who accepts as a descriptive definition of meaning the difference — whatever it may be — between a given mark, sound, or movement *as such* and *as sign* of something other than itself.

Whenever a mark, sound, or movement is employed successfully as a linguistic sign (i.e., to make a linguistic reference), whether that sign be a word or a sentence (i.e., whatever it is that one takes the unit of linguistic reference to be — word or phrase, subject of a sentence, whole sentence: whatever), it seems clear that its status as a piece of discourse involves three factors. *First*, there is the linguistic expression itself, which occurs outside the organism: let us call this the extraorganismic factor X. *Second*, there is the object that X is a sign of, the significate of X, what X refers to or is about: let us call this the objective or signified factor O. *Third*, there is the factor within the organism using or apprehending X as a sign of O, the organism's "understanding," on the basis of which factor precisely X is, over and above a mere mark, sound, or movement occurring extraorganismically, a *linguistic* mark, sound or movement signifying or referring to O: let us call this the intraorganismic factor C, inasmuch as it is the cause, here and now, of X's actual functioning status as sign of the object O. For, if C does not occur in connection with the perception of X, clearly, X will not be perceived by the organism in relation to O as a sign thereof.

It is thus C, the intraorganismic factor, that holds, in the final analysis, the key to the analysis of meaning. I say, "in the final analysis," for it is clear there there are many ancillary considerations that may be pursued in connection with C — for example, the analysis of the conventions of use surrounding the occurrence of X as evocative of C (the province of ordinary language analysis) or the analysis of the behavior of the organism consequent upon the occurrence of C (the province of psycholinguistics and behavioral psychology). But just as clearly, such pursuits *are* ancillary, and the heart of the problem lies in C itself. X functions as a sign of O on the basis of C, the intraorganismic factor whereby the language user apprehends O as object signified by X.

Notice here that *the being of O as an object for the user of X is also dependent upon the factor C. Even supposing that O exists in the world independently* of C, it exists here and now as something actually signified by X dependently upon C. As an object of discourse, therefore, as something signified by X, O has its being dependently upon C. In the analytic tradition, the tendency has been to give physical objects pride of place precisely because here, at least, we tend to have confidence in the reality of that about which we discourse. But, from the standpoint of C, this tendency suppresses a fundamental insight. Whenever an object exists as an object of discourse, it is not its supposed physical reality that is decisive, for the physically real object as physically real is thought to be such on the grounds that it seems to have being *independently* of discourse. But an object of discourse as such has its being *dependently* upon discourse, regardless of whether it *also* has an independent or physical being.

To get clear about what is at stake here, let us proceed for the moment on the assumption that the object O is a really existing thing factually given in the physical world quite apart from discourse. The advantage gained by making this assumption is simply that in the stipulated case — the case where O exists in fact independently of discourse — it is clear that not only are C and X really distinct as well as really related — (really related, that is, inasmuch as it is by virtue of C that the organism is aware of O), but also that the distinction between O as something existing in the physical world — O as thing, let us say — and O as something apprehended by a given organism — O as object, let us say — is precisely the difference, for purposes of discourse, between O as related in its existence to a given organism and O as unrelated to that organism, a difference made by the presence or absence in the organism of C. When C exists, O exists as apprehended as well as in fact; when C does not exist, O exists in fact but not as apprehended. C, therefore, is the basis of the cognitive relation R between an organism A and an object O. (Here we have a preliminary answer to the problem posed by the privacy of C vis-à-vis the public character of O: just as one and the same thing can serve as the term of several different relations, so one and the same object can be the term of relations founded on the C's existing in diverse individuals. One and the same object O can stand at the term of several different relations R founded on the different C's existing in different individuals. Thus the public character of O is reconciled with the privacy of C by the diversity of status between O and C: O exists as the term of the relation R, whereas C exists as the fundament or basis of that same relation R. C and O differ as fundament and term of a relation differ. C and O are located in physically disparate subjects, but several subjects can be related to one and the same term.)

Let us now reintroduce into the picture the linguistic factor — word or sentence or whole treatise — X, which, in conjunction with C, refers to O. Our preliminary assumption about O as a thing need not be altered, for X, obviously, insofar as it is a mark, sound, or movement (or a series of marks, sounds and movements), is also a thing existing in fact independently of any C here and now. This is an important point, but one whose significance has generally not been interpreted rightly by the philosophers of language.

Up to now, we have spoken of C and X as co-occurrent, the former intraorganismically and the latter extraorganismically, whenever X actually refers, here and now, to O. From this point of view it seems sufficient to say that X is able to be referred to O owing to the fact that O is apprehended by the user of X thanks to C. But this appearance of sufficiency is an illusion, for it glosses over the fact that X, precisely as linguistic, is every bit as much

an object — a term of a C-based relation — as O itself
is. C and X, as the thought and the word, do not belong
on one side of discourse, and O, object and thing, on the
other side. On the contrary, C belongs on one side and
X and O belong on the other, for X and O have in common the character of being objects, while C is known to
exist only analytically, as the basis that must be posited
for the difference between one and the same thing now
existing only in fact, now existing also in apprehension.
Here we arrive at a conclusion whose consequences are
definitive: the difference between X as physical and X as
significant or linguistic, is the same as the difference between O as thing and O as object of discourse.

The importance of the point demands that we spell
it out in detail. Whenever a given individual, A, let us
say, uses 'X, the X too is something that he is aware of,
and so 'is an object of apprehension — something A is
aware of — in its own right, as well as and as a necessary
condition for X's being a sign of O. Both X and O must
be apprehended as objects in order for either to function
as a sign of the other. This means that, since C is posited
precisely and only as the intraorganismic factor making
the difference between A's actually being aware or not
being aware of a given object here and now, before (logically, not always temporally) X is used to refer to O,
there are not one but two C's involved, one whereby X
exists as apprehended and one whereby O exists as apprehended. Strictly speaking, then, *the sign character of X
relative to O is due to the establishment of an association not between C and X but rather between X as one object and O as another
object*, which association in turn results in the formation of
a third C, which is the "idea" or "concept" neither of
X nor of O disjunctively but of the two conjunctively. It
is *this* C, properly speaking, that X evokes when it functions linguistically as a sign of O.

The situation can be clarified, perhaps, by a sequence of diagrams:

Diagram I: A is aware of O by virtue of C_1, the idea of O, prescinding from the question of how C_1 was formed.

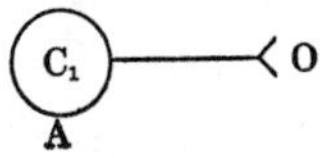

Diagram II: A is aware of X by virtue of C_2, the idea whereby X exists as something A is aware of.

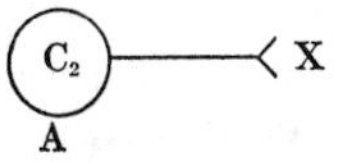

Diagram III: A is aware of X and O together, making possible the formation of an idea of the two as a unity — a unity of thought.

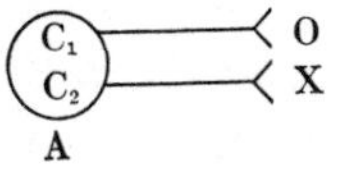

Diagram IV: A is aware of X and O not only together, but also as connected, by a connection consequent upon the idea, C_3, whereby X and O exist as something A is aware of "linguistically."

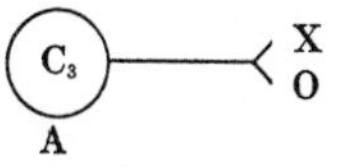

Viewed in this way, there is no chance of committing the blunder of thinking that thoughts and words are two separate processes, each of which would be just what it is if one or the other were to be removed. On the contrary, discourse — the whole of thought, language, and object — is profoundly one, so unified that the intraorganismic thoughts and the extraorganismic words and objects are what they are precisely and only to the extent that each is simultaneously. For, inasmuch as the objects of cognition as such exist dependently on the thought from the standpoint of being, object and thought co-exist in perfect proportion to one another from a temporal standpoint. The object cannot be as apprehended save when and as an idea of it exists, and an idea as idea cannot be save as giving an existence of presence to an object. In a certain sense, therefore, only upon the formation of C_3 in our sequence of diagrams do we have the existence of discourse properly speaking.

This reveals a profound import to the contemporary expression, ''universe of discourse.'' For, from the standpoint of the concept or idea, words are not opposed to objects as words are to things. On the contrary, words and things known are equally objects, but objects differing in status *primarily as regards their manageability*, as Gulliver had occasion to observe at the Academy of Lagado in Balnibarbi (Swift 1726: 3rd voyage, ch. 5 *ad finem*). Thus, words and sentences call things to mind and order our thoughts about things, but, equally, things suggest words and patterns of words. For both words and things exist, in discourse, in an objective unity derived from the concepts or ideas which give them their being — which ''constitute them,'' the phenomenologists say — as cognized or known.

A linguistic remark can fail to be understood — Q, on hearing X, may think of N rather than O. Or a perceived object may suggest no words to the perceiver but present itself, as it were, mutely. But in any case, whenever anything enters our consciousness, it does so by virtue of an intraorganismic occurrence C. (This analysis strongly supports the suggestion of Sebeok 1981d: 12, that much conceptual confusion today ''comes about from considering language as primarily a communicative tool,'' whereas in fact ''language must have evolved as an . . . instrument for modeling man's *Umwelt* in the mind

[*Innenwelt*]." Chomsky 1979: 35-36 makes much the same point.)

Having said this much, let me add in conclusion some remarks of a more contentious nature, anticipating what seem to me some of the more important consequences of the above analysis for the doctrine of signs.

First of all, what has been said already points to the utter peculiarity of the intraorganismic factor C, the concept or idea: unlike objects, including words, that are also signs, ideas cannot fail to give presence to something besides themselves. Inasmuch as a sign is anything that makes present in awareness something besides itself, ideas are pure signs: they do nothing but signify, i.e., make present the objects of awareness — be they words or things or whatnot — that the ideas themselves are not. Unlike the objects which are also signs, ideas cannot fail to signify. They alone, among all the furniture of the world, signify by necessity. For them, to be and to signify are simply one. The object of which we are directly aware, be it word or thing apprehended disjunctively or conjunctively, is, in every case, just what C *qua* C is not. If we were or could be directly aware of C, it would not be C, but something else, for C is just that factor which makes us aware of something that it itself is not. No matter how the matter is approached, careful attention to the function of C in relation to X and O reveals that, while C can be known to exist by a reflexive analysis of discourse, it can under no conditions be directly observed or apprehended. This is a point of some importance which was well understood by the older scholastics and by a few recent philosophers — notably Jacques Maritain and F. H. Bradley (1922: I, 22) — but which seems never to have been adverted to in a systematic way by anyone in the contemporary analytic or phenomenological traditions excepting Heidegger.

Its importance can perhaps be better illustrated by a closer scrutiny of our choice of the terms "idea" and "concept" to designate the intraorganismic factor C, for according to a celebrated theory widely held in current scientific and philosophical circles (e.g., Quine 1960: 264; Brown 1958: 82-83, 102-103) — the so-called "identity hypothesis" — the intraorganismic factor C is in fact a state of the brain of the organism A which uses X to discourse about O. What I have called an "idea" or "concept," according to this view, is more properly called an event or state of the central nervous system — an identification that must be made because, if the postulation of such intraorganismic factors "is going to prove fruitful," as Charles Osgood remarks (1953: 410), "and serve as anything more than a label for ignorance, properties must be attributed to them."

We can agree with Osgood on the importance of assigning properties for C, but to ascribe to C the properties of a nervous event or state is possible only to the extent that the above-described manner in which C functions relative to X and O has been systematically misunderstood. If what I have said is the function of C in discourse be admitted, then the view that "mental states are brain states" must be false (Rasmussen 1980). A brain state is something that is observable in principle. Therefore C as such is not a brain state but must be other than and superordinate to any state of the central nervous system; for, as we have seen, since an idea (C as C) cannot be save as giving an existence of presence to something which it itself is not, an idea as idea is intrinsically unobservable. It can be objectified only by inference, never by observation (cf. Poinsot 1635: 185a33-b25). To repeat an earlier remark: "careful attention to the function of C in relation to X and O reveals that, while C can be known to exist by a reflexive analysis of discourse, it can under no conditions be directly observed or apprehended" — not even (Deely 1975a: 92-93) by a second party (such as a neurosurgeon).

Physical marks, sounds or movements, when functioning in discourse, undergo — thanks to C — a singular and mysterious "elevation" (as Cajetan puts it, 1507: q. 14 art. 2 nn. 4, 7; q. 79 art. 2, n. 14), during which they exist in a higher way than is proper to them as observable, physical occurrences; and they do so inasmuch as they are the objective effects of the intraorganismic factor C — the concept or idea — within the speaker and hearer of language, a factor which, as it functions in discourse, is itself no more directly inspectable than the significance it causes. This is the point of view proper to a would-be philosophy of language; it is on this point that an account of meaning can properly turn. Here we may apply another of Cajetan's remarks (1507: q. 14 art 1. n. 7):

> From this it will appear how crude is the thinking of those who treat of sense and the sensible, of understanding and the understandable, as also of the processes of sensation and understanding, according to the canons of judgment applicable to material events. *Et disces elevare ingenium, aliumque rerum ordinem ingredi* — you must learn to raise up your mind, and enter into quite a different order of occurrences.

The point is not to deny that brain states are somehow correlative with and indeed necessary conditions for the existence of ideas (cf., for example, Griffin 1981: 24-30). It is simply to point out (cf. Poinsot 1635: 185b26-186b40, esp. 186b3-16) the error of reductively identifying C, as that which is conditioned, with a brain state, as that which doubtless conditions C. From this point of view, more recent talk of a "correlation version of the identity hypothesis" represents a considerable step away from confusion and toward theoretical clarity — although the ideological reluctance to abandon clear-cut materialism is flagged by the amusingly antinomic character of the new expression (since correlates are precisely not identical, are two not one, even when existentially inseparable, which is what is really being proposed about "brain" and "mind" in the new expression), like the car dealers who refer straightfacedly to "mandatory op-tions.'' Whatever difficulties one may have with the terminology of ideas and concepts, nonetheless, they are as nothing compared to the difficulties consequent upon the failure to grasp this principle: the conditioned as such is always other than its necessary and even sufficient conditions. This is a principle semiotic analysis is particularly unlikely to lose sight of in the nature of the case. It is thus particularly encouraging to see semioticians coming directly to terms with this important area of research (e.g., Perron 1981), which will surely be one of the most important for an ultimate synthesis of the *doctrina signorum*.

(Further to this discussion, see Part I, Section 5, note 9 below, pp. 168 ff., and Part II, Section 2, note 2, p. 198.)

NOTES

NOTES FOR PART I

Notes to Part I, Section 1

1. Romeo (1976: 75, 77, 79 n. 13) reacts in particular against the view of Kleinpaul 1888: 103, that Hippocrates is "der Vater und Meister aller Semiotik," on the quite correct grounds that the medical practitioner by the nature of the case is "an applied semioticist" who profits "from the spadework of theoretical semioticists." In the terms to be introduced in the present study, this is to say that medical semiotics forms part—an ancient and most privileged part, to be sure—of the interdisciplinary field of semiotics, in contrast to the foundational doctrine which provides its ultimate coherence.

2. This fertile notion in contemporary semiotics can be traced back at least to the colloquium "L'Archéologie du Signe," organized by Professors Eugene Vance and Paul Zumthor at the Centre Culturel International de Cérisy, Cérisy-la-Salle (Normandy), France, August 2-12, 1977.

3. "On the subject of the chronology of logic and its division into periods there is this to be said: this history begins in Europe in the 4th century B.C., in India about the 1st century A.D. Previously there is in Greece, India, and China, perhaps also in other places, something like a pre-history of logic; but it is a complete mistake to speak of a 'logic of the Upanishads' or a 'logic of the Pythagoreans'. Thinkers of these schools did indeed establish chains of inference, but logic consists in studying in-

145

ference, not in inferring. No such study can be detected with certainty before Plato and the Nyāga; at best we find some customary, fixed and canonical rules of discussion, but any complete critical appreciation and analysis of these rules are missing'' (Bochenski 1970: 11). This suggests that an archeology of semiotic consciousness comparable to the present effort might be done for the East, replacing the *Organon* with the *Nyāya-sūtra,* for example. But this once again indicates how really vast is the task of the thorough "history of semiotics" one day to be written. Cf. Baer 1980: 132.

4. First presented as an evening lecture at the first International Summer Institute for Semiotic and Structural Studies (ISISSS) at the University of Toronto in June of 1980, I had occasion to refine the thesis and ideas of this book in a research group at the second ISISSS at Vanderbilt University in June of 1981. It was on this second occasion that discussion, particularly through the remarks of Eugen Baer, Richard Lanigan, and Gray Cox, brought home to me the express strictures to be placed on the starting point I have chosen here for projecting a framework of semiotic development when one looks backwards from this starting point toward the pre-Socratic era—strictures I was already contemplating owing to private correspondence with Luigi Romeo. I am particularly indebted to these four individuals for the remaining paragraphs of this section and to the major studies of Richard Lanigan (1972, 1977) for leading ideas on the import of semiotic for speech communication and philosophy of language generally.

5. Bochenski precedes his table (1970: 26) with the following remarks on the logicians of the ancient period, i.e., the period ending with Boethius: "Aristotle, the first historian of philosophy, calls Zeno of Elea the 'founder of dialectic', but the first two men, so far as we know, to reflect seriously on logical problems were Plato and Euclid of Megara, both pupils of Socrates. And as Aristotle himself ascribes to Socrates important services in the domain of logic, or rather of methodology from which logic later developed, perhaps Socrates should be considered to be the father of Greek logic.

"Aristotle was a pupil of Plato, and his logic undoubtedly grew out of the practice of the Platonic Academy. Aristotle's chief pupil and long-time collaborator, Theophrastus, provides the link between the logical thought of his master and that of the Stoa.

For contemporaneously and parallel with Aristotelian logic there developed that derived from Euclid, of which the first important representatives were Megarians, Diodorus Cronus, Philo of Megara and others; later came the Stoics, who were closely connected with the Megarians, having Chrysippus as their most important thinker.

"After the death of Chrysippus, disputes arose between the Peripatetic and Megarian-Stoic schools, the latter now represented by the Stoics alone, and syncretism became prominent. Even then logicians were not lacking, the more important among them being apparently the commentators on Aristotle's logical works (Alexander, Philoponus), many Skeptics (especially Sextus Empiricus), these in the 3rd century B.C., and finally Boethius (5th-6th century A.D.)." Detailed historical discussion in Dumitriu 1977: I, chs. 4-13.

6. Bochenski 1970: 2: ". . . we find that there is one thinker who so distinctly marked out the basic problems of this residual domain that all later western inquirers trace their descent from him: Aristotle. Admittedly, in the course of centuries very many of these inquirers—among them even his principal pupil and successor Theophrastus—have altered Aristotelian *positions* and replaced them with others. But the essential problematic of their work was, so far as we know, in constant dependence in one way or another on that of Aristotle's *Organon*. Consequently, we shall denote as 'logic' primarily those problems which have developed from that problematic."

Notes to Part I, Section 2

1. "What most men in later centuries have called logic is the study of questions such as Aristotle discussed in the works of his *Organon:* and the novelty of the Stoic contribution, as we see it in retrospect, is not any new demarcation of subject-matter, but an emphasis on relations of propositions as distinct from relations of universals or concepts" (Kneale and Kneale, 1962: 737). Cf. Mueller 1978: esp. 6-8. Contrast the special pleading in Mates 1961: 2-3, an otherwise quite scientific monograph.

2. I cite Weisheipl 1965: 62-66. "The *Institutiones* of M. Aurelius Cassiodorus, a junior contemporary of Boethius, was written as a manual of divine and secular literature for the

monks of Vivarium about the year 544-5. The first book is a compendium of Sacred Scripture, exegesis, hagiography and religious discipline; the second book is a summary of the seven liberal arts; grammar, rhetoric, dialectic, arithmetic, music, geometry and astronomy. This second book, which became exceedingly popular in later centuries, is drawn largely from Boethius, Cicero, Donatus, Quintilian, Varro and St. Augustine. At the beginning of his summary of dialectics (lib. II, c. 3) Cassiodorus discussed the definition and division of philosophy, a procedure which was frequently followed throughout the Middle Ages. The schematic classification of philosophy given by Cassiodorus is simply that of Boethius, but in one popular recension, probably of the eighth century, this classification is attributed to Aristotle:

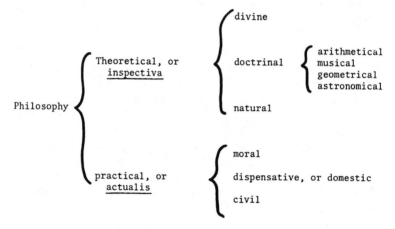

Natural philosophy discusses the nature of each thing which is produced naturally; doctrinal philosophy is the science which considers abstract quantity, i.e., quantity which has been mentally separated from matter or from the other accidents; philosophy is called 'divine' when it considers the ineffable nature of God or when it discusses spiritual creatures. Cassiodorus briefly defined each of the doctrinal, or mathematical sciences as well as the practical. The rest of the second book is devoted to the seven liberal arts. In the early Middle Ages the second book of Cassiodorus' work seems to have been copied separately and expanded by scholars desiring a fuller compendium of the arts.

"The encyclopedic *Etymologiae, libri XX* of St. Isidore of Seville was composed early in the seventh century and enjoyed great popularity as a reference work throughout the Middle Ages. A summary of the seven liberal arts was given in the first three books: I, grammar; II, rhetoric and dialectics; III, arithmetic, geometry, music and astronomy. Following Cassiodorus and Boethius, Isidore discusses the definition and division of philosophy at the beginning of his compendium of dialectics (lib. II, c. 3), but he gives two divisions of philosophy. The first is the familiar Stoic classification, which St. Augustine attributed to Plato, namely the division of philosophy into physics, ethics and logic. According to Isidore, Plato divided physics, or natural philosophy into arithmetic, geometry, music and astronomy. The division of logic into dialectics and rhetoric is also attributed to Plato, while the division of ethics according to the four cardinal virtues is said to have originated with Socrates, who first established moral science. St. Isidore's version of this classification can be represented briefly as follows:

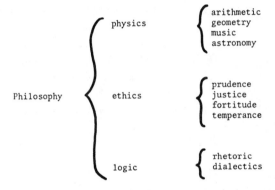

For Isidore the whole of theological teaching can also be adapted to this classification, for it discusses nature (Genesis and Ecclesiastes), ethics (Proverbs and other books) as well as logic (Canticle of Canticles and the Gospels). The second division of philosophy given by Isidore is taken directly from Cassidorus without alteration.

"St. Augustine, Boethius, Cassiodorus and St. Isidore served as the principal sources for all later discussion of the seven liberal arts and the tripartite division of philosophy. As the early Middle Ages were unaware of the numerous Greek works on natural science, metaphysics and ethics, repetition of the Boethian and Stoic classification of the sciences had little significance and no practical value for teachers of the arts. Misunderstanding of the original divisions and confusions of the issues involved were the inevitable result of not having the Aristotelian Corpus. This confusion can be seen in writers from the ninth through the twelfth century. Alcuin of York selected the Stoic division from Isidore as the point of departure for his *De dialectica*, presumably because it included the mention of dialectics, while the Boethian division did not. Rabanus Maurus likewise took the Stoic division, but he included under physics seven arts: arithmetic, astronomy, astrology, mechanics, medicine, geometry and music. Scotus Erigena combined the Boethian and Stoic classification when he divided philosophy into (i) *activa* or ethics; (ii) physics, or natural science, subdivided into the quadrivial arts; (iii) theology, which discusses God; (iv) logic, or rational philosophy, which shows the rules by which the other 'parts of wisdom' are to proceed.

"In the twelfth century a more thorough synthesis of the two ancient classifications was presented in the various *Didascalia*, or general introductions to the *artes*. These summary treatises follow the general pattern of the traditional *Disciplinarum libri*, discussing the nature and classification of learning, and briefly explaining the nature of each art. The best known of these is the *Didascalion* of Hugh of St. Victor (1096-1141). In this remarkable treatise seven mechanical arts are introduced as parts of philosophy in order to balance the seven liberal arts; all seven liberal arts, including grammar, find a place in this classification; and it is a suc-

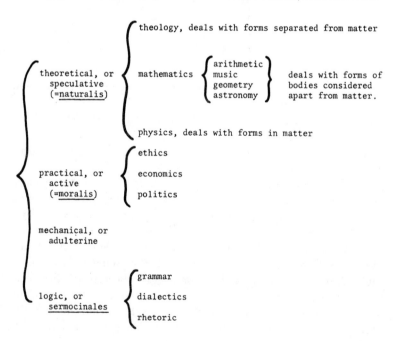

cessful combination of the Boethian and Stoic divisions of science. 'Philosophy is divided into theoretical, practical, mechanical and logical; these four branches embrace all scientific knowledge' (*Didascalion*, II, c. 1). Except for the mechanical arts, the basic division of scientific knowledge is that of the Stoics. In this case 'physics' is taken to be equivalent to 'theoretical' and coextensive with Boethius' tripartite classification of speculative philosophy:'' *(See Diagram on preceding page).*

3. Notice that in this scheme Natural Philosophy is conceived in such a way as to subsume the subject matter of metaphysics—as St. Thomas put it (c. 1269: I, 1, n. 2), "ita quod sub naturali philosophia comprehendamus et metaphysicam," a point that is of some importance for understanding the development of university curricula in the renaissance, particularly in the Iberian schools. See our chart of the Curriculum of Arts in the 17th century at the University of Alcalá in Section 3 of this essay.

4. "It was a question much debated in antiquity," the Kneales note (1962: 737), "whether logic should be accounted a branch of philosophy, as the Stoics said, or merely a preliminary to philosophical studies as the peripatetics maintained." With the glibness that has become the hallmark of academic philosophy in Britain in this century where basic issues are concerned, the Kneales see in this debate "little more than a quarrel about words." In fact, the very definition of philosophy and its relation to the order of mind-independent being was at stake in this quarrel. See Bird's discussion of the Kneales on this point (1963: 500-502).

See also Dumitriu's useful historical discussion (1977: I, 146f., and II, 50ff.) of "The place of logic among the other sciences," and his "General Conclusions" (1977: IV, 259ff., esp. 263-266).

5. This way of summarizing the *Isagoge* is deliberately aligned with the realist orientation which spontaneously permeated the concerns of the Greek and Latin ages, notwithstanding sophisticated contrary trends that develop in later Latin times (especially after William of Ockham) and triumph in the idealism of classical modern philosophy. It was this orientation which inclined the Latins to see in Porphyry's essay, as they did, and as will be discussed in Section 3 below, a preliminary to the study of reality itself. The more common current way of discussing the

Isagoge (when it is discussed at all—cf. Geach 1968: 23-24 par. no. 18) as a purely semantic exercise in discriminating the relations of predicates to subjects wholly within a linguistic context abstractly taken is accurate and legitimate as far as it goes, but is not the whole story, for "subjects" in philosophical discourse are not only syntactical loci (though they are always this) but sometimes ontological units of nature as well (and this in various senses). Joseph 1916: 68 makes the point thus: "The distinctions which we have to consider" in discussing the predicables, "therefore, do not afford a classification of things, but of concepts . . . considered in relation to one another.

"But things are known to us through these concepts, and an enquiry into the relation of concepts is an enquiry into the nature of things." See Poinsot 1631: 104b31-108b33 (Appendix A of 1983 edition of Poinsot 1632), 1632: Q. 3, esp. Art. 6, for a summary overview of this matter in Latin times. See also the following note.

6. The list of predicables includes, according to Warren's discussion (1975: 11; but cf. Joseph 1916: 66-67), only four terms in Aristotle himself (*Topics,* Book I, chs. 4-6, esp. ch. 5, 101b37-102b26), namely, definition (ὅρος, ὁρισμός), genus (γένος), property (ἴδιον) and accident (συμβεβηκός). But a definition for Aristotle is attained by a difference (διαφορά) added to a genus, which gives a species (εἶδος). Whether therefore Porphyry's substitution of the two terms (difference and species) in the list for Aristotle's one term (definition) is a clarification or somehow rather a doctrinal perversion "mixing and confusing logic with metaphysics," as Moody 1935 and others allege, is a question we can only mention here. Warren 1975: 11 note 3 has a preliminary discussion with references; Joseph 1916: 106-110 deals with the question on more strictly logical grounds in lively detail. My own view of the logical and ontological issues intertwined in the notion of "species" as natural kinds has been set forth at length in another context: see Deely 1969.

7. "L'influence de Boèce . . . au Moyen Age . . . a été par ses traductions, ses commentaires et ses traites de logique (qui remplacèront, pour une part, ses traductions et commentaires non transmis), l'introducteur d'Aristote en Occident. Certes, il n'a introduit, et encore partiellement, que la seule logique; mais celles-ci, et davantage encore les écrits personnels de Boèce, contenaient bon nombre de notions physiques et metaphysiques,

que les lecteurs médiévaux s'empressèrent de saisir au passage''
(Cappuyns, 1937: col. 376).

8. The distinction between words and ideas is commonly
challenged or repudiated outright in current circles of English-
speaking philosophers. Yet from a semiotic point of view it appears to be a sound and fundamental distinction, in the ways I
have tried to indicate in Appendix II above.

9. This must be said, for of course, to say nothing of the influence of Megarian-Stoic logic (as Bochenski, 1970: 106 terms
it), ''in addition to literal commentaries . . . Boethius had written
treatises of his own on categorical and hypothetical syllogisms and
on dialectical and rhetorical arguments (or 'topics'), adding to
these a commentary on Cicero's *Topics*'' (Moody 1967: 528). See
entry for Boethius in the References, below.

Notes to Part I, Section 3

1. ''Being as first known,'' like the ''blooming buzzing confusion'' James reflected upon (1911: 50, where he attributes the
expression to ''someone''), the Latins regarded not as an abstract
genus but as a primitive apprehension of the knowable as such in
a confused and indistinct or quasi-potential manner, according to
the everywhere accepted maxim, ''anima est quodammodo omnia.'' Understanding, they reasoned, proceeds naturally from
potency to act, from the imperfect to the (relatively) perfect. The
proportionate object of such a progression must likewise be
something confused and imperfect, inasmuch as the more distinct
as such is more perfect than the confused, and the notion of being
as manifested in any particular object of awareness has a more
confused—a more ''potential''—intelligibility as indistinctly
mingling every character actually found or findable in that object.
This ''being'' as the most primitive of intellectual apprehensions,
the ''prima ratio cognoscibilis seu primum cognitum formale
respectu nostri intellectus'' (as Poinsot 1633: Q. 1, Art. 3 formulated it), is also the richest of all notions, embracing every particular intelligible object in the amplitude of analogy according to
a totally confused and undistinguished awareness. Material entities as particular beings, for example, thus, are experienced
''factually'' only because being has been previously grasped in a
way that is very different from conceptualizations of the logical

order. This is the meaning of the "primo in intellectu cadit ens."

Out of this primitive awareness there arises in the course of changes experienced (movements, etc.), and by way of opposition to being, the idea of non-being. In the earliest phases of apprehension, this idea originates via the senses (and feelings of "disappointment") out of the basic awareness of differences in the sensibly varying situation, perhaps out of experiences of opposition in particular. This polarity from experience provides the understanding with the first materials for a judgment, that "being is not non-being," or, as they more concretely formulated the primitive possibility, "this is not that." In this very act, the understanding grasps (again for the first time) distinction, which in turn enables grasp of the first principle of intelligible discourse and ground of endless further judgments of a logical kind, namely, the principle of contradiction: it is not possible to both be and not be at the same time in the same respect (as, e.g., in Aquinas c. 1268-1272: IV, lect. 6, n. 605, "impossibile est esse et non esse simul").

As the direct outcome of the judgment that being is not non-being, the principle of contradiction participates in its non-alternative or necessary character. Unable on the inward side to affirm and deny the same thing under the same aspect ("demonstration is addressed not to the spoken word but to the discourse within the soul, and though we can always raise objections to the spoken word, to the inward discourse we cannot always object"—*Organon*, c. 348-47b: 76b24-27), the senses likewise manifest outwardly that entities are one way or another but not both in a given aspect, giving rise to the notion of being undivided or unity. But what is experimentally undivided in itself is in that very experience given as divided from others, whence the grasp of plurality, of many beings each of which is itself one. At this level the tautological judgment becomes possible—"every being is what it is"—and also the recognition of an "outside," i.e., outside of our subjectivity (i.e., independently existing in respect of our being as knowers), world. (To anticipate the analyses of Part II, it is this recognition that sets anthroposemiosis apart in principle from zoosemiosis as such. As it might be said: "In its most perfect function, which is not to manufacture ideas but to judge, the understanding seizes upon existence exercised by things.")

These seven elements, then—being, non-being, distinction, contradiction, unity, plurality, identity—are the foundation for the notion of "truth as conformity" (the basis for the prior possibility of such conformity being something else again, as

Heidegger best understood: see Deely 1971c, and Section 5 note 9 below); and their sequence, being the same for all in its necessary features, is what lays the ground of possibility for intersubjective agreement in the results of judgments as well. We have here, so to speak, the intellectual infrastructure of cultural reality in its difference from the purely social world. Idealism in the modern sense (that the mind knows only what the mind itself makes) is precluded in the setting of such an analysis "by the fact that the knowing subject is discovered [or, more exactly, discovers itself] only within a world of change subject to the law of contradiction" (Ashley 1973: 291-292). This law of contradiction itself, moreover, along with the other logical concepts, "such as 'something,' 'identity,' 'non-identity,' 'agreement,' 'disagreement,' 'characteristic,' 'relation,' and 'connection' " (cf. Aquinas c. 1268-1272: V, lect. 11, n. 912), is "rooted in our concrete dealings with beings. The elementary rules of logic owe their compelling force to our habitual knowledge about the identity, unity, inner indivision of being and its difference from other beings. In other words, the logical evidences are based [or rather, arise out of] a certain experience of being as being" (Strasser 1963: 263).

To summarize in the formula of an author of the period (Aquinas c. 1269-1272b: q. 66, 5 ad 2), wisdom has the function of knowing the "ratio entis et non entis . . . et aliorum quae consequuntur ad ens" (the "rationale of being and non-being . . . and the notions following therefrom").

2. Church (1948: 148) writes: "In Scholastic logic, first intentions were properties or classes of, and relations between, concrete things. Second intentions were properties or classes of, and relations between, first intentions.

"This suggests the beginning of a simple hierarchy of types, but actually is not so, because no 'third intentions' were separated out or distinguished from second. Thus the general concept of *class* is a second intention, although some particular classes may also be second intentions.

"Thomas Aquinas defined logic as the science of second intentions applied to first intentions."

This is a useful summary, but several cautions must be entered regarding it. In the first paragraph, to speak of first intentions as "classes of concrete things" is problematical. For the scholastics, all classes as such belonged to the order of second intentions.

In the second paragraph, therefore, to suggest that the

scholastics had no analysis of type hierarchy on the grounds that "no 'third intentions' were separated out" is a serious misunderstanding, as can be seen from a reading of Poinsot 1632: 292a33ff. The Latins expressly recognized that one second intention can and does frequently serve to found another and that other yet another (as in the predicable hierarchy of genus and species, for example), "and yet these are all called second intentions, even though one is erected upon the other, and not a third or a fourth intention, because they all pertain to an object as cognized, while to be cognized is always a second state of a thing."

(In the third paragraph, the "science of . . ." would be roughly formal logic as such, the "application to . . . ," material logic, a distinction we will take up shortly in the text above.)

A much better summary of the scholastic position has been made by Simon (1955: x-xi): "Things admit of more than one way of existing. Over and above the primary existence that they enjoy in nature, things enjoy, as objects of understanding, a new existence—objective, intelligible, intentional—which brings forth in them a new system of properties. The object of logic is constituted by the properties which accrue to things by reason of the new existence that they enjoy as objects of the human mind. In opposition to the real properties or 'first intentions' of things, these logical properties are called 'second intentions' in scholastic language. The laws of second intentions are the rules of reasoning, and the art of reasoning is the same as the science of second intentions." Although this summary makes no mention of a competing view on the matter that develops later in the Latin age (namely, the view that the syncategoremata or "logical constants" are the subject-matter of logic—see Bochenski 1970: §26, pp. 153-162), it is sufficiently accurate for the present discussion, because the later view is included within the first, inasmuch as the syncategoremata are readily seen and were seen by all the Latins as belonging to the order of second intentions, and they necessarily structure logical practice. Not until late modern times with the advent of "logical algebra" in its various forms are the syncategoremata subjected in practice to a further interpretation which divorces them from the order of "being as known intellectually," second intentions in the scholastic sense. (See, for example, the spirited controversy between Veatch 1951 and Copi 1951—which Veatch carries on more or less throughout his many writings on logic—of which Clark 1952: 96 says: "Veatch demonstrates that the objects of modern logic are not 'second intentions,' as such.") Hence Bochenski is able to observe (1970:

156) "that in fact the *entire* [sic] practice of medieval logic corresponds to the Thomist conception of the object of logic [i.e., of
its subject matter, which is about], even though this conception
was not the only one. For scholastic logic essentially consists of
two parts: the doctrine of the properties of terms, and the doctrine
of consequences. The properties of terms are evidently second intentions in the Thomist sense; and one must think of consequences in the same light, since the logical relationships they exhibit (e.g., between antecedent and consequent) are not real
things." Bochenski (*ibid.*: 155) further relates this point of universal Latin practice to the earlier Stoic doctrine of the λεκτόν:
"Thus according to Thomas the subject-matter of logic is such
'secondarily understood things' or 'second intentions,' belonging
to the domain of being in thought, and so *lecta*. Not all *lecta*,
however, but a special kind, such as those corresponding to the
meaning of logical constants. It is to be stressed that according to
Thomas, as for the Stoics, the subject-matter of logic is nothing
psychical, but something objective, which yet exists only in the
soul." This shows how ill-founded is "the tendency of recent
philosophers," as Mueller observes (1978: 8), "to reject the
Aristotelian way [of interpreting a propositional logic] as
'psychologism'." But, more importantly, it shows as well that the
complication of the controversy, medieval or modern, leaves
unaffected the issues foundational for semiotic as such, which is
our principal concern.

3. The beginning student today is no more likely to possess
a knowledge of Aristotle's categories than of Porphyry's
predicables. It would be useful therefore to insert at this point a
brief schema exhibiting what those categories are and a typical rationale or manner of their derivation, particularly as it relates to
the logical analysis of discourse, and without going into any of the
controversies over whether the standard list of ten categories
should be decreased or lengthened. It is helpful to bear in mind
that the Latin word for "category" is *praedicamentum*, which is
from the same root as "to predicate" ("*praedicare*"). Thus the
Latin term carries a connection between being and discourse in
this area that is lost in our language. In any event, the categories
of Aristotle, i.e., his classification of the fundamental ways in
which being is able to exist in the world of nature, or, alternative-
ly (and slightly more exactly), of "the broadest of all terms that
can be predicated *univocally* of a subject" (Simon 1971: 521), can
be "deduced logically" from the diverse ways of speaking about

things. The following derivation is based on Aquinas 1268-1272: V, lect. 9, nn. 889-893, and 1268: III, lect. 5, n. 322, and can be regarded as representing a characteristic Latin understanding of the matter.

The CATEGORIES or "PREDICAMENTS" of Aristotle, logically derived:

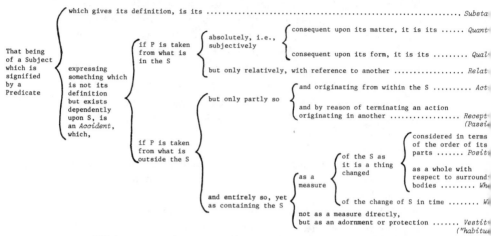

Without entering, as explained above, into the controversies surrounding this so-called "deduction"—which are extensive (e.g., on the notion of categorial "where" alone, cfr. Nys 1942: II, 376-397), have never achieved generally satisfactory resolution, take on a quite new dimension in the modern era (a fact semiotic expressly takes into account: Deely 1977: 47-48, 57 note 4), and are far from over (perhaps the best starting point for a post-modern discussion would be Heidegger 1927: 3)—it may yet be said, in line with our observations above on *ens rationis*, and as is clear from our schema (p. 26 above) on its contrast to *ens reale*, that even a glance at the thoroughly "traditionally-minded" work of Simon 1970: esp. Ch. IV, pp. 89ff., suffices to reveal how fundamental is the role of mind-dependent being in enabling us to grasp what the ancients considered to be the most universal feature of natural experience and Aristotle made the point of departure for his "realist" philosophy of nature, namely, the feature of movement or change in the physical environment. If semiotic places us, as it does, at the intersection of nature and culture, that is because semiosis in humankind is precisely their interpenetration and common fulfillment.

4. As points of interpretation go, consensus on this one is exceptionally broad. E.g., cf. Ackrill, 1963: 71 note: ". . . it is im-

portant to recognize from the start that the *Categories* is not primarily or explicitly about names, but about the things that names signify. . . . Aristotle relies greatly on linguistic facts and tests, but his aim is to discover truths about non-linguistic items.'' Compare this with the assessment of Poinsot 1632: 500b36-501a2: ''The distinction of the categories was introduced for this, that the orders and classes of diverse natures might be set forth, to which all the things which participate some nature might be reduced, and on this basis the first thing that must be excluded from *every* category is mind-dependent being, because being which depends for its being on being cognized (so-called mind-dependent being) has not a nature nor a true entity, but a constructed one, and therefore must be relegated not to a true category, but to a constructed one. Whence St. Thomas says (in q. 7, art. 9 of his *Disputed Questions on the Power of God*) that only a thing independent of the soul pertains to the categories.''

5. Aquinas, c. 1269-1272a: ''Proemium,'' opening paragraph: ''. . . hominum genus arte et rationibus vivit: in quo videtur Philosophus tangere quoddam hominis proprium quo a caeteris animalibus differt. Alia enim animalia quodam naturali instinctu ad suos actus aguntur; homo autem rationis judicio in suis actionibus dirigitur. Et inde est quod ad actus humanos faciliter et ordinate perficiendos diversae artes deserviunt. Nihil enim aliud ars esse videtur, quam certa ordinatio rationis quomodo per determinata media ad debitum finem actus humani perveniant.

''Ratio autem non solum dirigere potest inferiorum partium actus, sed etiam actus sui directiva est. Hoc enim est proprium intellectivae partis, ut in seipsam reflectatur: nam intellectus intelligit seipsum et similiter ratio de suo actu ratiocinari potest. Si igitur ex hoc, quod ratio de actu manus ratiocinatur, adinventa est ars aedificatoria vel fabrilis, per quas homo faciliter et ordinate huiusmodi actus exercere potest; eadem ratione ars quaedam necessaria est, quae sit directiva ipsius actus rationis, per quam scilicet homo in ipso actu rationis ordinate, faciliter et sine errore procedat.

''Et haec ars est *Logica*, idest rationalis scientia. Quae non solum rationalis est ex hoc, quod est secundum rationem (quod est omnibus artibus commune); sed etiam ex hoc, quod est circa ipsum actum rationis sicut circa propriam materiam.

''Et ideo videtur esse ars artium, quia in actu rationis nos dirigit, a quo omnes artes procedunt. Oportet igitur Logicae partes accipere secundum diversitatem actuum rationis.''

6. The notion of "natural language," which has not to my knowledge been adequately explored yet as such (see Part II of this book), must not be confused with the notion of "ordinary language" which has been so abused in contemporary philosophy after Wittgenstein. "Ordinary" language is a chimera opposed to the language of technical and specialized pursuits, and used by certain "linguistic" philosophers after the manner of a talisman to make philosophical problems "disappear." I call it a chimera, because in truth it has no proper existence as such, being in truth only inadequately distinct from the technical vocabularies and constantly modified by them. (Thus Marcus 1979: 35-36 observes that the "paradox" of artificial languages, considered in terms of their semiotic status, "consists of the fact that they become very natural when their pragmatics are old enough.") "Ordinary language," in short, is a sociological phenomenon, not primarily a philosophical one, and decidedly relative to the culture and consciousness of specific ages. Natural language, by contrast, is the semiotic web constituting a linguistic community at any given time in its totality and diachronically as well as synchronically. Ivo Thomas (1967: 960), speaking of what might be called early anticipations of so-called "classical logic" (which will be discussed in Section 6 of this essay) as it appeared more or less full blown in the Port-Royal Logic, writes as follows: "It was about 1440 that the first recorded voice of the new age, or non-age, in logic made itself heard. L. Valla, a renowned humanist scholar, then rejected the third figure of the syllogism on the grounds that women, children, and nonlogicians generally, do not argue that way. Perhaps this is the first time that ordinary language was claimed as the standard of logical doctrine. Evidently all sense of syllogistic as a deductive system had been lost; indeed Valla said that conversion, Aristotle's chief means of deduction, is only a 'remedy for sick syllogisms.' R. Agricola's *De dialectica inventione* swung the ambivalent 'topical' tradition firmly into the path of rhetoric, in contrast with Abelard. P. Melanchthon, writing in 1521, expounded Cicero's syllogism before Aristotle's. Older doctrines were quickly dropped or ridiculed. G. Savonarola kept telling the 16th century in numerous re-editions that anyone arguing from a conjunction to one of its parts was *dignus explosione*.

"In mid-16th century, vernacular logics began to appear, e.g., T. Wilson's *The Rule of Reason* (1551) and the *Dialectique* (1555) of Peter Ramus. This last writer's views on logical reform provoked widespread and long-lasting controversy. His simplified syllogistic and novel terminology occasioned long commentaries on very little and a new technical scholasticism. Aristotelians found little to discuss besides the iniquities of Ramism and the fourth figure of the syllogism, few recognizing that this was a matter to be settled by definition. Sextus Empiricus appeared in Latin in 1569, but led to no rediscovery of Stoic logic.

"There was an occasional break in the clouds. J. Hospinianus (1515-75) thoroughly investigated syllogistic on a combinatory basis, and G. Cardano illustrated his *Dialectica* with geometrical arguments. J. Junge (*Logica Hamburgensis*, 1638) showed a deductive interest in the syllogism and some appreciation of Aristotle's logic of relations. In 1662 A. Geulincx pleaded for the restoration of medieval doctrines. In that year the 'Port Royal Logic' of A. Arnauld and P. Nicole was published. Antirhetorical and anti-Ramist, the authors idolized geometry and did much to tighten up syllogistic theory. At the same time they opened the way to introducing epistemological and psychological discussions into books of logic."

7. Ashworth 1974: 2, after deftly summarizing the accepted conventions established regarding the role and place of Petrus Hispanus in the development and history of Logic, continues: "If one looks up 'Petrus Hispanus' in Risse's invaluable *Bibliographia Logica*, one finds that no editions appeared in Spain or England, a few in Paris, some in Germany, Poland, the Netherlands and Belgium. Deventer leads with sixteen editions between 1485 and 1528. After 1528 there are only seven editions, the last in 1639, and *all* were printed in Venice."

8. Thus Fonseca 1564: "Praefatio": "Adeo inops fuit politioris Literaturae superior aetas, ut cum omnes, qui Philosophiae studia consectabantur, Aristotelici haberi vellent, paucissimi essent, qui Aristotelem evolverent. Arbitrantur enim Aristotelicam doctrinam planius, et expeditius in summulis quibusdam, ac quaestionibus, quas diligentiorum industria pepererat, quam in suo auctore contineri."

9. E.g., Thomas 1967: 960: "H. Aldrich, in his *Artis logicae compendium* (1691), correctly tabled 24 moods of the syllogism in 4 figures and methodically proved all others invalid." Five additional valid moods can be added to the nineteen mentioned above by drawing particular conclusions in cases where the premises admit universal conclusions to be drawn, a move justified by the consideration that a subaltern proposition makes the same asser-

tion or denial as its universal diminished in force, and so must be admitted if the universal would be admitted. The valid argument forms whose conclusions are thus diluted or "weakened" are called the *subaltern moods*.

Notes to Part I, Section 4

1. Eco (ISISSS lecture of 6/6/80) has pointed out that this famous text, everywhere cited and made much of, as a matter of fact does not fit in very well with the main thrust of the context in which it appears, as though it were an *obiter dictum*, hardly a proof text of something well thought through or established.

2. Simon 1955: note 4, 613-615, using no punctuation (including quotation marks) other than Simon's own: The word translated by 'idea' is *species*, in psychology and epistemology one of the most embarrassing expressions of the scholastic language. Against the use of 'idea' for *species* it can be objected that we have no other word than 'idea' to translate the Latin *idea* [ee-day-uh], whose meaning will be hard to convey if the word to which it is intrusted conveys also another notion of very frequent occurrence. In our opinion, this difficulty is inevitable and ought to be taken care of as best we can in each particular case. We have no choice, for 'idea' alone [Simon is sometimes given to such overstatement, as noted in Deely 1983: EA] can express with the needed vividness the meaning of the Aristotelian εἶδος and of the scholastic *species*.

The scholastic usage of *species* in psychological and epistemological contexts is fixed by Aristotelian sentences the most famous of which is: οὐ γὰρ ὁ λίθος ἐν τῇ ψυχῇ, ἀλλὰ τὸ εἶδος. *On the Soul* 3. 8. 431ᵇ29. J. A. Smith (*The Basic Works of Aristotle* [New York: Random House, 1941]) translates: ". . .it is not the stone which is present in the soul but its form." This is a perfectly accurate translation, but the word 'form' is of no help in our endeavor to figure out precisely what is present in the soul when the stone is perceived. The theory of cognitive "forms," which, in Aristotle, involves much obscurity, has been greatly clarified by St. Thomas and his commentators. With particular reference to its treatment by Cajetan and John of St. Thomas, it can be outlined as follows: Knowing is a certain way of being, primarily distinguished by the paradoxical ability of the knower to be not only what it is but also what other things are. (*On the Soul* 3. 8. 431ᵇ20, "Let us now summarize our results about the soul and repeat that the soul is in a way all existing things.'' Translated by J. A. Smith.) The mode of existence according to which the soul is all things is described as immaterial, spiritual, objective, *intentional*, transsubjective, in opposition to the mode of existence according to which things are just what they are, and which is called material, *physical*, natural, entitative, subjective. Here, as elsewhere, existence is intelligibly prior to what bears it, and the contrast between, say, the stone and its ''form'' must be understood in relation to an intelligibly antecedent contrast, viz., that between the physical and the intentional ways of existing. ''Notice, Cajetan writes (*Com. on Summa theologica*, i. 55. 3), that there are two genera of beings. Some are primarily designed to exist, although, secondarily, they may happen to represent other beings, and these we call *things*. But some beings are primarily designed by nature to represent other beings: and these we call intentions of things, and sensible or intelligible *species*. The reason why it is necessary to posit these two genera is that the cognitive must be not only itself but also others, and the intellective, all things, as established [by St. Thomas' exposition] in i. 14 [i.e., c. 1266] and by the consensus of the philosophers, who agree that like is known by like. Now the natures of things cannot be present in the cognitive with their own entity. It is not the stone which is present in the soul. Again, the knower cannot, by its finite substance alone, be so excellent as to have in itself the means of assimilating the natures of the knowable things, distinctly and according to their proper features. Thus it was necessary for nature to establish the intentional being, by means of which the knower is the knowable.''

The intentional form of Aristotelianism (εἶδος) has sometimes been confused with the simulacrum of the Epicureans (εἴδωλον). In the terms of Cajetan's exposition, it is clear that the Epicurean simulacrum remains a *thing*, i.e., an entity of the first genus, which is defined by the existential function of existing. The simulacrum is a small thing, which inconspicuously accomplishes feats that big things could not conceivably accomplish, viz., getting through the pores of the skin, reaching the subtle center of the body, etc. But just as the intentional 'to be' of the Aristotelians is by no means a physical existence, so their ''intentions'' and ''sensible and intelligible *species*'' are no things. They are defined by their being related to 'to be intentionally' as things are related to 'to be physically.' To designate such entities, there is only one word, the word 'idea.' The two systems described by Cajetan are the system of the things and the system of the ideas.

We commonly use 'ideas' not in its Augustinian and scholastic sense of creative pattern, but in the sense of intelligible "*species*." Much can be learned about Aristotelian psychology and theory of knowledge by extending the use of 'idea' to the *species* of all cognitive powers. [Indeed! See our discussion of "conceptus" in this work and in Deely 1983.] There are ideas in the intellect and in the imagination and in the memory and in the external senses. Aristotelian views on sensation, so wretchedly expounded most of the time, become intelligible when we understand that Aristotelianism is the philosophy which posits ideas not only in the intellect and in the imagination and in the memory but also in sight and hearing and touch. Other philosophies know of ideas born in the soul, e.g., intellectual representations consequent upon images, images consequent upon sense impressions. But *Aristotelianism knows of ideas that are initial in an absolute sense and are not born in the soul but in nature.* The sensorial idea is the Aristotelian answer to the problem of the initial connection between physical nature and the soul. Those things are impossible to explain if we translate *species sensibilis* by sensible 'species' or 'form' or anything short of the thought-provoking power of the word 'idea.' [Second last emphasis supplied. See further Simon 1970: 47-50; Maritain 1959: 103-104, 114-128.]

Notes to Part I, Section 5

1. "It cannot be said of Peirce—as of some of today's representatives of formal logic and the 'logic of exact science','' Apel observes (1981: 19), "that he had no sense of history, no consciousness of the fact that all thought is mediated through tradition. The opposite is true. From the beginning of his Kant studies in 1855, Peirce formulated his systematic thought in a continuing dialogue with the great Western tradition of thought. His need to take proper account of history went so far that, as early as in his works of 1868, he introduced the terms that he planned to use— for example, 'intuition,' 'hypothesis,' and 'contemplation'—with long excurses on the history of terminology. Later, in the propagation of the 'Ethics of Terminology,' Peirce's concern was not just the logical clarity of definitions, but reflection on precisely his own starting point in the history of philosophical language.'' Apel also notes, a little further on (*ibid.*, p. 20), that Peirce in his philosophizing "calls into question basic presuppositions shared by both Hume and Kant, presuppositions of the entire modern pe-

riod of philosophy [cf. note 9 below concluding this Section]. He does this, inspired by his knowledge of the history of logic, while orienting himself to the Aristotelian Middle Ages and, simultaneously, retaining certain basic presuppositions of the modern critique of knowledge.''

2. Bouissac (1979: 209) describes a romantic caricature of this heritage as well. ''The Cartesian fallacy, which holds individual inner evidence to be a criterial value, implies the belief that deep introspection served by a reasonably coherent discourse necessarily leads to the 'truth.' Hence the production of scores of mostly unreferenced texts, spelling out the meanderings of a reflexive experience . . . .'' Cf. Bouissac 1976.

3. Boehner 1957: ix-xi: ''Scholastic philosophy found its mature expression during the thirteenth and fourteenth centuries. The scholasticism of the thirteenth century was predominantly receptive and constructive in its tendencies. Its chief exponents were mainly interested in absorbing the wealth of philosophical learning that came to them from Greek and Arabic sources, and in constructing articulate systems comprising the thought of their time. Their work can perhaps best be called 'synthetic'. By contrast, fourteenth-century scholasticism was occupied in sifting, revising and adapting its rich legacy of ideas. Its chief exponents focused their attention on the structure of the traditional philosophy itself; they tested its basis and examined the solidity of its parts. Their philosophy may therefore be characterized by the term 'critical'. These labels must not, however, be taken as mutually exclusive. Neither the thirteenth nor the fourteenth century was without originality; and while in the thirteenth century a sound sense of criticism was visibly active and alive, the fourteenth proved itself by no means incapable of building systems.

''In one aspect the two centuries are two parts of a single whole—the period of classical scholasticism. There is a tendency on the part of historians who have mainly studied the thirteenth century to look upon them as two distinct or even opposing periods. In their view the thirteenth century is unmistakably the golden age, the fourteenth a period of decline and decadence. Yet it remains an historical fact that there was a unity of civilization and religion ensured by an agreement in holding the dogmas of the Catholic faith, dogmas which it was their main endeavour to elucidate. There was the unity of an unbroken academic tradition guaranteed by the use of common textbooks, viz. the writings of

Aristotle, the *Sentences* of Peter Lombard and others, which had to be read and publicly interpreted by anyone aspiring to academic degrees.

Within this unity there was a lively discussion of the various conflicting solutions of the common problems, but, in contrast to the terminological confusion of modern philosophy, this discussion was grounded on the use of a generally accepted common technical language.'' What Boehner observes here is true as far as it goes, but it does not go far enough. The ''period of classical scholasticism,'' as Boehner describes it, extends in fact all the way to the middle of the 17th century. Boehner's preference for the 14th century is at least as arbitrary as the preference of those historians he criticizes for puffing the 13th century. The epoch of natural philosophy is as cultural life goes a ''natural'' unity in the Latin West, and needs to be studied as such. When sufficient work has been done, the ''standard historiographies'' will be revised accordingly.

4. ''Signa formalia sunt similitudines, seu species quaedam rerum significatarum in potentiis cognoscentibus consignatae, quibus res significatae percipiuntur. Huius generis est similitudo, quam mons obiectus imprimit in oculis: item ea, quam amicus absens in memoria amici reliquit; item ea, quam quis de re, quam nunquam vidit, effingit. Dicuntur autem formalia signa, quia formant, et quasi figurant potentiam cognoscentem. Signa instrumentalia sunt ea, quae potentiis cognoscentibus obiecta, in alterius rei cognitione ducunt. Huius generis est vestigium animalis in pulvere impressum, fumus, statua, et alia huiusmodi. Nam vestigium est signum animalis, a quo impressum est: fumus vero, ignis latentis: statua denique Caesaris, aut alicuius alterius. Haec dicuntur signa instrumentalia, vel quia his quasi instrumentis, conceptus nostros alijs significamus: vel quia quemadmodum artifex, ut instrumento moveat materiam; necesse est, ut moveat instrumentum, sic potentiae ad cognoscendum aptae, ut hoc signorum genere rem aliquam cognoscant, necesse est, ut haec signa percipiant. Hinc colliges apertissimum discrimen inter haec signa, et superiora: illa siquidem non sunt a nobis necessario percipienda, ut ipsorum perceptione in rei significatae cognitionem veniamus: haec autem nisi percipiantur, nemini alicuius rei cognitionem adducent.'' Comparative translation in Romeo 1979: 194-195, based on other editions than my Venice, 1611.

5. In Greek and Latin cultures, Bacchus crowned with ivy during his debauches made of ivy a universal symbol of drunken-

ness·and revelry. Similarly, the common use of cypress boughs in ancient funeral rites and of cypress trees to mark burial sites made cypress a signifier of death.

6. Translation basically by Romeo, 1979: 201 note 1. Bosserel's lectures, MS 133 of the University of Graz, are published as an Appendix to Ferreira Gomes 1964: 779-861, neither of which sources had I access to at the time of the June 24 ISISSS '80 lecture. For information and text on this point, I was at the time entirely dependent on Romeo 1979: esp. 190, 198-200, and 201 note 2. The text itself as published in Ferreira Gomes, vol. II, p. 800, reads: "significare autem est aliquid potentiae cognoscenti repraesentare, ut sensui, phantasiae, intellectui.

"Dividuntur signa duplici divisione. Prima in formalia et instrumentalia. Formalia sunt similitudines, seu species quaedam rerum significatarum in potentiis cognoscentibus quibus res significatae percipiuntur, ut similitudo amici, et haec signa non habent opus cognosci sicut ut videam oculo non necesse habeo ipsum oculum videre quo video.

"Instrumentalia sunt quae potentiis cognoscentibus obiecta non solum ipsa cognoscuntur, sed etiam in alterius rei cognitionem ducunt, ut vestigium animalis, fumus, rugae in fronte.

"Secunda naturalia et ex instituto. Naturalia sunt quae apud omnes idem significant, ut gemitus et risus. Ex instituto, quae ex hominum voluntate, et quadam quasi conventione significant, ut voces et characteres, et quae apud omnes populos usurpata sunt, ut hedera, cupressus.

"Nota quod etiam naturalia possint esse formalia, haec non omnia. Conceptus enim et gemitus sunt naturalia, gemitus tamen non formale, sed instrumentale."

7. "Atque ut alte, et a capite significandi modos, repetam, Significare nihil aliud est, quam potentiae cognoscenti, aliquid repraesentare. Cum autem omne, quod aliquid repraesentat, sit signum rei, quae repraesentatur, efficitur, ut quicquid rem aliquam significat, sit signum eius." The text does not seem right here. Cf. translation in Romeo 1979: 194: "In order to trace the modes of signification back to their most remote origin, 'to signify' is simply to depict something to a cognoscitive being. Everything representing something is a sign of what is represented, hence whatever represents something is at the same time a sign."

8. "Signa vero ex instituto sunt, quae ex hominum volun-

tate, et quadam quasi compositioni significant. Quorum rursus duo sunt genera. Nam quaedam significant ex impositione, ut-pote voces quibus homines colloquuntur, et scripta, quibus ab-sentes inter se communicant: alia ex consuetudine, et communi usurpatione: quo pacto ea, quae pro foribus appenduntur, signi-ficant res venales. Eorum porro, quae ex impositione significant, duplex est significatio, propria, et impropria. . . . Fere autem ver-ba ad aliquem modum (τϱόπον Graeci vocant) traducta, et immu-tata, impropriam habent significationem: ut quae per Metaphor-am, Catachresim, Metalepsim, et Metonymiam immutantur.''

9. The treatment above of Poinsot's contribution, in counter-point to the traditional elements and positions against which he reacted in the fashioning of his *Treatise on Signs*, does not bring out clearly the difference between his semiotic (as the foundational doctrine of what a sign is) and his semiotics (as the development of that understanding in terms of the classification and treatment of specific types and contexts of signs). In order to bring out this difference, therefore, both because of the near-complete unavail-ability at present of Poinsot's work, and because of the extreme skepticism evinced by Scruton (speaking for many contempo-raries) toward, as George Kennard put it in a letter of 20 Decem-ber 1981, ''any generic doctrine of signs purporting to cover two distinct species, words and ideas, and clouds into the bargain,'' I will enter here, in effect, an excursus recounting summarily this earliest ''generic'' semiotic (so to speak). I will do so strictly in terms of its own essentials, but precisely and only as they unfold *systematically*—not in counterpoint to other views but from its own point of departure as determined by the matter-at-issue, namely, semiosis. As far as I understand these matters, it is the angle of vision afforded by *this* standpoint that positions one best to see how semiotic requires a revolution in philosophy, classical and contemporary alike—which is not to deny the necessity of other standpoints as well for completing the picture. In this excursus, then, points covered in the text above will be resumed in an order which better reveals their integration in the overall thematic unity of the doctrine of signs as it was integrally envisaged in the mind of this — so far as is presently known — its first systematiser.

Briefly, then, Poinsot begins his *Treatise on Signs* by drawing attention to a central feature of semiosis that must, in his opinion, be a first concern of semioticians to safeguard and give adequate account of, namely, the fact that, in our experience, signs bring together natural and social phenomena. The sign, he points out

(Book I, Question 1, 646b26-45), is something neither preclusively natural nor preclusively social, but both inclusively. For while all signs as such acquire their signification and exist actually only within some living being's experience, nonetheless, within that very experience, the connection between signs and what they signify sometimes seems to have roots outside our experience of their connection (the case of "natural" signs), and other times seems to have no reality other than the one derived from the experience itself of social interaction (the case of customary and stipulated signs). Thus the first task of the semiotician, in Poinsot's judgment, is to secure a standpoint superior to the division of being into what exists independently of our cognition (*ens reale*, "mind-independent being"), and what exists dependently upon cognition (*ens rationis*, "mind-dependent being"). For Poinsot, semiotic must take its stand, in the felicitous description of Sebeok (1975b), squarely "at the intersection of nature and culture" (see Deely 1975a, 1978a).

This new, wholly experiential point of departure selected for Poinsot's philosophical account of signs (Ransdell 1980: 181 speaks similarly of the "basic phenomenological stance" endemic to semiotic) sets him on a path toward reconciling the seemingly opposed orders of nature and culture which have generally been considered irreconcilable in modern thought at least since the famous *Critique of Pure Reason* of Immanuel Kant (1781, 1787). Kant's conclusions in this regard merely systematized and made unmistakable inclinations that had been at work from the beginnings of modern thought in its manner of treating knowledge (see Deely 1978c). But his simple description of semiotic's initial task also amounts to a revolution within the perspective of natural philosophy or "physics" traditional in Poinsot's day. For the sole concern of that tradition was to uncover and explicate the structure of *ens reale*, which they thought to have achieved, after Aristotle, with the division of mind-independent being into *substances* or natural units of independent existence (see Ashley 1973) with their *accidents* or various properties and characteristics. Thus, the division of being into the Aristotelian categories of substance and the various types of accident was generally thought to be the permanent achievement of ontology in the Latin age.

Poinsot's approach to semiotic simply undercuts this categorial scheme, not in the sense of showing it to be false, but in the sense of going below it and beginning with an analysis of experience prior to the possibility of the working out of *any* such, Aristotelian ("realist") or Kantian ("phenomenalist") equally (see

Deely 1977). Comparatively to the traditions of ancient Greek
and medieval Latin philosophy alike, Poinsot establishes a *fundamental ontology* in just that sense which Heidegger (1927: 3; 1929)
calls for in our own time, namely, an "ontology" which accounts
for the categorial interconnections and lays bare the ground of the
prior possibility of truth as a "correspondence" between thought
and being. Poinsot finds this fundamental ontology in our experience of *the ways in which things appear to be relative*. The simplicity
of his analysis on this point is nothing short of ingenious, although
his terminology and style of expression is so history-laden with the
concerns of a previous tradition of discussion in this area, going
back continuously some eleven hundred years (to the work of
Boethius—discussion in Krempel 1952), that it makes for exceedingly difficult access on the part of contemporary readers separated by more than centuries from contact with that then-living
tradition. I will try to recapture the central insights of concern
here by some simple examples before introducing the minimum
of technical terms.

Consider the case of a room in which all the furniture has just
been moved in, but not yet arranged, and that same room after
each item of furniture has been put into proper place. Literally,
no thing has been altered in the two cases — each thing in itself,
each item of furniture, remains just as it was, assuming no
damage in the rearrangements; and yet the simple fact of arrange-
ment makes all the difference in the world between the two cases.
It is not *in the things* that a difference has been made, but *in between*
them. Moreover, this "in between" difference is there in both
cases, whether or not anyone happens to be contemplating it. We
have here the matter of what Poinsot calls "predicamental" or
real (physical) relations.

Now consider further the case of the unarranged room while
its owner is deciding how to arrange it. Suppose, for simplicity's
sake, that that person completely thinks out in advance the exact
position for each item, and only then proceeds to place the furnishings accordingly. At the moment when everything has been
thought out but nothing yet placed, there exists in thought a network of objective but entirely mind-dependent ("mental") relations (*relationes rationis*); yet once the furnishings have been moved
accordingly, this very same network has been made to exist in the
physical order of what stands independently of cognition! Thus
Poinsot observed (following in this Aquinas c. 1266: q. 28, and
Cajetan 1507 before him) that as a mode of reality relation is
unique in that its essence (*esse ad aliud*, "being between") is sepa-

rate from its cause or ground of existence (*esse in alio*, "the character or feature upon which a relation is founded"), which is not the case for any other mode of reality. Poinsot sees in this the ultimate reason for the possibility of semiosis: relation in what is proper to it, namely, suprasubjectivity or intersubjectivity (*esse ad*), is indifferent to realization now in nature, now in thought, now in both (Deely 1971b, 1972a, 1972b). Relation in this sense, precisely as indifferent to the opposition of what depends upon and what is independent of cognition, Poinsot calls *relatio secundum esse*, "relation according to the way it has being" or "ontological relation" (see Deely 1974, 1983).

Consider now the case of some "individual" being, whether "natural"—say, a dinosaur—or "artificial"—say, a lamp in the newly arranged room. Such individuals are emphatically not relations in the being proper to them (*secundum esse*)—they exist subjectively as something in their own right, not just between other things sustaining them in a derivative way. And yet, if we seek to *explain* why they are as they are or how they might be altered from their present state, we find it necessary to refer to what the individuals in question themselves are not. Thus, even the individual entities and "natural units" of experience existing in their own right—even substances in Aristotle's scheme, the most absolute of the subjective entities—are seen to be *relative* when it comes to the question of how they come to be or of how they are to be accounted for. Relativity in *this* sense, precisely as infecting the whole scheme of categories of cognition-independent existents, Poinsot termed *relatio secundum dici*, "relation according to the way being must be expressed in discourse," or (synonymously) *relatio transcendentalis*, "transcendental relation."

With this division of being, then, into transcendental and ontological relation, Poinsot has two simple "categories" which are exhaustive and exclusive, but whose terms are entirely matters of *direct experience* (unlike Aristotle's division of being into substance and accident, which was also exhaustive and exclusive, but directly experienced only on the side of certain accidents: comprehensive discussion in Powell 1982), and whose relevance to the doctrine of signs is immediate: for all authors agree, and indeed experience makes quite unmistakable, that every sign as such is a *relative* being (something making known another than itself); and since, by the prior terms of the analysis of relative being, we know that there are only two irreducible types of relativity, it remains only to apply that analysis to our experience of semiosis in order to determine in what precisely a sign consists (the *formalis ratio signi*, as Poinsot puts it), that is to say, what is it that constitutes a sign in its proper being?

The answer to this question is ontological relation, an answer which enables Poinsot to resolve a number of aporia which have plagued accounts of signifying from ancient times down to the present (Deely 1976, 1978b), and which turn out to be decisive for epistemology and philosophical thought generally.

To mention only some of the most salient points, this resolution enables Poinsot to explain the indifference of discourse to physical reality (the possibility of lying, scientific posits—like Eudoxus' spheres—that prove to be mythical, talk about the past or future, fiction, etc.) and, at the same time, the power of discourse to express a factual situation (see Deely 1975b). In sharp contrast to the direction his contemporary Descartes was even then giving to what was to become the modern mainstream of philosophy, Poinsot was able to provide an analysis of ideas as signs which short-circuited the potential problem of how we can come to know any reality external to our own minds. He did so by showing that ideas in their existence as "private" (*esse in*) are mere transcendental relations serving to ground in their proper being (*esse ad*) relations to objects which by definition are in every case suprasubjective and accessible to many, in the same way that any two or more things can be related to something in common. Communication and public life, immediate components of common experience, are thus verified theoretically by the terms of Poinsot's semiotic, as is also the possibility of a science of nature which attains its object by the critical control of objectivity through the isolation of variables.

In this same line, Poinsot is able to secure the distinction between *representation* and *signification*, showing that, while every sign involves representation fundamentally, yet formally the sign in its proper being goes beyond the representative on which it is as such founded to lead awareness to another than itself. In technical terms, the representative element in signification is a transcendental relation, whereas the signification proper is in every case an ontological relation, and a categorial or "real" one when the conditions for relation to obtain in the physical order—principally the cognition-independent or "subjective" existence of its term—are fulfilled. Thus, while the concept as a similitude (or "representation") is but a remote connection with existing entities, as Descartes and Hume brought out so forcefully, it is not in this capacity that ideas (understood semiotically) provide the objects of apprehension, being in this capacity but transcendental relatives founding ontological relations, which latter alone are the proximate means for apprehending objects, whether real or not. As Powell summarized (cited in Deely 1983: EA III.C.2.(f)):

> Thanks to these innovations Poinsot can be seen as a bridge for a philosophy of realism between medieval philosophy of real individual substance and modern philosophers of empiricism and of social world. Empiricism is satisfied in terms of realism by making transcendental relations and predicamental relations the empirical origin of realism in philosophy. Social world is made intelligible in terms of realism by the univocity *as known* of real and unreal relations in language as customary signs.

Or again (Powell, *ibid.*):

> Poinsot wrote many purely traditional treatises as well as this one, but this *Treatise* contains in the concept of *formalis ratio signi* a moment when medieval realism of individual substance was passing into modern philosophies of empiricism and social world. We do not claim that Poinsot's concept of the *formalis ratio signi* is the only such moment. But the "formalis ratio signi" *defined* as *relatio secundum esse* expresses both the 'realist reason' of medieval substance philosophy and the 'subjective empiricist reason' of modern philosophies.

These remarks, confined to the central point of the doctrine (the foundation of semiosis in the nature of relative being), it should be noticed, have made no mention at all of the distinction between formal and instrumental signs. This well illustrates that the distinction, however important, derives from, and does not constitute the foundation of, Poinsot's semiotic. Given the novelty of the perspectives opened up by the notion of formal signs once it has been introduced, however, it is perhaps not surprising that this has been the one element of Poinsot's semiotics that was fastened upon (even in the absence of any understanding of his unique way of grounding that distinction in the relative) in the polemical climate of the last quarter century or so, by philosophers interested primarily in a "realist" epistemology and logic — e.g., Maritain (1924, 1943, 1957, 1959, etc.), Oesterle (1944), Adler (1967), Simon (1961), Veatch (1952), Parker and Veatch (1959), Wild (1947).

The strictly limited success met with by these attempts to appropriate Poinsot's conception, I venture, traces directly to the fact that each of these authors attempts to employ the distinction of formal signs directly, as if it were independent of Poinsot's prior account of relative being. Yet it is precisely that prior account which gives to the distinction its proper force (see Deely 1974: 875-6 note 26), and sets its use apart in Poinsot's context from the earlier discussions of the time. Indeed, in the case of Wild and Adler, so "independent" is the use made of the notion taken from Poinsot, in terms of its semiotic origin, that they deploy it against the background of a view of the reality of relation that is the contrary opposite of the one Poinsot regards as indispensably propaedeutic to the possibility of *any* finally coherent theory of signs (Wild 1956: 558; Adler 1968: 582)! In any event, when the notion of formal sign is detached from the account of the relative being constitutive of *all* signs, and is treated rather, not as a particular instance of *this* being (the intraorganismically founded instance), but as something posited independently, as it were, and cut out of whole cloth, it is bound to appear as an extremely interesting but essentially arbitrary *ad hoc* construct (as Ransdell 1966: 143 expressly noted), lacking proper philosophical justification and hence finally unconvincing in its own right. This is a point Poinsot, in taking over the terminology, gave a great deal of thought to, as Herculano de Carvalho (1969: 139) well points out.

This veneer of arbitrariness is what the semiotic foundation of this division removes, as is brought out in the following diagram, based on an original 1975 sketch drawn up in discussion of these matters by the Adlerian psychologist P. Lawrence Belove:

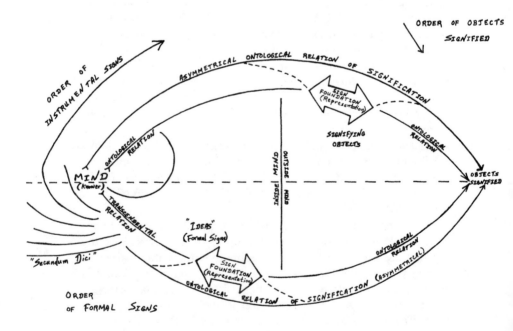

It is in such a light that we may expect the distinction of formal signs to play the central role it is capable of playing in the full-scale reassessment of the history of post-seventeenth-century thought that is long overdue in all that concerns the theories of mind, knowledge, and truth. For, given the distinction between representation and signifying as Poinsot construes and applies it to the distinction of formal from instrumental signs, we can see that, ironically enough, the conclusion of Locke's famous *Essay*, where he marks out the domain of semiotic and identifies ideas as signs (Book IV, Chap. XXI, esp. par. 4), is in principle at variance—contradictory variance—with the doctrine of ideas as objects with which he introduces the *Essay* (Introduction, par. 8) and on which he grounded the body of its expositions—which doctrine, moreover, be it noted, is basically consistent with the thrust of Descartes' *cogito* (a fact more fundamental than the rejection of innate ideas), and became the commonly accepted doctrine in the modern mainstream, rationalist and empiricist alike.

How precisely is the doctrine of ideas as signs contradictory to the modern doctrine of ideas as objects directly cognized? Even here in passing this contradiction is worth a closer look.

Consider how signs function in our experience of what is essential to them as signs: they bring into awareness something other than themselves, what they themselves are not. (By defining ideas as that which the mind is directly aware of, Descartes, Locke, and those after them must posit *something else* on the basis of which the "idea-objects" are presented. What this "something else" would be—the mind itself precisely as acting, perhaps, as opposed to any results of such acting—they do not discuss in any express detail. It is this, however, that constitutes the idea as we are defining it and as Locke proposed that it should be considered, namely, as a sign.) Immediately we are struck by how much closer to unreflected usage in the natural languages such a formula brings us when applied to ideas than does the standard modern formula which makes of ideas objects in their own right. When we think of some natural or cultural entity—a tree, say, or a flag—we are not aware of any "mental state" as such. Rather, we are aware of a tree or a flag, something an idea most certainly is not. At the same time, it is clear that a tree we are looking at, in order to be present not merely in the physical world but in our awareness as well, requires for this relative-to-an-observer existence some factor within the observer on the basis of which the tree existing in nature *also* exists as the term of his or her awareness of it. This intraorganismic factor on the basis of which a

given object, concrete or abstract, perceptual or conceptual, real
or unreal, exists for an individual as something of which that individual is aware, i.e., as a terminus of his or her cognition, is
what an "idea" is seen to be in semiotic perspective. Of course,
any object, once cognized, may further become a sign in its own
right for the one cognizing it, as a certain tree may lead the
biologist on to consider an entire evolutionary history, or the
lover to recall a former tryst.

Note the procedure here: The basis for positing the existence
of ideas is our awareness of objects, not, as in modern philosophy
(cf. Hume 1748: 680) or the introspective psychology that preceded behaviorism, the other way around. Conformably with our
spontaneous interpretation of experience and in line with the
"opinion strangely prevailing amongst men" (Berkeley 1710:
524), we affirm *first* the indubitable experience of apparently cognition-independent things, both natural and artificial, of which
we become aware; and *from the fact of that awareness* we infer the
existence of ideas.

In other words, in approaching cognition from a semiotic
point of view, the first requirement is to distinguish between signs
which make possible the existence of objects cognized—ideas in
the generic sense—and signs which must be perceived as objects
even in order to function as signs. Both types of signs, those which
are such precisely because they are not what we directly appre-
hend, and those which are such precisely as part of what we are
directly aware of, function *as* signs in exactly the same way,
namely, to bring to awareness another than itself. This precisely
is the relativity constitutive of the sign in its proper being. But
signs of the former sort, ideas (or "concepts and images"), are
not known or knowable through direct perception. On the contrary, they are cognized, if at all, only on reflection, and as the
foundation or ground in the knower of what is apprehended directly. As private, i.e., inasmuch as each organism forms its *own*
ideas, they are not objects at all, but the foundation or basis for
relations of cognition to objects, which, owing to the indifference
of relation to its subjective ground, may be real or unreal.

Thus, solipsism is overcome at a stroke, and the semiotic approach to cognition explains the possibility of communication in
the same way that any two things can be related to a common
third. Ideas as belonging to an individual are private, but as signs
they relate that individual to objects that are other than private
states, objects that still other individuals may also form "ideas

of,'' and so enter into communication about through the use of extraorganismic elements—such as sounds, marks, or gestures— as signs (see discussion in Appendix II above). Signs of this latter sort, being fundamentally objects first of all, may or may not be successfully used to signify in any given case—as the first-time visitor to a foreign culture learns all too well. Their being as signs depends on their being as objects, and their being as objects depends on their ontological difference from the being as signs of ideas, the intraorganismic factor identified above.

In short, the definition of ideas as objects of awareness, which Descartes made the center of his *Meditations* (1641) and with which Locke began his *Essay* (1690), the definition which unremittingly influenced the classical modern formulation of theories of knowledge and psychology, especially in the work of Hume with its impact on Kant (awakening him from one "dogmatic slumber" only to induce another far deeper), is incompatible with common experience and incompossible with the definition of ideas as signs which Locke proposed on concluding the *Essay*. If, as the very brief remarks foregoing strongly suggest, the concluding proposal is more sound than the opening one, it is not too much to say that the introduction of the semiotic point of view into the account of cognition portends a revolution for philosophy and psychology alike, and an end to the modern era of solipsism and reductionism.

How this is so may be further briefly indicated. Resuming the last part of our discussion from Appendix II above, let us ask whether ideas as semiotically conceived, that is, as signs, might not be simply states of our nervous system. The answer is that ideas and neural conditions cannot be so identified, for the reason that brain states are in principle (under appropriate instrumentation) sense perceptible, while, by contrast, ideas in principle—that is, in order to be ideas and to function according to the rationale of their admission as real—are not sense perceptible, but are rather that on which every sense perceptible object as actually perceived here and now depends. Let us call them "mental events" in contrast to "physical events," that is, in contrast to items of possible sense apprehension. Thus, in a semiotic perspective, the same reasoning that leads us to affirm the reality of ideas as mental in contradistinction to brain states as physical, also requires us to preclude the reduction of the mental to the physical, and to preclude as well identification of the mental with that of which we are directly aware in cognition. The reduction and identification are alike incompatible with the semiotic (sign) structure of apprehension itself as underlying all observation and constituting its ground.

Moreover, this analysis removes the principal ground on which behaviorists and analytic philosophers have repudiated the existence of ideas, namely, the ground that we have no direct awareness of them in our experience as something distinct or separable from the objective "physical" being of the marks seen and expressions heard. Indeed, the thrust of this argument is heuristically just what the semiotic analysis of ideas would lead us to expect. In short, the line of argument from which contemporary Anglo-American analysis of language rejects the existence of ideas in the modern sense, supports the acceptance of the existence of ideas in the semiotic sense, i.e., as making present in our consciousness objects which they themselves are not. The recent attempts of mainstream philosophers to explain away the mental somehow in terms of the physical is shown by semiotic analysis to be misguided. That same line of analysis demonstrates the wrongheadedness of the more enduring modern tendency to close thought within its own constructions, with the result of making experience of communication unintelligible or merely apparent at best. What the analysis of cognition from a semiotic point of view quickly reveals is that the solipsistic and reductionist tendencies of mainstream modern and contemporary philosophy and psychology have as their common root an inadequate understanding of the phenomenon of signifying which is at the heart of cognitive life.

The counter to both these tendencies, accordingly, and the opening of a new era of understanding, can be found in a careful establishment of the foundations of the doctrine of signs (semiotic in the strict sense) and in the extension of such analysis to all the phenomena of which signs make up part (the interdisciplinary field of semiotics). The possibilities of such a work and perspective seem to have been first secured systematically as early as 1632 in the *Treatise on Signs* of John Poinsot, while the actual project has begun to go forward only in most recent times.

Thus, when Locke conjectured, in the same breath with which he proposed *semiotic* as a distinct domain, that perhaps if "*ideas* and *words* [formal and instrumental signs, in the language of Poinsot] as the great instruments of knowledge . . . were distinctly weighed, and duly considered [precisely *as* signs, i.e., semiotically], they would afford us another sort of logic and critic, than what we have been hitherto acquainted with," he spoke truly, indeed, and as a prophet; but a prophet whose vision had in substance been realized by an earlier contemporary of another land and culture, in a work that would wait some three hundred years to be heard outside the Latin world, when the project of semiotic, compassing the very foundations and origin of experience and knowledge, would at last in our own time be ventured in earnest in the national languages, thanks to the work of Peirce, Saussure, and a hundred others.

Intricacies of Poinsot's semiotic applied to the other classifications of signs current in his day, of course, could also be discussed—e.g., how his account of the being proper to signs shows that the standard dichotomy between "natural" and "conventional" signs is unworkable, requiring a trichotomy in its place (Deely 1978a; cf. Rollin 1976)—to say nothing of intricacies of its application to classifications current today (e.g., Deely 1980b), or of its inclusion of other forms of biological life (zoosemiotics: see Deely 1975a, 1983: Sixth Semiotic Marker). But enough has been said for present purposes to demonstrate that the dominant interest of the work is the prospective significance of a seminal treatment, illuminating possibilities of a future age; and amply to justify the assessment of Sebeok (1975a: 3), that Poinsot "appears, in retrospect, to have forged the most solid, lasting link between the Scholastic semioticians—an intellectual milieu in which this keen thinker was still profoundly at home—and the emergent doctrine of signs envisaged, labelled, and foreshadowed by John Locke half a century later in 1690."

Notes to Part I, Section 6

1. Peirce himself has emerged in social consciousness as "the real founder and first systematic investigator" of contemporary semiotic (Sebeok 1974: 5) somewhat belatedly; and for a long time, especially in the European context, the perception of Peirce's semiotic was mediated by the everywhere-known semiotic writings of Charles Morris, "author," as Fisch 1979: 159 remarks, "of the classic works, from 1938 to 1964, which were collected in his *Writings on the General Theory of Signs* (The Hague: Mouton, 1971)." In fact, that Peirce's semiotic is far different from the views of Morris is by now becoming a common theme (e.g., Rochberg-Halton and McMurtrey 1981), and Morris himself did not think of himself as a Peirce exegete, being much more behaviorist and "psychological" (after Mead) in his approach to

semiosis. Thus, although his work does not directly fall in the line of development of "logic as semiotic" that we are following here, mention must be made of the great contribution Morris made to the social awareness of the idea of a foundational doctrine of signs as something to be developed in our time, both because of his early connection (especially abroad) with interest in Peirce, and because—from the standpoint of sociology of knowledge looking over the first half or so of the twentieth century, if not from the point of view of the doctrine itself of signs—"Morris' place as the most important representative of twentieth century semiotics has been generally recognized" (Rossi-Landi 1978: 3).

2. Bochenski 1970: 14 writes of this logic that "One *could* understand it as a distinct variety, since while it consists of fragments of scholastic logic (taking over for example the mnemonic *Barbara*, *Celarent*, etc.), yet these fragments are interpreted quite unscholastically, in an ancient rather than scholastic way. But the content of this logic is so poor, it is loaded with so many utter misunderstandings, and its creative power is so extremely weak, that one can hardly risk calling something so decadent a distinct variety of logic and so setting it on a level with ancient, scholastic, mathematical and Indian logic."

3. E.g., *Topics*, Book I, ch. 12, 105a11-13: "There is on the one hand Induction, on the other Reasoning. Now what reasoning is has been said above [in ch. 1, 100a25: "an argument in which, certain things being laid down, something other than these necessarily comes about through them"]: induction is a passage from individuals to universals."

Aristotle treats of the 'logical mechanism' of induction in a variety of places, principally, in addition to the *Topics*, Book I, ch. 12 (where he has in mind primarily "Baconian" or "incomplete" induction), the *Prior Analytics*, Book II, ch. 23, esp. 68b27-29 (read in conjunction the *Historia Animalium*, Book II, ch. 15, 506a20ff., and the *De Partibus Animalium*, Book II, 676b26ff., esp. 677a15-61), and the *Posterior Analytics*, Book I, ch. 18. It is safe to say that a sophisticated and sensitive, and indeed sympathetic, reading of the *Organon* is essential to an intelligent commentary on Aristotle's thought in this area. Thus Joseph 1916: 391-392 writes: "The critics of whom Bacon is the coryphaeus, recognizing with Aristotle that we discover universal truths by induction, attacked him for saying that we only discover them by complete enumeration, which he had not said; and finding the name Induction given to no other formally valid process than this, supposed he had nothing else to say of the processes by which such truths are reached. Bacon himself attempted to systematize the process of discovering and proving them in a way which undoubtedly possesses value, and no less undoubtedly owes much to Aristotle; but as the Aristotelian doctrines on which it is based do not occur in the *Organon* in connexion with ἐπαγωή , he hardly realized how much he was borrowing.''

4. Except for a rationalist even more radical than Descartes, therefore, one who believes that *all* our intellectual apprehensions *without exception* are inborn in the individual, it is not only empiricists who are ''faced,'' as Max Black puts it (1967: 170), ''with the problem of accounting for the crucial step from knowledge of experiential particulars to reasoned acceptance of empirical generalizations sufficiently powerful to serve as the major premises of subsequent logical and mathematical deduction.'' The problem is a quite general one, and Black's ascription of it peculiarly to ''empiricists'' seems singularly unwarranted.

5. Comparing the technical development of terms in renaissance scholasticism with the ancient usage of Aristotle himself, Maritain (1923: 273-274) remarks on this point: ''*(a)* The analogy uniting *abstraction* and *induction* is thus apparent. Abstraction concerns the *first operation of the mind* and starting from singular facts of sense experience leads the mind to ideas and concepts (*universal* as objects of simple apprehension).

''Induction bears upon the *third operation of the mind*, and leads the mind to universal propositions (*universal as objects of judgment*) starting either from singular data of sense experience or from previously abstracted data and universals that are less universal than the proposition in question (particular instances).

''*(b)* For Aristotle the word *induction* had a much more general sense. It went far beyond—while comprising—inductive inference or induction as we have been understanding it here, and was applicable to every passage from the plane of sensible facts to that of universal propositions, even in the case in which, in a single sensible example (but transcending all sense experience and without any inductive reasoning whatsoever) the intelligence sees immediately from its very terms, a self-evident truth such as the principle of identity or of causality. Thus understood induction is neither an inference properly so-called, nor an argument nor proof: it merely leads the mind to a connection of terms whose intelligible necessity it perceives immediately, without reasoning. It is in this sense that Aristotle says that only by induction may we attain to universal truths: ἡ μὲν δὴ ἐπαγωγὴ ἀϱχῆς ἐστι καὶ τοῦ καθόλου (*Ethic. Nic.,* VI, 3, 1139b28); ἀδύνατον δὲ τὰ καθόλου θεωϱῆσαι μὴ δι᾽ ἐπαγωγῆς (*Anal. Post,.* I, 18, 81a40; Aquinas 1269-1271a: I, lect. 30)." Cf. Poinsot 1631: Q. 8, Art. 2 (Reiser ed. 198a19-200b32).

6. Joseph 1916: 394: "Bacon wrote in the dawn of modern science, and proclaimed with splendid confidence its future triumphs. His predictions have been fulfilled, perhaps to the extent, though not on the lines, that he anticipated. *Spes est una,* he wrote (1620: I. 14.), *in inductione vera*; and as men watched the continuous progress of the inductive sciences, they came to think that induction was really some new form of reasoning . . . . To praise induction became a sign of enlightenment; but the praise of it ran ahead of the understanding."

7. "It should now be apparent how great is the too frequently committed blunder of representing the opposition of the syllogism and induction as the simple opposition of two movements proceeding in contrary directions on the same road. Such a representation betrays a complete misunderstanding of the true nature of this opposition and even risks confusing the syllogism with inductive *descensus.* The opposition between the syllogism and induction is much deeper: it is a fundamental opposition. The very paths which they pursue are different. One moves entirely upon the intelligible plane; the other leads from the plane of sense experience to the intelligible plane, from the plane of the particular or the singular to the plane of the universal (or inversely). The syllogism is based entirely upon the connection of two terms with a same third term (the middle term). Induction replaces the middle term by an enumeration of parts and is entirely based upon the connection of individuals or of parts with the universal whole" (Maritain 1923: 267).

8. This becomes especially clear when one considers that the same conclusion can be reached by either of the three routes. E.g., Maritain 1923: 267: "a conclusion such as: 'iron conducts electricity' may be inferred *either* in virtue of an inductive *ascensus,* starting from actual facts: 'this piece of iron, and this one, and that one, each conduct electricity,' *or* in virtue of an inductive *descensus,* starting from the universal 'metal,' for example: 'metal

conducts electricity, and to say metal is to say iron, and silver, and copper, etc.,'' *or* in virtue of a syllogism starting from the same universal 'metal' but proceeding by the force of an altogether different kind of inference: 'every metal conducts electricity, but iron is a metal, therefore, etc.' '' Cf. Joseph 1916: 399; and see discussion in following note.

9. Maritain 1923: 276-278: "take note here that the conditions for a 'sufficient' enumeration vary according to the case. For instance, in relation to an essential predicate such as *mortal* it would, strictly speaking, be sufficient to cite *one single case*: 'Peter is mortal, therefore man is mortal' (if we know through some other source that this is a question of an essential predicate, and that the fact that a living being is mortal or immortal depends upon the inmost constitution of its nature) . . . .

"We should note, too, before everything else that the enumeration is *sufficient* when we have considered a sufficient number of parts to know *in a certain or in a merely probable manner* that the universal which represents them in relation to the predicate in question is indeed the universal under consideration. What is true of the enumerated parts will then be *certainly* or *probably* true of this universal whole.

"It is obvious, in considering induction in itself, abstracting from certain particular conditions or limit-cases (as those of *complete* enumeration of which we shall speak below) that, in itself, it admits of a certain zone of probability. For example, when we said: 'Iron and copper and gold and silver . . . conduct electricity,' it is certain that, in relation to the Pr. 'conductor of electricity,' iron, copper, gold, silver and their like, are the constitutive parts of a certain universal whole X. But is this universal whole really the subject *metal* itself, or is it not a more restricted universal: 'metal answering to such and such determined physical or chemical conditions,' so that a metal might be found which did not answer to these conditions and therefore did not conduct electricity? We cannot affirm this with absolute certitude, and the inductive minor: 'The universal which represents iron, copper, gold, silver, etc., in relation to the predicate conductor of electricity is the universal metal,' is but a *probable* proposition.

"The reason for this is that, in virtue of the very structure of induction, the mind in this reasoning does not identify two concepts by means of a third, a procedure which produces perfect certitude—it identifies two concepts (S. and Pr. of the Conclusion) by means of an enumeration of singular or particular subjects each of which it identifies with the predicate-concept, and from which it ascends to a concept (the subject-concept) which represents them all in relation to the predicate under consideration. By the light of abstraction, the mind immediately seizes this universal subject as a whole realized in these singular subjects. But with the exception of certain special conditions, it seizes it neither as belonging *solely* to these singular subjects and their like, nor as being unable to comprise anything beyond them.

"Thus, by its very structure, induction admits of the possibility (destroyed only in certain particular cases) of a deficiency on the side of matter. But, as we saw above, this does not prevent it from being a true and formal inference (*as inductive*). Let us keep in mind that *inductive* inference is other, and has another end than *syllogistic* inference, and that the mind does not *see* the same way in induction as it does in the syllogism. In showing to the mind, in the middle term, the *reason* for the identity of the extremes, the syllogism compels it to see this identity, by the light of the premises. In showing to the mind, in the enumeration of parts, the *matter* wherein the extremes are identified, induction compels it to see, by the light of abstraction, the universal subject to which the predicate belongs (perhaps on the condition that it restrict this subject). Thus it *authorizes* rather than *necessitates* the mind to posit the conclusion."

10. It is instructive to read Cohen and Nagel 1934: 273-279 side-by-side with Maritain 1923: 269-271, 281-282, even allowing for the latter's excessively polemical tone. Further complexities implied by the older view in relation to probabilities and necessities in our knowledge of the physical world are nicely brought out in highly original ways by Cahalan 1981.

11. A similar vision had inspired Ramon Lull, or Llull (c. 1232-1316), who like Leibniz dreamed of a logic in which calculation would hold the central place. "Lull even designed machines, formed of superimposed rotating discs, by which his calculus could be worked out mechanically," Moody notes (1967: 530), "an enterprise which perhaps earns him the right to be called the father of computer programming."

"The desire to bring about the conversion of Muslims and Jews, as well as pagan Tartars, which inspired Lull's ceaseless activity, also inspired his writings," Hillgarth writes (1967: 107-108). "Despite the clear analogies between the two systems, Leibniz took over only part of Lull's ideas, omitting Lull's original purpose of the Art as a means of converting infidels." Apparently, Hillgarth does not know the story of Guilielmus Pacidius, whom Leibniz created for the express purpose of "the complete reunification of mankind, through Christianity."

It should also be noted that Lull was the first Christian philosopher of the middle ages to use a language other than Latin, namely, Catalan, and sometimes Arabic, for his major works.

12. Hence Geach's complaint (1968: 134) that "the essential objection to the doctrine of *suppositio* is the way new sorts of *suppositio* keep on turning up," in contrast to (*ibid.*, 106) "what is set forth so perspicuously in the modern notation of quantifiers and bound variables." Bochenski 1970: 17 remarked in this connection: "highly relevant to the question of the continual progress of logic throughout its history is the fact that the earlier varieties are not simply predecessors of contemporary logic, but deal in part with the same or similar problems though from a different standpoint and by different methods." A case in point is precisely the doctrine of quantification vis-à-vis the doctrine of *suppositio*. "The scholastic doctrine of supposition," Bochenski flatly states (*ibid.*), "is evidently richer in important insights and rules than the semiotic so far developed by mathematical logic." Moreover, the semiotic level at which supposition is aimed must always be presupposed by the technical levels: see Part II, Section 1. "This sort of logic could not have been imagined by the Greeks," Dumitriu says of mathematical logic in a kind of romantic overstatement (1977: IV, 259). "Their ideal was not to construct machinery; the ideal type of man in the Greek period was the hero and the sage . . . . If it had been discovered in Greek times, it would probably have been considered merely as a curiosity."

13. If this is understood, it will also be seen that, far from providing a tool for adjudicating philosophical disputes, as has been commonly supposed, philosophical dispute precisely is taken as settled whenever and as long as one has recourse to logistic methods, most notably propositional functions and quantifiers. This point is beginning to be recognized among contemporaries, so that one may hope its importance will eventually sink in. (See extended discussions from very different standpoints in Deely 1975b: esp. 266-267; Küng 1967: esp. 8-9; and Strawson 1952: esp. 193-194.) For example, Dummet (1973: 671) points out that even Frege, that most formidable formalist who "had a poor opinion of natural language," and inclined to regard it as a hin-

drance to "correct" logical analysis, "often found himself com-
pelled to admit that, misleading as it is, he was forced to give explanations in terms of natural language." In this same line,
Dummet, without any realization of the magnitude or consequences of the point, had already conceded at the outset of his attempt to portray Frege's views as a new and solid foundation for
the whole of philosophy, that (*ibid.*, p. xix), when it came to de-
fending the soundness of his views, Frege had to abandon his
preferred standpoint in the use of symbols, i.e., the constructivist
standpoint of contemporary formal logic. It is indeed a gain that
he found it essential to a "theory of meaning" that we recognize
in effect three distinct realms (cf. Part II, Section 2 below), and
that the objective realm—in which formal logic as such exclusively moves—does not reduce to either the psychical or the physical. But this was hardly a gain as original with Frege as Dummett
seems to think (see, for example, discussion in Section 4 note 2
above; also Deely 1972a: 232 note 34; Part II Section 2 below;
etc.) Nor can formal logic alone, in the nature of the case, ever
account for the constant interpenetration of these three realms in
semiosis, the spinning across time of the semiotic web that is the
élan of every life form and specifically the *humanitas* of the *animal
rationale*. This is why, in sharp contrast to Peirce, a "philosophy
of language" developed in terms of Frege's philosophy of logic
can never succeed as a general semiotic, even though it points in
that direction. For the scientistic pretentions of his approach must
be abandoned precisely to the extent one undertakes to philosophically justify them—the pursuit and its justification lack com-
plementarity, relating rather as contraries; whereas with Peirce,
as Apel 1981: 194 put it, "the transcendental semiotic foundation
of Peirce's philosophy, the a priori of the communication community, itself opens the way for a complementary, nonscientistic interpretation of Peirce."

It would appear, in short, that the "Fregean revolution in
philosophy," to the extent that it is separable from the formalistic
gains which have to do with the study of validity as a specialized
pursuit, can succeed only to the extent that it defeats itself, owing
to the fact that the search for an adequate notation of itself leads
beyond the bounds in principle of *any* notation system, *especially*
the kinds that are central to the deployment of artificial languages, precisely because a notation system as such, like the communicative function itself of language (Sebeok 1981d: 12; Chomsky 1979: 35-36; (Appendix II, pp. 138-139 above), is a derivative
phenomenon, a "secondary modeling system." (See further dis-

cussion in Part II below). A curious revolution indeed, one whose success will *consist in* feeding on its own children. That is the price discourse exacts of those who think to defeat its historical essence rather than harness and work from it. We confront here one of the dividing lines between sound and unsound approaches to semiotic foundations, or, as perhaps we might say, the difference between those who employ means permitting them to see but not to enter the Promised Land, and those destined to enter and cultivate the land itself.

14. Bochenski 1970: 16-17: "Calculation, again, is certainly a useful tool for logic, but only as facilitating new insights into logical interconnection. It is undeniable that such insights, e.g., in the logic of relations, have been reached by its means, and the convenience and accuracy of this instrument are so great that no serious logician can now dispense with it. But we would not go so far as to say that calculation has *at every point* allowed mathematical logic to surpass the older forms. Think for example of two-valued propositional logic: the essentially new features introduced by *Principia Mathematica* are quite unimportant when we compare the scholastic treatment.

"Once again the matter reduces to our insufficient knowledge of the earlier forms of logic. For years people spoke of a supposed great discovery by De Morgan; then Lukasiewicz showed that his famous law was part of the elementary doctrine of Scholasticism. The discovery of truth-matrices was ascribed to Peirce, or even Wittgenstein; Peirce himself found it in the Megarians. D. Ingalls found Frege's classical definition of number in the Indian Mathuranatha (17th century). And then we are all too well aware that we know, as has been said, only fragments of Scholastic and Indian logic, while much more awaits us in manuscripts and even in unread printed works. The Megarian-Stoic logic, too, is lost, except for a few poor fragments transmitted by its opponents.

"Also highly relevant to the question of the continual progress of logic throughout its history is the fact that the earlier varieties are not simply predecessors of contemporary logic, but deal in part with the same or similar problems though from a different standpoint and by different methods."

Similar conclusions are reached by Dumitriu 1977.

15. Here we must note Bochenski's judgment (1970: 268) of the unique place of Frege in the pantheon of modern and con-

temporary "symbolic logicians": "His *Begriffsschrift* can only be compared with one other work in the whole history of logic, the *Prior Analytics* of Aristotle. The two cannot quite be put on a level, for Aristotle was the very founder of logic, while Frege could as a result only develop it [cf. the more extreme view of Thomas 1967: 96]. But there is a great likeness between these two gifted works. The *Begriffsschrift*, like the *Prior Analytics*, contains a long series of quite new insights, e.g., Frege formulates for the first time the sharp distinction between variables and constants, the concepts of logical function, of a many-place function, of the quantifier; he has a notably more accurate understanding of the Aristotelian theory of an axiomatic system, distinguishes clearly between laws and rules, and introduces an equally sharp distinction between language and meta-language, though without using these terms; he is the author of the theory of description; without having discovered, indeed, the notion of a value, he is the first to have elaborated it systematically. And that is far from being all.

"At the same time, and just like Aristotle, he presents nearly all these new ideas and intuitions in an exemplarily clear and systematic way. Already in the *Begriffsschrift* we have a long series of mathematico-logical theorems derived from a few axioms 'without interruption' (*lückenlos*), as Frege says, for the first time in history. Various other mathematical logicians at the same time, or even earlier, expounded similar ideas and theories, but none of them had the gift of presenting all at once so many, often quite original, innovations in so perfect a form.

"It is a remarkable fact that this logician of them all had to wait twenty years before he was at all noticed, and another twenty before his full strictness of procedure was resumed by Lukasiewicz. In this last respect, everything published between 1879 and 1921 fell below the standard of Frege, and it is seldom attained even today. The fate of Frege's work was in part determined by his symbolism. It is not true that it is particularly difficult to read, as the reader can assure himself from the examples given below; but it is certainly too original, and contrary to the age-old habits of mankind, to be acceptable."

16. "Perihermenias" is bound to be, for a while anyway, an especially clarifying term for semiotic historiography in any pre-modern period. In the renaissance, as indeed very early in the Latin population we have tried to focus on above, this twofold Greek title ("Peri Hermenias") came to exist semiotically in single term form, early (at least pre-1477), as Zigliara (1882:

1-3) shows in his prefatory remarks, in the spelling "peryermenias," as also in the spelling "peryarmenias" and "periermenias." This already is a semiotic phenomenon to be noted and considered carefully, as Dr. Herzfeld pointed out in discussions (see p. xiii above). For in Greek, the late Latin single word, as used for example in Poinsot 1632, was definitely *binary* in both semantic and syntactic structure, and the Greek original binary term was from the earliest days of the integral naturalism in philosophy devolving from Aristotle a subject of substantive controversy, as can be seen from Zigliara, 1882: 7 note γ: "*Interpretatio, secundum Boethium* etc. Haec Boethius habet Prooemio Edit. prim. in lib. *De interpretatione* (Opp.-Basileae 1570, pag. 215). *Interpretatio* (ἑρμηνεία) *est vox significativa, per seipsam aliquid significans.* Et quia non solum *propositio* (quae est vox complexa), sed etiam *nomen* et *verbum* (quae sunt voces incomplexae) aliquid per seipsa significant, sequitur quod, iuxta sententiam Boethii, ab eodem expressam (*ib.*), *nomen* et *verbum* subjectum Peri hermeneias constituant non solum prout sunt partes *enunciationis* seu propositionis, sed etiam secundum se sumpta.—Sed Boethio haud consentit s. Thomas, recte notando quod ille interpretatur, proprie loquendo, qui exponit aliquid esse verum vel falsum. Ergo *interpretatio* proprie non erit quaelibet vox per se significans, sed quae et per se significat et simul per se continet enunciatque verum vel falsum. Hoc autem proprium est vocis complexae seu orationis, imo solius *orationis enunciativae*, quatenus haec distinguitur ab oratione optativa et imperativa et aliis, ut in hoc ipso numero optime dicit Angelicus. Unde colligitur quod titulus περὶ ἑρμηνείας, qui de verbo ad verbum vertitur *De interpretatione*, philosophice reddi iure merito potest, *De enunciativa oratione*. Hinc Ammonius in prologo sui Commentarii in librum *Peri hermeneias* dicit: '*De interpretatione* librum inscripsit, perinde quasi hoc modo, an *De enunciativa* inscribas *oratione*, nihil intersit: ἐπέγραψε τὸ βιβλίον περὶ ἑρμηνείας, ὡς οὐδὲν διαφέρον ἢ οὕτως ἐπιγράφειν, ἢ περὶ τοῦ ἀποφαντικοῦ λόγου'(Venetiis, 1546, interprete Bartholomaeo Sylvanio, fol. I, col. 3. - ib. graec. ed. cit. Aldi Pii Manutii).

"Attamen quamvis oratio enunciativa constituat subiectum huius tractatus, non de illa solummodo hic agitur, sed etiam de nomine et verbo, aliisque ad ipsam enunciativam orationem pertinentibus. Ratio est quia proprium scientiae est cognitio sui subiecti ad quod tanquam ad suum finem ordinatur. Non autem possibile est cognoscere naturam cuiusque subiecti nisi cognoscantur partes ex quibus constituitur (sicut ad cognoscendam hominis naturam necesse est cognoscere eius partes, tum physicas, nempe animam et corpus organicum, tum metaphysicas, scilicet *animal-itatem* et *rationalitatem*); neque plene iterum cognoscitur ipsum sub-iectum, cognita ipsius natura, nisi etiam cognoscantur eius pro-prietates, seu propriae passiones, quae naturam ipsam subiecti consequuntur (eo modo quo capacitas sciendi in homine sequitur eius naturam rationalem). Atqui partes seu principia ex quibus constituitur oratio enunciativa sunt *nomina* et *verba*. Ergo et de istis et de proprietatibus enunciationis, prout ordinantur ad principale subiectum quod est ipsa enunciativa oratio, determinat liber iste Peri hermeneias.

"Quibus constitutis, non est difficilis solutio quaestionis, quae quoad titulum περὶ ἑρμηνείας, praefixum huic libro ab ipso Aristotele, uti videtur, penes veteres agitabatur, quamque iterum recentiores versant. Aspasius enim et Alexander Aphrodisiensis, uti refert Boethius in Prologo secundae Ed. Commentarior. in hunc librum (pag. 291-2), *de oratione* hic tractari ab Aristotele iux-ta titulum affirmabant: nam si proferre aliquid oratione, ut aiunt ipsi, interpretari est, *De interpretatione* liber veluti de oratione perscriptus est. Unde Alexander imperfectum addebat esse titu-lum praefixum; quia cum ἑρμηνεία sonet orationem quamcum-que, nonnisi de oratione enunciativa, idest de oratione in qua continetur verum vel falsum in libro est sermo. 'Sed, *respondet Boethius*, qui (Alexander) semel solam orationem interpretationis nomine vocari recipit, in intellectu quoque ipsius inscriptionis (*nempe* περὶ ἑρμηνείας) erravit. Cur enim putaret imperfectum esse titulum, quoniam nihil de qua oratione disputaret adiecerit; ut si quis interrogans quid est homo, alio respondente animal, culpet ad dicat imperfecte illum dixisse quid sit, quoniam non sit omnes differentias persecutis? . . . Eodem quoque modo et de ora-tione, si quis hoc concedat primum, nihil aliud interpretatione dici nisi orationem, cur qui de interpretatione inscripserit, et de qua interpretatione dicat non addiderit, culpetur? Satis est enim eum libri titulum etiam de aliqua continenti communione fecisse, ut nos eum et de *nominibus* et *verbis* et de *orationibus*, cum haec om-nia uno interpretationis nomine continerentur, supra fecisse docuimus, cum hic liber ab eo (*Aristotele*) de interpretatione nomi-natus est' (Loc. supra cit. ex II Edit.). Neque Alexandro neque Boethio subscribit s. Thomas: titulus non est imperfectus, quia ἑρμηνεία non orationem quamcumque, sed illam quae continet verum vel falsum seu *enunciativam* proprie significat; neque est titulus communis nomini, verbo et orationi, quia ἑρμηνεία non est λέξις, nempe dictio vel oratio quaecumque per se significans, sed significans verum vel falsum, ut dictum est: proindeque non comprehendit nomina et verba praecise quia per se significant aliquid, sed quatenus sunt partes τῆς ἑρμηνείας, orationis videlicet interpretativae seu enunciativae, a qua, sicut a principaliori subiecto liber denominatur (Cf. Albert Magn. in lib. I *Perihermeneias* tract. I, c. 1, p. 237).

"Theodor. Waitz, *Aristotelis Organon graece*, p. I, pag. 323, Lipsiae 1844,—recitat et approbat sententiam Aquinatis aientis, nomen et verbum magis interpretationis principia esse quam interpretationes; verum loquens postea de Gumposch ait: 'Titulum libri plane ineptum judicat (Gumposch) quem equidem ferri posse putaverim, quum ἑρμηνεία de communicatione sermonis intelligitur, cuius principia in hoc libro traduntur' (Ib. pag. 324). Adde quod haec s. Thomae explicatio videtur haud satis conformis ipsi Aristoteli. In libro enim *De respiratione* cap. XI ait: 'In quibusdam lingua et ad percipiendos sapores et ad formandum sermonem, καὶ πρὸς τὴν ἑρμηνείαν, (*natura*) utitur.' Hoc loco, sicut et II *De anima*, cap. VIII, n. 10, ἑρμηνείαν pro sermone usurpat Aristoteles; et pro elocutione sumit in libro *De rhetorica* ad Alexandrum capp. XXIII et XXIV. Quibus cohaerenter s. Isidorus in libro II *Originum* seu *Etymologiarum*, cap. XXVII, *De perihermeniis Aristotelis* loquens, ait: 'Omnis elocutio conceptae rei interpres est; inde Perihermeniam nominat (*Aristoteles*) quam interpretationem nos appellamus.'—Hisce de causis nuperus auctor libri *De logica Aristotelis* existimat titulum Peri hermeneias verius verti *de sermone*, non quidem generice accepto, prouti nempe est signum quodlibet sensibile manifestativum passionum animae (ut sumitur loco citato ex libro *De respiratione*), sed prouti strictiori sensu assumitur ad efformandas diversas propositiones.

"Quae omnia, deducta ex ipso vocabulo περὶ ἑρμηνείας non infirmant, meo iudicio, sententiam s. Thomae. Etenim cum, philosophice loquendo, verum sit nomen et verbum, ex quibus enunciatio componitur, esse potius principia interpretationis quam interpretationes, sequitur quod interpretatio, ἑρμηνεία, proprie orationem in genere et magis etiam proprie orationem enunciativam designet.—Praeterea concedimus quod elocutio conceptae rei interpres est; sed ea de qua in hoc tractatu agitur, elocutio est non rhetorica sed philosophica vel dialectica (ut ex Alexandro refert Boethius loc. cit.), quae est idem ac enunciatio, qua mens conceptam rei veritatem aut falsitatem manifestat. Et ideo *sermo* manifestativus conceptuum mentis suam perfectionem propriumque finem non attingit nisi in enunciatione. Unde merito s. Thomas dicit ἑρμηνείαν hoc est *interpretationem* sumi ab Aristotele pro *enunciatione* in titulo huius libri.—Aegidius Colum-

na, s. Thomae discipulus doctissimus: 'Hic, *inquit*, intendit deter-
minare de compositione simplicium quidditatum, scilcet de enunciatione sive interpretatione. Et in hoc patet subiectum huius libri
scilicet interpretatio . . . Et, si obiiciatur: interpretatio est locus
dialecticus; ergo non est subiectum in hoc libro; dicendum quod
locus dialecticus est prout unum nomen exponitur per alia nomina; ut *philosophus* per hoc quod est *amator sapientiae*. Sed in hoc
libro est subiectum prout est idem quod enunciatio. Unde neque
nomen per se, neque verbum dicitur interpretatio, quae sunt
partes interpretationis; et interpretatio idem est quod enunciatio'
(In lib. *Periherm*, Exposit. in princ.—Venetiis per Simonem De
Luere 1507 fol. 47, verso, col. I). Nempe Aegidius vestigia premit
Magistri, quem, ut in Praefatione diximus, sub nomine *Expositoris*
frequentissime citat.''

It is not hard to conjecture well in view of all this why Poinsot, in commenting on the "perihermenias" books as he did, re-
sorted flatly to *substitute* his general treatise for the traditional, i.e.,
Thomist, *commentary* grounded in the logic of terms and of propositions, when construing "perihermenias" in a way "philosophice reddi jure merito potest" yet at the precise opposite end of
the spectrum from the contextually literal *commentary* which St.
Thomas had undertaken (*circa* 1269) but had not yet completed
at the time of his death in 1274. How strong the line of interpretation begun by Aquinas was can be gathered from the fact that
it became for a while almost customary for other Dominicans up
to Cajetan's time (i.e., early 16th century) to set themselves to
complete St. Thomas' unfinished commentary as he would have
himself completed it in life, as appears in Spiazzi's summary
(1955: xi-xii): "Opus istud *Peri hermeneias*, quod apud graecos
unico libro continetur, in duos libros a latinis interpretibus divi-
sum passim reperitur: quorum primus priora novem capita, reli-
qua quinque (X-XIV) alter complectitur. Hanc divisionem se-
quutus S. Thomas integrum primum librum exposuit, sed in
alterum nonnisi duas lectiones scripsit super primam partem
capitis X.—Piani editores hanc in fine notam ponunt: *Com-
mentariorum d. Thomae Aquinatis, quae ob eius mortem incompleta
manserunt, finis*. At mortem non fuisse in causa cur opus non com-
pleverit S. Doctor contendit Echardus, inquiens, vel quod nimiae
occupationes obstiterunt, vel potius iuvenis ille et sapiens Praepo-
situs forsan praesens plura non postulavit, religionique habuit
maioribus intentum in his tyronum propriis diutius distinere.—
Addit De Rubeis quod *opus incompletum mansit, nec ab alio suppletum*:
quae ultima verba quo sensu dicantur a viro eruditissimo haud

facile intelligitur. Eum namque non latuit a Caietano nostro fuisse suppletum, quod in Commentariis S. Thomae desideratur: quod Caietani supplementum pluries typis editum huic Editioni adnectimus. Verum et longe ante Caietanum nonnulli incompletum Angelici opus supplere moliti sunt. In Veneta *Peri hermeneias* editione 1477, fol. 21 verso, legitur: *Explicit sententia libri peryermenias secundum sanctissimum doctorem Thomam de Aquino.* Deinde fol. 22 recto: *Hoc quod sequitur est secundum expositionem Gratiadei de Esculo, Ordinis Praedicatorum. Et per eum completur lectura haec: nam S. Thomas non plus fecit morte praeventus.* Incipit: *Deinde cum dicit: Similiter autem se habet, distinguit enunciationes, quae accipiunt pro subiecto nomen finitum universaliter sumptum* etc. Denique fol. 32 verso: *Explicit supplementum in librum secundum Periermenias secundum Gratiadeum de Esculo Ordinis Praedicatorum.* Floruit Gratiadeus, iuxta Leandrum Albertum, ad annum 1341, et eximius fuit, inquit Echard, et celebris sua aetate philosophus et theologus (*Scriptor. Ord. Praedic.* ad ann. 1341, tom. I, pag. 603). Supplementum Gratiadei extat etiam in alia Veneta editione 1495, sed additur *ex commentariis* eiusdem Auctoris *in eosdem libros Aristotelis* excerptum fuisse (fol. 15 verso). Denique in tertia editione pariter Veneta 1496, fol. 15 recto dicitur: *Plures eiusdem Ordinis* (Praedic.) *doctores clarissimi suppleverunt,* quae nempe deerant Commentario S. Thomae. Revera in codice Urbinate post ultimam S. Thomae lectionem, haec leguntur fol. 233 verso: *Hucusque scripsit S. Thomas de Aquino Ordinis Praedicatorum. Ea vero quae secuntur scripsit frater Robertus de Vulgarbia Ordinis eorumdem Praedicatorum.* Incipit: *Similiter autem se habet. In hac parte multiplicat oppositionem in universalibus* etc. Desinit fol. 241 verso, col. 2: *Vel de eodem in diversis tempore.* Tum: *Laus tibi Christe. Explicit expositio secundi libri Periarmenias S. Thomae de Aquino. Sed finita fuit per magistrum Robertum de Vulgarbia Ordinis eorumdem Praedicatorum. Finis.* Fragmentum huius supplementi, sed sine auctoris nomine, habetur etiam in cod. Vatic. 2115; ex quo eiusdem antiquitas constituitur: codex enim est labentis saeculi XIII. Codex Parisiensis 16154 habet et ipse fragmentum, sine nomine auctoris, alterius supplementi cuius specimen exhibeo in fine Commentarii S. Thomae.''

Notes to Part I, Section 7

1. In the philosophical tradition, apart from the work of Poinsot as discussed above (esp. note 9 to Section 5), the most suggestive indications of this perhaps are to be found in the

"Logic" of Hegel (1812, 1830), which takes its departure from the identity in becoming of being and non-being and makes of this triad a "dialectic" compassing the whole of philosophy and human science. It is my suspicion that the interplay of *ens reale* and *ens rationis* at the heart of semiosis is precisely what Hegel's system is centered upon in its own, peculiarly obscure and convoluted, way.

2. A clarification of the manner of this penetration has recently been effected by Brooke Williams in a brief terminological discussion (1981: 309-310) of her use of "semiotic" in the context of feminist thought: "in speaking of a 'semiotic' beyond feminism, I am using a word in a way which, although common, has to my knowledge never been defined. It is a third-level spin-off of the original usage traceable to Locke. In his *Essay* of 1690, 'semiotic' means quite precisely the foundational doctrine of signs as these underlie and structure the whole of our experience and consciousness. Derivative from this usage but in contrast to it is the contemporary use of semiotics as an umbrella term for that whole range or field of specialized and interdisciplinary inquiries, which have stemmed from the inspiration of seeing all things anew.

"In the interplay between these two terms, 'semiotic' and 'semiotics,' a third term has arisen, a new use of 'semiotic' as a label for a given specialized study within the field of semiotics (such as the architectural semiotic of the Gothic cathedral). *It is in this sense* that feminist thought—like any other symbolic structure when viewed on its own and precisely in terms of its signifying—also constitutes a semiotic, not in the foundational sense, but in a sense which is aware of its foundations in knowledge and experience precisely as they are works of interpretation through signs."

NOTES FOR PART II

Notes to Part II, Section 1

1. A similar general *caveat* must be entered concerning the tendency of much of cultural, literary, and linguistic semiotics to coalesce around the notion and methods of so-called "structuralism." It is a great mistake (and a useless one) to pretend that the whole of semiotics can be encompassed by models derived from linguistics. Starting from Saussure's observation that human language provides the most important and best known area of signification, certain authors manage to turn this observation into the far different claim that only a linguistic model of semiosis is viable for the understanding of any human experience, a gratuitous assertion taken to its "logical extreme" (so to speak) by Roland Barthes in particular (1964: 10-11; cf. Hawkes 1977: 123-150), but effectively subscribed to also by A. J. Greimas and many others.

Besides being an unnecessary claim—there are many corners of human experience which are so far *best* illuminated by structuralist analysis (e.g., in the studies of Lévi-Strauss), and nothing is added to this valuable achievement by claiming for the methods of its accomplishment exclusive validity over all areas—this extreme of glottocentrism has the stultifying effect of carrying over into semiotics the tired debate of modern philosophy between "idealism" and "realism," just at the moment when we should be moving to transcend the terms of this debate in a definitive way.

Fortunately, therefore, as has already been suggested, it is

quite possible to distinguish within structuralism between methodology and ideology, as between what is essential and what is
superfluous cultural baggage. As an *ideology*, structuralism tends
toward the "crude extreme," as Herzfeld has called it, of a semiotic version of anthropomorphism—a "pathetic fallacy" writ
large. As a *methodology*, in sharp contrast to such philosophical
crudity, structuralism is a powerful and effective tool for dissect-
ing and illuminating a broad range of anthropological data.
Basing itself on an oppositional model derived from linguistics
(and already there are many possibilities for such derivation),
structuralist analysis applies the terms of this model to various
artifacts or elements of human experience, thus assimilating the
chosen object analogously to the notion of a "text" in the literary
sense, and generating in the process of such comparative assimilation a kind of back-and-forth communication between what I
will call shortly (Section 3 of Part II) the linguistic and post-
linguistic levels of experience. But if one seeks to understand pre-
linguistic structures in this way (to say nothing of endo- or phyto-
semiotic exchanges, etc.)—when it comes to the study of things
humans and animals have in common that don't follow upon language—then the analysis becomes viciously circular, approximat-
ing indeed to the ideal type of a Kantian theory of reason wherein
the mind makes what it knows *as* known.

To give structuralism its proper place within the field of
semiotic endeavor and inquiry, in short, it must be said that it
forms *a part*, and a very important part, of anthroposemiotics
(that is, of the analysis of specifically human sign systems), as a
tool for the analysis of cultural phenomena. I say "a part of anthroposemiotics," inasmuch as structuralism as such cannot account for natural signs as such even as they occur therein (cf. my
essay review of Eco 1976); but that doesn't mean that structural-
ists, the practitioners of structuralist analysis, must perforce deny
that natural modes of semiosis exist, even when they more or less
ignore them for methodological reasons (since they can't adequately apply their models thereto). Here the practitioners face a
choice (cf. Merrell 1975): to bring as semioticians sufficiently critical parsimony to their definitions of code, etc., to avoid illegiti-
mate conclusions methodologically induced from inappropriately
selected data, or to pursue their method in an ideological, pro-
crustean way, blind to the limits inherent in its modular base.

The first option leads to continued advances in the field of
semiotics, the second right back by an unexpected detour into the
stale idealist controversies of modern philosophy and into the

stalemate of the concomitant pre-semiotic "theories" of knowledge and mind. It is to structuralism in the first context that we owe some of the most vital and fruitful currents of semiotics today, currents which have gone far in reconceptualizing and transforming traditional disciplines along semiotic lines.

A student of mine, Ms. Felicia Kruse, who has studied structuralist semiotics under Professor John Lyne of the University of Iowa, suggested to me a diagrammatic representation of the situation, from which I have devised the following:

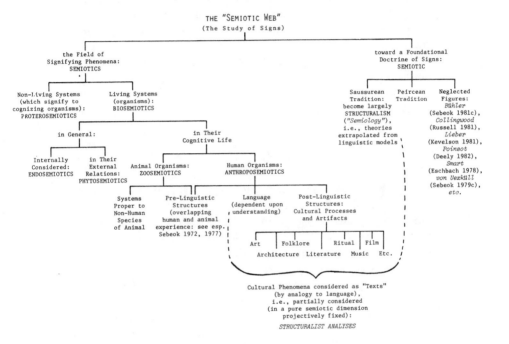

Notes to Part II, Section 2

1. The thesis that cognition requires a semiotic perspective for revealing what is proper to it receives striking, if indirect, confirmation from the fact that the characteristically modern and contemporary pre- or even anti-semiotic approaches to cognition from the time of Descartes, both in philosophy and psychology, have led to insoluble dilemmas of solipsism. The general historical argument on this point is outlined in note 9 of Section 5 above, with much detailed filled in in Deely 1978c and 1981b.

2. This comparatively "unreal" element at the heart of all semiosis has been nicely indicated by Wilden 1981: 2: "Information can be stored and transmitted only by being inscribed on a matter-energy base: waves, particles, and molecules, for instance; natural and synthetic substances; memories, mementos, and monuments. But information is not of the same order of reality as its base. Unlike energy, which as far as we know is always conserved whatever its transformations, information is created and replicated, and neutralized and destroyed, in everyday human and natural activities. Thus the many different kinds of bases or markers that carry information are constrained by the 'laws' of physics—by the accepted axioms of physics—but information as information is not.

"Matter-energy and information, therefore, are not just different in kind; they are, above all, distinct in level of relationship."

How these distinct levels interplay in the structuring of experience is reflected upon in Hanke 1972.

Notes to Part II, Section 3

1. So far as I have been able to determine, this distinction I am proposing between linguistic and post-linguistic systems does not appear anywhere in previous semiotic literature. This strikes me as somewhat improbable, so I should not be surprised to later learn that it does have a true counterpart in some book or essay as yet unknown to me. Nevertheless, I must report that the only distinction found so far even analogous to the one I am proposing is Jurij M. Lotman's distinction between primary and secondary modeling systems, first called to my attention by Jean Umiker-Sebeok in conversations preparatory to an earlier version of this essay (Deely 1980a): see Daniel P. Lucid (1977: 7ff.), J. Lotman (1977a: 95-98, 1977b: *passim*), Ann Shukman (1977: 122-124), and Daniel Laferrière (1977). But this distinction as it is employed in Soviet semiotics, though unquestionably related to the distinction being proposed here, is not the same distinction, being intrinsically glottocentric (and hence too narrow for the present purpose), and indeed not yet clear in its foundations. Laferrière comments (1977: 29-30): "As Shukman observes (122), the notion of secondary modelling system, which arose only as an operational concept during the first (1964) summer school in Kääriku, and which still remains to be satisfactorily elaborated by Lotman, assumes that language is not only the semiotic system

par excellence, but that consciousness is itself a primarily linguistic phenomenon.'' Lengthy discussions with experts versed in the Soviet literature, notably Dr. David Danow of the University of South Carolina and Dr. James Peters of the University of Missouri, served only to confirm the ambiguity as to the grounding and the more narrowly literary "structuralist" thrust of Lotman's usage.

My choice of terminology for expressing the proposed distinction was a difficult one. "Paralinguistic" would have been my preferred term for what I am here calling "post-linguistic," but previous appropriation of this term by linguists (see Sebeok, Hayes, and Bateson 1964; Crystal 1974) made this choice likely to create endless and needless misunderstandings. The final choice of "post-linguistic" was influenced more than anything else by Charles Morris' discussion of what he called "post-language symbols" (1946: 46-49). But whereas Morris is naming a particular group and functioning of signs as such, the structures I am referring to incorporate and generate signs without being in themselves semiotic, even though they owe their origin to semiosis and normally are permeated by semiotic dimensions.

2. James (1909: 279-280; see also 1890: I, 196ff., II, 8, etc.) among the moderns came perhaps the closest to a semiotic understanding of this matter, finding it necessary to break with the characteristically modern views in order to do so: "Every examiner of the sensible life *in concreto* must see that relations of every sort, of time, space, difference, likeness, change, rate, cause, or what not, are just as integral members of the sensational flux as terms are, and that conjunctive relations are just as true members of the flux as disjunctive relations are. This is what in some recent writings of mine I have called the 'radically empiricist' doctrine (in distinction from the doctrine of mental atoms which the name empiricism so often suggests). Intellectualistic critics of sensation insist that sensations are *dis*joined only. Radical empiricism insists that conjunctions between them are just as immediately given as disjunctions are, and that relations, whether disjunctive or conjunctive, are in their original sensible giveness just as fleeting and momentary (in Green's words), and just as 'particular,' as terms are. Later, both terms and relations get universalized by being conceptualized and named."

3. Julian Huxley, in his classic study (1942: 414), went so far as to say that Cott "has shown that concealing and revealing

coloration, when properly investigated, remain the paradigm of adaptive studies, and has thoroughly turned the tables on captious objectors.''

4. The ''sensory core'' we have distinguished within perception (Table II above) consists of the impressions produced in the organs of sense by the action here and now of the surrounding environment on the organisms. Never given as such in our experience, which is always of perceptual wholes, pure sensations are known only derivatively and by an analysis which proceeds from the realization that unless there were such first elements or data at the base and core of perception, we would find that all knowing in every respect entails an infinite regress, and so could have no point of origin (cf. Price 1950: 3, 7, 149, 155).

Now sensations are always given with and by perceptions, that is to say, within an elaborate and detailed network of objectivity that is the work of memory and imagination as well as of the so-called external senses. Moreover, the perceptual field is not only determined by the individual experiences of an organism, but, even more profoundly, by the anthropoid history of the higher organisms (which alone concern us at present) as it has been built into their genetic constitution over the centuries by the complex processes of ''natural'' or evolutionary selection. Thus, a given organism has a ''natural'' perception of certain objects as friendly or hostile, alluring or repulsive, prey or predator, etc., and these naturally given determinations of perception—sometimes called ''instinct''—precisely consist in the catching of a given element of experience within a net of ''unreal'' or cognition-dependent relations whereby the perceiver apprehends its objects not principally according to what they are ''in themselves,'' as it were, but rather according to what they are *so far as the perceiving organism is involved.* The same remarks apply to cognition-dependent relations attached to objects not by the a-prioris of organic constitution (the organism's genetic and selective history), but by the simple *learnings about* things built up through experiences the organism undergoes.

Now outside the human species, and indeed often enough inside the human species, this difference between relations obtaining among objects *so far as the actions or behavior of the individual organism is concerned* and relations obtaining among objects prior to *or* independent of the self-interests of the perceiver in the perceived—this is never thematized, never disengaged as such as an explicit component of a categorial scheme. Yet, prior to such a

thematization, in all our direct experiences of objects, the objects
are given in an apparently unified way which in fact conceals the
profound differences between an object as a thing in its own right
and an object as an element of experience being accounted for by
the perceiver in terms entirely born of its own needs and desires.

Thus, all objects of direct experience, from an independent
viewpoint, are known to be at best an imperfectly discriminated
amalgam of what is, in terms of cognition-independent being,
being and non-being, i.e., cognition-independent and cognition-
dependent interwoven networks of objectified relations.

The discrimination of relation as such, as a mode of being
distinct from and superordinate to related subjects, seems to take
place only upon a comparative analysis—not always self-
conscious and transparent to itself, be it said—which is also able,
in principle at least, to further distinguish among relations so discriminated between those whose entire actuality is the work of the
perceiving organisms (whether idiosyncratically, by custom, or
by social institution) and those which obtain physically as well as
through our experience. This relative discrimination of cognition-dependent elements in the objective structures of experience
and (in further refinements) beyond the experimentally given—
never wholly secure, to be sure, because never exhaustive (caught
as we are in time which throws up new structures in direct apper-
ception faster than we can reflexively disengage their pure elements)—is what underlies the possibility of a system of signs containing irreducibly stipulated components demonstrably understood as such by the controlled flexibility human beings display
in imaginative discourse and, perhaps especially, fairy tales.

This peculiar capacity for thematizing and critically reas-
sessing under various circumstances the line between reality and
unreality, exhibited in the partially controllable indifference of
our discourse to what is and what is not the case, is found nowhere
else in the animal kingdom, certainly not in the recent "sentences" constructed by our neighbors in evolution, the chimpanzees. It is an activity unique to and in some ways definitive of
human understanding. (See Deely 1975a, and notes following.)

5. In 1632, Poinsot, in his *Tractatus de signis* (642a24-29;
301a1-306b45, esp. 304b11-306a5; 747a33-b2), expressly regarded such an approach as an essential propaedeutic to the doctrine of signs. Among contemporary authors known to me, one,
a student of Poinsot's thought, has made a serious attempt at developing this way of interpreting human understanding. His pre-

liminary conclusions, some of which were cited in epigraphic form at the opening of the previous section and in the opening paragraphs of this section, are equally interesting in the area of zoosemiotics proper (Maritain 1957: 90): "So far we have spoken of genuine language. Let us point out that the word 'language,' when referring to animals, is equivocal. Animals possess a variety of means of communication but no genuine language. I have observed that animals use signs. But, as I also pointed out, no animal knows the relation of signification or uses signs as involving and manifesting an awareness of this relation.

"The full import of this is best realized in connection with the use of conventional signs by animals"—e.g., in the case of bees (von Frisch 1950), or, I would add, in the more indirect but no less intriguing case of the balloon flies (Kessel 1955).

Non-linguistic animals "use signs—and they do not know that there are signs."

6. If one considers the difference between the post-linguistic and the pre-linguistic systems, and the fact that the post-linguistic structures, when they acquire a semiotic dimension, as they invariably do (if indeed they don't have it from the outset), can be understood in the way that is essential to them *as* post-linguistic *only by linguistic animals*, then it is also clear that as they redescend below the linguistic interface, as they are experienced by the non-linguistic animals, signs designating them function in a completely different way. The post-linguistic meaning never survives as common to the two levels. The *materially same* sign designating a post-linguistic structure in those of its elements that are accessible in pure perception pre-linguistically is *formally diverse* from its designating what is actually proper to those elements *as* post-linguistic.

Take the case of civil government. Consider the notion of a president—the President of this country. If I were the Premacks, I would teach my chimpanzee each time, say, Richard Nixon walked into the room, to put on the board plastic symbols indicating "Here comes the President." Now, if I were the Premacks, I would forthwith claim that I had taught Sarah or Washoe or whichever chimp the meaning of the word "president." But the fact of the matter is that the animal doesn't see a *president*. Indeed, a president, *as such*, never appears *to the eyes*. The chimp doesn't have clue one as to what is referred to by the term "president," as it designates something distinct and distinguishable from the given concrete individual. When the chimp associates the word "president" with Richard M. Nixon, and when a human being says, "Richard M. Nixon was the President of the United States," the materially same sound or symbolic marker for "president" is functioning in a completely different sense, once above the linguistic interface as well as below it, the other time below it only. To stipulate the meaning of a word, to teach it to a chimpanzee by standard associative techniques, and then to assert that the word is functioning in the chimpanzee's sign system in precisely the stipulated sense is a particular version of "Clever Hans" that I would call the fallacy of linguistic anthropomorphism.

7. Here can be seen the point of Wilden's formula (1981: 10) that "language has ecological validity," being neither a copy nor a misrepresentation in its proper being, but rather "a part of human reality." This is also why the system of language, to be best understood, should not be conceptualized as a whole unto itself, but *as an interface*, a perceptually diaphanous network of unreal relations intervening as such between the specifically human language users and the layered manifolds of experience they seek to understand. It is in such a light that the relation of linguistics to the philosophy of language within semiotics might well be further examined.

REFERENCES

(HISTORICALLY LAYERED BY AUTHORS)

AND

INDICES

EXPLANATION OF REFERENCE STYLE

The reference style adopted for this book reflects by design the synthetic and historical perspective proper to the philosophical understanding of semiosis. All sources used in the course of the work are here listed in full, arranged alphabetically by author, as is standard bibliographical technique in existing style sheets, but with the twist of dating these sources in a linear column under the names according to the period of composition (in the case of ancient authors) or original publication (in the case of modern authors) of the works cited, with dates of modern editions used or translations consulted being given internal to the reference. Before a date, the prefix c. means *circa* or "approximately"; a. means *ante* or "before"; p. means *post* or "after"; i. means *inter* or "between" ("in the interval"). The abbreviation q.v., of course, means *quod vide*—"which see" or, in our case, "complete information under the author and year referred to." Annotations are added to a given reference as seems useful.

This system, called the historical layering of sources, conveniently and directly reflects the period of origin of the contributions to the dialogue under way. By this manner of reference, the relationship of conceptual thought to experience and the experimental continuities underlying the material differences of philosophical languages are brought to the foreground, helping to develop the reader's sensitivities to the historicity built into the human condition.

It is perhaps not too much to hope that this device will eventually establish itself as a standard bibliographical technique, supplanting the cumbersome and historically confused systems that have become rooted in academe, regularly creating such absurdities as "Galen 1821" or "Dante 1963."

ACKRILL, J. F.
   1963.   Translations of *Aristotle's Categories and De Interpretatione* (Oxford: Clarendon), with notes.

ADLER, Mortimer J.
   1967.   *The Difference of Man* (New York: Holt, Rinehart, & Winston), esp. p. 320 n.8, p. 327 n.10, p. 331 n.11. In this work, Adler uses "the ideas without the terminology" of Poinsot, or so he would have it.
   1968.   "Sense Cognition: Aristotle vs. Aquinas," *The New Scholasticism* XLII (Autumn): 578-91.

AGRICOLA, Rudolf.
   1480.   *De inventione dialectica.*

ALBERTUS MAGNUS. (Chronology for this reference is based on Weisheipl 1980a, b.)
   c.1250-1264.   *Liber Primus et Liber Secundus Priorum Analyticorum*, in the *Opera Omnia Alberti Magni*, ed. Auguste Borgnet, Vol. 2 (Paris: Vivès, 1890), pp. 459-809.
   c.1264-1270.   *Libri Topicorum*, in the *Opera Omnia*, ed. Auguste Borgnet, Vol. 2 (Paris: Vivès, 1890), pp. 233-524.

ALDRICH, H.
   1691.   *Artis Logicae Compendium.*

ALSTON, William P.
   1964.   *Philosophy of Language* (Englewood Cliffs, N.J.: Prentice-Hall, Inc.).

APEL, Karl-Otto.
   1981.   *Charles S. Peirce. From Pragmatism to Pragmaticism*, trans. John Michael Krois (Amherst: University of Massachusetts Press).

AQUINAS, Thomas.
   c.1255-1259.   *In librum Boetii de Trinitate expositio*, cura et studio M. Calcaterra, in *Opuscula Theologica*, ed. Raymundus M. Spiazzi (Turin: Marietti, 1954), Vol. II, pp. 313-389. For the dating of this work I have followed Maurer 1958: vi, q.v.
   c.1265-1267.   *De Potentia*, cura et studio R.P. Pauli M. Pession, in *Quaestiones Disputatae*, Vol. II (ixth ed., rev.; Turin: Marietti, 1953), pp. 7-276.
   c.1266.   *Summa theologiae prima pars*, ed. P. Carmello cum textu ex recensione leonina (Turin: Marietti, 1952).
   c.1268.   *In octo libros physicorum Aristotelis expositio*, cura et studio P. M. Maggiolo (Rome: Marietti, 1954).
   c.1268-1272.   *In duodecim libros metaphysicorum Aristotelis expositio*, ed. M. R. Cathala et R. M. Spiazzi (Turin: Marietti, 1950).
   c.1269.   *In decem libros ethicorum Aristotelis ad Nicomachum expositio*, cura et studio Raymundi Spiazzi (3rd ed.; Turin: Marietti, 1964).
   c.1269-1272a.   *In libros posteriorum analyticorum expositio*. Cum textu ex recensione leonina cura et studio R. M. Spiazzi (Turin: Marietti, 1955).
   c.1269-1272b.   *Summa theologiae pars prima secundae*, Carmello ed. bound with 1266 entry above.

c.1269-1274. Uncompleted commentary (after Book II, lectio 14: see note 16, pp. 188ff. above, and see entry for Cajetan 1496) *In Aristotelis libros perihermenias expositio*, pp. 5-144 of the Spiazzi edition based on the leonine text (1882) of this commentary together with that of St. Thomas on the *Posterior Analytics* (Turin: Marietti, 1955). English trans. in Oesterle 1962: pp. 17-137.

ARISTOTLE.
  c.360-330 B.C. *Organon*, in R. McKeon, ed., *The Basic Works of Aristotle* (New York: Random House), 1-212. Chronologizing based on Gauthier 1970, as follows:
    c.360.   *Categories*, 1-37 (complete; Edghill trans.).
    c.353a.   *Topics*, 187-206 (incomplete; Pickard-Cambridge trans.).
    c.353b.   *Refuting Sophisms*, 207-212 (incomplete; Pickard-Cambridge trans.).
    c.348-7a. *Prior Analytics*, 62-107 (incomplete; Jenkinson trans.).
    c.348-7b. *Posterior Analytics*, 108-186 (complete; Mure trans.).
    c.330.   *On Interpretation*, 38-61 (complete; Edghill trans.).
        It should be noted that, in some ways more consistent than the Latin development of Aristotle's notion of Logic as the instrument common to *all* thought, it was the custom in the Arabic tradition of Aristotelian commentary to include the *Rhetoric* (composed c. 335-4) and the *Poetics* (c. 335-4) as part of the *Organon* itself, corresponding, as it were, to the logic involved in practical knowledge (see our first diagram in the text above). Cfr. Lanigan 1969.
  c.348-347a. B.C. (Bks. I-VI, VIII), 353 B.C. (Bk. VII). *Physics*.
  c.348-347b. B.C. *The History of Animals*.
  c.348-347c. B.C. *On Generation and Corruption*.
  c.345-344. B.C. (Bks. II-IV), 330 B.C. (Bk. I). *On the Parts of Animals*.
  c.335-334a. B.C. *Nicomachean Ethics*.
  c.335-334b. B.C. *Meteorology*.
  c.330 B.C. *On the Soul*.

ARNAULD, Antoine, and NICOLE, Pierre.
  1662.   *La Logique, ou l'Art de Penser* (Paris).

ASHLEY, Benedict.
  1973.   "Change and Process," in *The Problem of Evolution*, ed. John N. Deely and Raymond J. Nogar (Indianapolis, Ind.: Hackett Publishing Co.), pp. 265-294.

ASHWORTH, E. J.
  1974.   *Language and Logic in the Post-Medieval Period* (Holland: Reidel).

Saint AUGUSTINE of Hippo.
  c.397-426. *De doctrina christiana libri quattuor* ("On Christian Doctrine"), in *Patrologiae Cursus Completus*, ed. J. P. Migne, *Series Latina* (P.L.), Volume 34, cols. 15-122. The *édition Bénédictine* of 1949 (Paris: Desclée), in *Oeuvres de Saint Augustin*, Vol. 11, was also consulted.

AVERROES.
  p.1181(?). *Commentarium Magnum in Aristotelis De Anima Libros*, ed. F. Stuart
      Crawford (Cambridge, Mass.: The Mediaeval Academy of Ameri-
      ca, 1953).

AYER, A. J.
  1947. *Thinking and Meaning* (London: H.K. Lewis).

BACON, Francis.
  1620. *Novum Organum*, ed. Thomas Fowler (Oxford, 1889); English trans.
      ed. by Fulton H. Anderson, *The New Organon* (Indianapolis: Bobbs-
      Merrill, 1960).
  1623. *De Dignitate et Augmentis Scientiarum*, the first part of a planned work
      of which the above 1620 work formed the second part.

BAER, Eugen.
  1980. "Toward a History of Semiotics. The German Translation of B.H.
      Smart's *Sematology*," *Ars Semeiotica* III:1, 129-136.

BAÑEZ, Domingo (1528-1604).
  1618. *Institutiones minores dialecticae, hoc est summulae* (Cologne; posthumous
      publication).

BARTHES, Roland.
  1964. *Elements of Semiology*, trans. from the French by Annette Lavers and
      Colin Smith (New York: Hill and Wang, 1968).

BERKELEY, Bishop George.
  1710. *A Treatise Concerning the Principles of Human Knowledge*, complete and
      unabridged text in *The English Philosophers from Bacon to Mill*, ed.
      E.A. Burtt (New York: The Modern Library, 1939), pp. 509-579.

BIRD, Otto A.
  1963. "The History of Logic," *Review of Metaphysics* XVI, no. 3 (March):
      491-502. A gentlemanly, informed review of Kneale and Kneale
      1962 and the first edition (Notre Dame, 1961) of Bochenski 1970.

BLACK, Max.
  1967. "Induction," in *The Encyclopedia of Philosophy*, ed. Paul Edwards
      (New York: The Free Press), Vol. 4, pp. 169-181.

BOCHENSKI, I.
  1970. *A History of Formal Logic*, translated and edited "with the author's
      full concurrence" by Ivo Thomas from *Formale Logik* (Freiburg:
      Verlag Karl Alber, 1956) (2nd ed., with corrections; New York:
      Chelsea Publishing Company).

BOEHNER, Philotheus.
  1957. "Introduction" to *Ockham. Philosophical Writings*, edited and
      presented in bi-lingual format (London: Thomas Nelson and Sons,
      Ltd.), pp. ix-lix.

BOETHIUS, Anicius Manlius Severinus. (The presentation of Boethius' works in Migne p.1844 [q.v.], P.L. Vol. 64, is here chronologized and evaluated textually solely on the basis of Cappuyns 1937, q.v.).

a.509.   *Dialogi in Porphyrium a Victorino translati* (ante 363).

509-510. *Commentaria in Porphyrium.*

510.   *In categorias Aristotelis libri quattuor.*

511.   *In librum Aristotelis de interpretatione Commentaria minor.*

p.511a. *Interpretatio priorum Analyticorum Aristotelis:* version authored by James of Venice, c. 1128.

p.511b. *Interpretatio posteriorum Analyticorum Aristotelis*: version authored by James of Venice, c. 1128.

p.511c. *Interpretatio Topicorum Aristotelis*: also by James of Venice, c. 1128.

p.511d. *Interpretatio Elenchorum Sophisticorum Aristotelis*: version of James of Venice, c. 1128.

511-513. *In librum Aristotelis de interpretatione Commentaria major.*

512-513a. *De Syllogismo categorico libri duo.*

512-513b. *Introductio ad Syllogismos Categoricos* (in some mss., *Antepraedicamenta*). Perhaps a 2nd ed. of 512-513a, above.

p.513a. *De Syllogismo hypothetico libri duo.* (Probably completed *soon* after 513.)

p.513b. *Liber de divisione.* (Also probably soon after 513.)

513-515. *Commentaria in Topica Ciceronis.*

c.515.   *De Differentiis topicis.* The two tracts, *De rhetorica cognatione* and *Locorum rhetoricorum distinctio*, Migne p.1844, P.L. 64, cols. 1217-1222 and 1222-1223, respectively, are only extracts of Book IV.

c.520.   *De Trinitate*, or, properly, *Liber de Sancta Trinitate* (more fully: *Quomodo trinitas unus deus ac non tres dii*).
       Liber de diffinitione: Spurious (authored by Marius Victorinus, born c. 280-300, died c. 363).

BOOLE, George.

1847.   *The Mathematical Analysis of Logic, being an essay toward a calculus of deductive reasoning* (London: Cambridge).

BOSSEREL, J. B.

1615.   *Synopses in quibus doctrina dialectica R.^{i} P.^{i} Petri Fonseca ad Ordinem Aristotelicum revocatur, Anno Domini 1615* (University of Graz MS 133; reprinted in Ferreira Gomes 1964, II: 779-861).

BOUISSAC, Paul.

1976.   "The 'Golden Legend' of Semiotics," *Semiotica* 17/4: 371-384.

1979.   "A Compass for Semiotics," *Ars Semeiotica* II: 2, 205-221.

BRADLEY, F. H.

1922.   *The Principles of Logic* (2nd ed., rev.; London: Oxford University Press), 2 vols.

BROWN, Roger.

1958.   *Words and Things* (New York: The Free Press).

CAHALAN, John C.
    1981.   "Maritain's View on the Philosophy of Nature," in *Selected Papers from the Conference-Seminar on The Degrees of Knowledge*, ed. Robert J. Henle, Marion Cordes, and Jeanne Vatterott (Saint Louis: The American Maritain Association), pp. 185-218. The title and context of this paper, as indeed much of the author's partisan rhetoric throughout, risk putting off the reader by disguising a highly original and creative approach to the problem of necessity in our knowledge of physical nature. It would be fascinating and useful to see this author's views advanced in a neutral forum and developed entirely in their own terms.

CAJETAN, Thomas de Vio.
    1496.   *Commentaria in reliquum libri secundi peri hermenias*, in *Sancti Thomae Aquinatis Opera Omnia*, Leonine ed., Tomus Primus (Rome: 1882, ed. Zigliara), pp. 87-128. English translation in Oesterle 1962: pp. 139-255.
    1507.   *Commentaria in Summam Theologicam. Prima Pars* (Rome). Reprinted in the Leonine ed. of the *Sancti Thomae Aquinatis Doctoris Angelici Opera Omnia*, vols. 4 and 5 (Rome, 1888-1889).

CARDANO, Girolamo (1501-1576).
    p.1554. *Dialectica.*

CAPPUYNS, M.
    1937.   Entry "Boèce" in *Dictionnaire d'Histoire et de Géographie Ecclésiastiques*, tome neuvième (Paris: Librarie Letouzey), columns 347-380.

CARNAP, Rudolf.
    1934.   *Logische Syntax der Sprache* (Vienna), published in English trans. by Amethe Smeaton, with additions, as *The Logical Syntax of Language* (London: Routledge & Kegan Paul, 1937).

CATON, Charles E.
    1967.   "Artificial and Natural Languages," in *The Encyclopedia of Philosophy*, ed. Paul Edwards (New York: Macmillan, 1967), Vol. 1, pp. 168-171.

CHAPMAN, R. F.
    1971.   *The Insects. Structure and Function* (New York: Elsevier).

CHATMAN, Seymour, ECO, Umberto, and KLINKENBERG, Jean-Marie, eds.
    1979.   *Panorama Sémiotique/A Semiotic Landscape*, Proceedings of the International Association for Semiotic Studies, Milan, June 1974 (The Hague: Mouton).

CHEVALIER, Ulysse.
    1907.   *Répertoire des Sources Historiques du Moyen Age. Bio-Bibliographie* (nouvelle ed. refondue, corrigée et aug.; Paris: Librairie Alphonse Picard et Fils), Deuxième Volume, entry for "Jacques clerc à Venise, traducteur," col. 2330.

CHOMSKY, Noam.
1968. *Language and Mind* (New York: Harcourt, Brace, & World).
1979. "Human Language and Other Semiotic Systems," *Semiotica* 25—
1/2, 31-44. This article is reprinted in Sebeok and Umiker-Sebeok
1980 (q.v.): 429-440.

CHURCH, Alonzo.
1948. The entry "Intention" in *The Dictionary of Philosophy*, ed. Dagobert
D. Runes (New York: Philosophical Library).

CLARK, Joseph T.
1952. *Conventional Logic and Modern Logic. A Prelude to Transition* (Woodstock, Md.: Woodstock College Press). Usefully annotated bibliography.

COFFEY, P.
1938. *The Science of Logic*, in two volumes (New York: Peter Smith).

COHEN, L. Jonathan.
1979. "Philosophy of Language and Semiotics," in Chatman, Eco, and
Klinkenberg 1979 (q.v.): 19-28.

COHEN, Morris R., and NAGEL, Ernest.
1934. *An Introduction to Logic and Scientific Method* (New York: Harcourt,
Brace & World).

COPI, Irving M.
1951. "The 'Intentionality' of Formal Logic," *Philosophy and Phenomenological Research* 11, pp. 366-372. Debate with Veatch 1951.
1982. *Introduction to Logic*, 6th ed. (New York: Macmillan).

COTT, H. B.
1940. *Adaptive Coloration in Animals* (London: Methuen).

CRYSTAL, David.
1974. "Paralinguistics," in *Linguistics and Adjacent Arts and Sciences*, Volume 12 of the *Current Trends in Linguistics* series, ed. by Thomas A.
Sebeok (The Hague: Mouton), pp. 265-295.

DEELY, John N.
1969. "The Philosophical Dimensions of the Origin of Species," *The
Thomist*, XXXIII (January and April), I, 75-149; II, 251-342.
1971a. "Animal Intelligence and Concept-Formation," *The Thomist*,
XXXV (January), 43-93.
1971b. "The Myth as Integral Objectivity," ACPA *Proceedings*, XLV:
67-76.
1971c. *The Tradition via Heidegger* (The Hague: Martinus Nijhoff).
1972a. "The Ontological Status of Intentionality," *The New Scholasticism*,
XLVI, 220-233.
1972b. "How Language Refers," *Studi Internazionali di Filosofia* 4: 41-
50.

1974.   "The Two Approaches to Language: Philosophical and Historical Reflections on the Point of Departure of Jean Poinsot's Semiotic," *The Thomist*, XXXVII, 4 (October), 856-907.

1975a.   "Modern Logic, Animal Psychology, and Human Discourse," *Revue de l'Université d'Ottawa*, 45, 1 (janvier-mars), 80-100.

1975b.   "Reference to the Non-Existent," *The Thomist*, XXXIX, 2 (April), 253-308.

1976.   "The Doctrine of Signs: Taking Form at Last," *Semiotica* 18:2, 171-193. (Essay review of Eco 1976.)

1977.   " 'Semiotic' as the Doctrine of Signs," *Ars Semeiotica* 1/3, 41-68.

1978a.   "Toward the Origin of Semiotic," in *Sight, Sound, and Sense*, ed. Thomas A. Sebeok (Bloomington: Indiana University Press), pp. 1-30. This work erroneously conjectured (p. 7) that "the explicit thematization and appellation of the division of signs into formal and instrumental may well have been original with Poinsot." Romeo (1979), working from Herculano de Carvalho, 1970 (q.v.), shows that while Poinsot's thematization in Book II, Question 2, of the *Treatise* was indeed original, the appellation of this contrast was already in use with Petrus Fonsecus' *Institutionum dialecticarum libri octo* (1564), a work with which Poinsot was certainly familiar. See Romeo 1979: 194-195, for a translation of Fonseca's summary remarks "about formal and instrumental signs."

1978b.   "What's in a Name?" *Semiotica* 22:1-2, 151-181. (Essay review of Sebeok 1976.)

1978c.   "Semiotic and the Controversy over Mental Events," ACPA *Proceedings*, LII, pp. 16-27.

1980a.   "The Nonverbal Inlay in Linguistic Communication," in *The Signifying Animal*, ed. Irmengard Rauch and Gerald F. Carr (Bloomington: Indiana University Press), pp. 201-217. This essay is an earlier version of Part II, Section 3, of the present book. In that Section, the "Tables" as originally hand-drawn by Brooke Williams are reproduced.

1980b.   "Antecedents to Peirce's Notion of Iconic Signs," in *Semiotics 1980* (Proceedings of the Semiotic Society of America), ed. Margot Lenhart and Michael Herzfeld (New York: Plenum), pp. 109-120.

1981a.   "The ISISSS Project: A Report on the First Annual International Summer Institute for Semiotic and Structural Studies," *Semiotic Scene*, Vol. IV, no. 2, 57-63.

1981b.   "Cognition from a Semiotic Point of View," in *Semiotics 1981* (Proceedings of the Semiotic Society of America), ed. John N. Deely and Margot D. Lenhart (New York: Plenum, in press).

1982.   "Neglected Figures in the History of Semiotic Inquiry: John Poinsot," in *History of Semiotics*, ed. Achim Eschbach and Jürgen Trabant (Amsterdam: John Benjamins).

1983(?). "Editorial Afterword" (EA), Semiotic Markers, notes, and indices to the bi-lingual edition of Poinsot's 1632 *Tractatus de Signis* (q.v.), including an exhaustive discussion of the "nationality" and proper name of this author.

DE MORGAN, Augustus.
  1847. *Formal Logic, or the calculus of inference, necessary and probable* (London).

DESCARTES, René.
  1641. *Meditations on First Philosophy*, trans. Elizabeth S. Haldane and G.R.T. Gross, in *The Philosophical Works of Descartes* (corrected reprint edition; New York: Dover, 1955), Vol. I, pp. 131-199.

DIELS, Hermann.
  1922. *Die Fragmente der Vorsokratiker* (Berlin: Weidmannsche Buchhandlung), 3 vols.

DUMITRIU, Anton.
  1977. *A History of Logic*, being a revised, updated and enlarged edition in 4 volumes of the single volume Roumanian work *Istoria Logica* (Bucharest: Editura Didactica, 1975), trans. Duiliu Zamfirescu, Dinu Giurcaneanu, and Doina Doneaud (Turnbridge Wells, Kent, England: Abacus Press):
    Vol. I.   Logic in Non-European Cultures. Logic in Ancient Greece. Rhetors and Commentators.
    Vol. II.   Scholastic Logic. Renaissance Logic.
    Vol. III. Methodological Logic. Development of Modern Logic.
    Vol. IV.   Mathematical Logic.

DUMMET, Michael.
  1967. "Frege, Gottlob," in *The Encyclopedia of Philosophy*, ed. Paul Edwards (New York: The Free Press), Vol. 3, pp. 225-237.
  1973. *Frege: Philosophy of Language* (New York: Harper & Row).

ECO, Umberto.
  1976. *A Theory of Semiotics* (Bloomington: Indiana University Press). Reviewed in Deely 1976.
  1983(?) Entry, "Aquinas," in the forthcoming *Encyclopedic Dictionary of Semiotics*, ed. Sebeok *et alii* (Bloomington: Indiana University Press).

ESCHBACH, Achim.
  1978. "Einleitung" to his translation from English of Benjamin Humphrey Smart, 1842 (q.v.), *Grundlagen der Zeichentheorie: Grammatik, Logik, Rhetorik* (Frankfurt am Main: Syndikat Autoren- und Verlagsgesellschaft), pp. 7-33.

FAY, Thomas A.
  1977. *Heidegger: The Critique of Logic* (The Hague: Martinus Nijhoff).

FERREIRA GOMES, Joaquim.
  1964. Introdução, Estabelecimento do Texto, Tradução e Notas for Fonseca 1564, q.v.

216   *References*

FISCH, Max H.
  1977.   "Peirce's Place in American Thought," *Ars Semeiotica*, 1/2: 21-37.
  1979.   "Charles Morris (1901-1979)," *Semiotic Scene*, III, 3 (September), 159-160.
  1980.   "Foreword" to *"You Know My Method"*: *A Juxtaposition of Charles S. Peirce and Sherlock Holmes*, by Thomas A. Sebeok and Jean Umiker-Sebeok (Bloomington, Indiana: Gaslight Publications), pp. 7-13.

FISCH, Max H., KETNER, Kenneth Laine, and KLOESEL, Christian J.W.
  1979.   "The New Tools of Peirce Scholarship, with Particular Reference to Semiotic," in *Peirce Studies*, Number 1 (Lubbock, Texas: Institute for Studies in Pragmaticism), ed. K. L. Ketner and J. M. Ransdell, pp. 1-17.

FONSECA, Petrus ("Pedro da").
  1564.   *Institutionum dialecticarum libri octo* (Coimbra: Apud haeredes Joannis Blauij). I was able to consult on microfilm the 1611 Venice edition "Apud Vincentium Florinum. MDCXI," which is the text cited in this essay. According to Ferreira Gomes 1964: vol. I, p. XLIV, an original of this edition can be seen in the library of the University of Munich. The most important edition of this work thus far is the bilingual presentation comparable to Poinsot 1632 (q.v.) of Joaquim Ferreira Gomes, *Instituições Dialecticas* (*Institutionum dialecticarum libri octo*), 2 vols. (Instituto de Estudos Filosoficos da Universidad de Coimbra, 1964). Discussion in Romeo 1979.

FREGE, G.
  1879.   *Begriffsschrift, eine der arithmetischen nachgebildete Formelsprache des reinen Denkens* (Halle).
  1892.   "Über Sinn und Bedeutung," *Zeitschrift für Philosophie und philosophische Kritik*, Vol. C, pp. 25-50.

GAUTHIER, René Antoine.
  1970.   "Introduction" to *L'Ethique à Nicomaque, traduction et commentaire*, par R.A. Gauthier et Jean Yves Jolif (12th ed., avec une introduction nouvelle; Paris: Beatrice-Nauwelaerts), Tome I, première partie.

GEACH, Peter.
  1968.   *Reference and Generality. An Examination of Some Medieval and Modern Theories* (emended edition; Ithaca: Cornell University Press).
  1972.   "History of the corruptions of logic," in *Logic Matters* (Berkeley: University of California Press), pp. 44-61.

GERHARDT, C. J.
  1961.   "Einleitung" to *Die philosophischen Schriften von Gottfried Wilhelm Leibniz*, ed. C. J. Gerhardt, Band VII (Hildesheim: Georg Olms), pp. 3-42, esp. 37ff.

GEULINCX, Arnold.
  1662.   *Logica Fundamentis Suis a quibus hactenus collapsa fuerat Restituta*.

GILSON, Etienne.
1937. *The Unity of Philosophical Experience* (New York: Scribner's).
1952. *La Philosophie au Moyen Age. Des Origines Patristiques à la Fin du XIVe Siècle* (2nd ed., rev. et aug.; Paris: Payot).

GRIFFIN, Donald R.
1981. *The Question of Animal Awareness* (revised and enlarged ed.; New York: The Rockefeller University Press).

HALVERSON, William H.
1976. *A Concise Introduction to Philosophy* (3rd ed.; New York: Random House).

HANKE, John W.
1972. "Sign and What Appears," *The New Scholasticism*, XLVI (Summer): 331-336. A brief but acute and stimulating reflection on the contrast between semiosis and material being.

HAWKES, Terrence.
1977. *Structuralism and Semiotics* (Berkeley: University of California Press).

HAWKINS, D. J. B.
1945. *The Criticism of Experience* (London: Sheed & Ward).
1946. *A Sketch of Mediaeval Philosophy* (London: Sheed & Ward).

HEGEL, G. W. F.
1812. *Wissenschaft der Logik: Erster Teil: Die Objektive Logik*, in *Sämtliche Werke* (Stuttgart: Frommann, 1958), Vol. 4.
1830. *Die Logik*, being the *Erster Teil* of *System der Philosophie*, in *Sämtliche Werke*, Vol. 8 (Stuttgart: Frommann, 1964), i.e., Part I of the 3rd edition of *Enzyklopädie der philosophischen Wissenschaften*, first published in 1816.

HEIDEGGER, Martin.
1927. *Sein und Zeit*, originally published in the *Jahrbuch für Phänomenologie und phänomenologische Forschung*, ed. E. Husserl. Page references in the present work are to the 10th edition (Tübingen: Niemeyer, 1963).
1929. *Vom Wesen des Grundes* (Frankfurt: Klostermann).
1947. *Platons Lehre von der Wahrheit, mit einem Brief über den Humanismus* (Bern: Francke).

HERBERT, Wray.
1981. "Semiotics: Fad or Revolution," in *Humanities Report* (publication of the American Association for the Advancement of the Humanities), Vol. III, no. 1 (January), 4-9.

HERCULANO DE CARVALHO, José G.
1969. "Segno e significazione in João de São Tomás," in *Estudos Linguísticos*, Vol. 2 (Coimbra: Atlântida Editora). Pp. 129-153 are exposition; 154-168 reproduce selected passages of Latin text. This careful essay, a most important piece of work on Poinsot's semiotic, stands along with the essay of Maritain, 1938, 1943, as a firsthand

presentation of Poinsot's views on the subject of signs. It is ex-
cerpted from Herculano de Carvalho 1970, q.v.

1970.   *Teoria da linguagem. Natureza do fenómeno linguístico e a análise das lín-*
guas (reprint with additions of 1967 work of same title, and now as
"Tomo I" with a second volume of the same name published in
1973; Coimbra: Atlântida). "Rarely acknowledged in the English-
speaking world" (Romeo 1979: 188-189), several chapters of this
work form "a basic introduction to general semiotics" (in particular, Chs. 5-8 "should be required reading as a challenging and
fresh outlook on language analysis within semiotics") written "on
the basis of and stemming from a wide view of the science of language within the western tradition of studies on the sign," and containing "considerations on both human and non-human communication." This richly learned study was a singularly fruitful result, according to Romeo, of the establishment in 1957 of a chair
for linguistics within the Faculty of Letters at the University of
Coimbra. It is no credit to the human condition that a political
situation should be able to make a scholar of such magnitude into
an official non-person, expelled from university life, and seques-
tered from "foreign" contacts. "Should Herculano de Carvalho's
Teoria be translated one day," Romeo muses (p. 189), "crossing
either the Channel or the Atlantic, doubtless it will have an impact
on a younger generation understandably tired of being led by the
nose by those astero-linguists who try to reinvent the wheel each
time a Ph.D. dissertation is 'published'. Let us hope his work will
not have to wait half a century for a Baskin."

HERSCHEL, Sir John.
1831.   *A Preliminary Discourse on the Study of Natural Philosophy* (London:
Longman, Rees, Orme, Brown and Green).

HERZFELD, Michael.
1981.   "The Music of the Hemispheres: ISISSS '80 in Review," *Semiotica*
34-3/4: 219-224.

HILBERT, D.
1905.   "Über die Grundlagen der Logik und der Arithmetik," *Verh. d. 3.*
Int. Mathem.-Kongr. (Leipzig), 174-185.

HILLGARTH, Jocelyn Nigel.
1967.   "Lull, Ramon," in *The Encyclopedia of Philosophy*, ed. Paul Edwards
(New York: Macmillan), Vol. 5, pp. 107-108.
1971.   *Ramon Lull and Lullism in Fourteenth Century France* (Oxford: Clarendon Press).

HUME, David.
1748.   *An Enquiry Concerning Human Understanding*, complete and unabridged text in *The English Philosophers from Bacon to Mill*, ed. E.A.
Burtt (New York: The Modern Library, 1939), pp. 585-689.

HUXLEY, Julian S.
1942. *Evolution: The Modern Synthesis* (London: George Allen & Unwin Ltd.)

JAKOBSON, Roman.
1979. "Coup d'oeil sur le devéloppement de la sémiotique," in Chatman, Eco, and Klinkenberg 1979 (q.v.): 3-18.

JAMES, William.
1890. *The Principles of Psychology* (unabridged and unaltered republication; New York: Dover), 2 vols.
1909. *A Pluralistic Universe* (New York: Longmans, Green, and Co.).
1911. "Percept and Concept—The Import of Concepts," Ch. IV of *Some Problems of Philosophy. A Beginning of an Introduction to Philosophy* (New York: Longmans & Green), pp. 47-74. This uncompleted book was worked on by James between March of 1909 and his death in August of 1910. It was edited and put into publishable form posthumously by Henry James, Jr., working with H. M. Kallen and R. B. Perry.

JEVONS, W. S.
1864. *Pure Logic, or the Logic of Quality apart from Quantity* (London).

JOSEPH, H. W. B.
1916. *An Introduction to Logic* (2nd ed., rev.; Oxford: Clarendon Press).

JOURDAIN, A.
1843. *Recherches critiques sur l'âge et l'origine des traductions latine d'Aristote* (Paris).

JUNGIUS ("JUNGE"), Joachim.
1635. *Logica Hamburgensis*.

KANT, Immanuel.
1781, 1787. *Kritik der reinen Vernunft* (Riga). References in the present work are to the N. K. Smith translation, *Kant's Critique of Pure Reason* (New York: St. Martin's Press, 1963), and to *Kant's Gesammelte Schriften*, issued by the Königlich Preussischen Akademie der Wissenschaften, Band III, *Kritik der reinen Vernunft*, 2nd ed. (1787) (Berlin: Druck und Verlag von Georg Reimer, 1911).

KESSEL, Edward L.
1955. "The Mating Activities of Balloon Flies," *Systematic Zoology*, 4, 96-104.

KEVELSON, Roberta.
1981. "Francis Lieber and the Semiotics of Law and Politics," in *Semiotics 1981* (Proceedings of the Semiotic Society of America), ed. John N. Deely and Margot D. Lenhart (New York: Plenum, in press).

KLEINPAUL, Rudolph.
1888. *Sprache ohne Worte: Idee einer allegemeinen Wissenschaft der Sprache* (Leipzig: Friedrich).

KNEALE, William and Martha.
1962. *The Development of Logic* (London: Oxford).

KRAMPEN, Martin.
  1981. "Phytosemiotics," *Semiotica*, 36-3/4: 187-209.
KREMPEL, A.
  1952. *La doctrine de la relation chez St. Thomas* (Paris: Vrin).
KRETZMANN, Norman.
  1979. *Pauli Veneti Logica Magna Prima Pars Tractatus de Terminis*, ed. with an English trans. and notes (Oxford: The British Academy).
KRISTELLER, Paul Oskar.
  1961a. "The Aristotelian Tradition," in his *Renaissance Thought* (New York: Harper), pp. 24-47.
  1961b. "Humanism and Scholasticism in the Italian Renaissance," in *op. cit.*, 92-119.
KÜNG, Guido.
  1967. *Ontology and the Logistic Analysis of Language* (rev. ed.; Dordrecht-Holland: Reidel). A remarkable and extremely valuable book which shows perhaps more of the limits of logistic philosophizing than any other single study—or than its author hoped.
LAFERRIERE, Daniel.
  1977. "Of Semioticians and Slavists," *Semiotic Scene*, Vol. I, no. 4, 28-33.
LANIGAN, Richard L.
  1969. "Aristotle's Rhetoric: Addendum to the Organon," *Dialogue* 11, no. 2 (November): 1-6.
  1972. *Speaking and Semiology* (The Hague: Mouton).
  1977. *Speech Act Phenomenology* (The Hague: Martinus Nijhoff).
LEIBNIZ, G. W. F. (The chronology and pagination references for the following list of Leibniz's works relevant to the present essay is based on the edition of Renate Vollbrecht, *Gottfried Wilhelm Leibniz Opera Philosophica quae exstant latina gallica germanica omnia*, instruxit J.E. Erdmann: Faksimiledruck der Ausgabe 1840 durch weitere Textstücke ergänzt und mit einem Vorwort versehen von Renate Vollbrecht. Meisenheim: Scientia Aalen, 1959. For the questionable dates, Gerhardt 1961 was further consulted).
  c.1666. "Dissertatio de arte combinatoria cum appendice," in Vollbrecht, pp. 6-44.
  1677. "Dialogus de connexione, inter res et verba," in Vollbrecht, pp. 76-78.
  1685-1686(?)a. "De scientia universali seu calculo philosophico," in Vollbrecht, pp. 82-85.
  1685-1686(?)b. "Initia scientiae generalis de nova ratione instaurationis et augmentationis scientiarum, ita ut exiguo tempore et negotio, si modo velint homines, magna praestari possint ad felicitatis humanae incrementum," in Vollbrecht, pp. 85-86.
  1685-1686(?)c. "De natura et usu scientiae generalis," in Vollbrecht, pp. 86-88.

1685-1686(?)d. "Synopsis libri, cui titulus erit: Scientia nova generalis pro instauratione et augmentis scientiarum ad publicam felicitatem," in Vollbrecht, pp. 88-89.

1685-1686(?)e. "Guilielmi Pacidii plus ultra, sive initia et specimina scientiae generalis etc.," in Vollbrecht, p. 89.

1685-1686(?)f. "Guilielmi Pacidii initia et specimina scientiae generalis," in Vollbrecht, pp. 90-91.

1685-1686(?)g. "In specimina Pacidii introductio historica," in Vollbrecht, pp. 91-92.

1685-1686(?)h. "Fundamenta calculi ratiocinatoris," in Vollbrecht, pp. 92-94.

1685-1686(?)i. "Non inelegans specimen demonstrandi in abstractis," in Vollbrecht, pp. 94-97.

1685-1686(?)j. "Addenda ad specimen calculi universalis," in Vollbrecht, pp. 98-99.

1685-1686(?)k. "De veritatibus primis," in Vollbrecht, p. 99.

1685-1686(?)l. "Definitiones Logicae," in Vollbrecht, pp. 100-101.

1696. "Schreiben an Gabriel Wagner vom Nutzen der Vernunftkunst oder Logik," in Vollbrecht, pp. 418-426.

1704. Completion of *Nouveaux Essais sur l'entendement humain*, ms. not published until 1765.

LEVY-BRUHL, L.

1899. "Essay on Descartes," added "as it appeared in the author's *History of Modern Philosophy in France* (Chicago: Open Court, 1899) by way of a general introduction" to *The Meditations and Selections from the Principles of René Descartes*, trans. by John Veitch and published by Open Court of Chicago in 1905 under the editorship of T.J. McCormack, pp. vii-xxx.

LOCKE, John.

1690. *An Essay Concerning Human Understanding*, ed. Alexander Campbell Fraser (Oxford, 1894; Dover reprint 1959), in 2 vols. The edition of P. H. Nidditch (Oxford: Clarendon Press, 1975) was also consulted.

LOMBARD, Peter.

c.1150. *Libri Quattuor Sententiarum* ("The Four Books of the Sentences"), in *Patrologiae Cursus Completus*, ed. J. P. Migne, *Series Latina* (P.L.), Vol. 192, cols. 522-963. (One of the very earliest printed editions of this formerly ubiquitous work appeared in Venice: Vandelin Spire, 1477.)

LOTMAN, Jurij M.

1977a. "Primary and Secondary Communication-Modeling Systems," in *Soviet Semiotics*, trans. and ed. by Daniel P. Lucid (Baltimore: Johns Hopkins University Press), pp. 95-98.

1977b. *The Structure of the Artistic Text*, trans. by Ronald Vroon (Ann Arbor: Michigan Slavic Contributions, University of Michigan).

LOTZE, Hermann.
    1843.   *Logik* (Leipzig; English trans. Oxford 1884).

LUCID, Daniel P.
    1977.   "Introduction" to *Soviet Semiotics: An Anthology*, ed. Daniel P. Lucid
             (Baltimore: Johns Hopkins University Press), pp. 1-23.

LULL, Ramon.
    1274.   Composition of the first version of the *Ars Magna*, the *Ars compen-
             diosa inveniendi veritatem*, which "has only once been published, by
             Salzinger" as the opening work in the 8-volume *Beati Raymundi
             Lulli Opera*, ed. Ivo Salzinger (Mainz, 1721-1742). "The Catalan
             original (*Ars abreujada d'atrobar veritat*) is lost but it certainly existed;
             it is referred to by Lull, *Ars demonstrativa*, c.1275." (Hillgarth 1971:
             8 n. 32.)

MARCUS, Solomon.
    1979.   "Semiotics of Scientific Languages," in Chatman, Eco, and Klink-
             enberg 1979 (q.v.): 29-40.

MARITAIN, Jacques.
    1923.   *Éléments de Philosophie. II. L'Ordre des Concepts. I. Petite Logique (Lo-
             gique formelle)* (Paris: Tequi). Citations and page references through-
             out the present work are from the English trans. by Imelda Cho-
             quette, *Formal Logic* (New York: Sheed and Ward, 1937).
    1924.   *Réflexions sur l'intelligence et sur sa vie propre* (Paris: Nouvelle Librairie
             Nationale).
    1937-38. "Sign and Symbol," trans. Mary Morris in *Journal of the Warburg
             Institute*, I, pp. 1-11. See also entries for 1938 and 1943.
    1938.   "Signe et symbole," *Revue Thomiste*, XLIV (April), 299-330.
    1943.   "Sign and Symbol," English trans. of 1938 entry above (q.v.) by
             H. L. Binsse in *Redeeming the Time* (London: Geoffrey Bles), text pp.
             191-224, Latin notes pp. 268-276.
    1957.   "Language and the Theory of Sign," in *Language: An Enquiry into
             Its Meaning and Function*, ed. Ruth Nanda Anshen (New York: Har-
             per), pp. 86-101.
    1959.   *Distinguish to Unite, or The Degrees of Knowledge*, trans. from the fourth
             French edition under the supervision of Gerald B. Phelan (New
             York: Scribner's). Original publication in French, 1932.
    1966.   *God and the Permission of Evil*, trans. Joseph Evans (Milwaukee: The
             Bruce Publishing Co.).

MATES, Benson.
    1961.   *Stoic Logic* (Berkeley: University of California Press).

MAURER, Armand A.
    1958.   "Introduction" to St. Thomas Aquinas, *The Division and Methods of
             the Sciences*, Questions V and VI of Aquinas, c. 1255-1259 (q.v.),
             trans. by Armand Maurer (2nd rev. ed.; Toronto: Pontifical Insti-
             tute of Medieval Studies), pp. vii-xxxvi.

McLAUGHLIN, R. J.
1981. "Language and Man: Aristotle Meets Koko," *The Thomist,* 45 (October), 541-570.

MELANCTHON, Philip.
c.1521. *Erotemata Dialectices* (Wittenberg).

MENNE, Albert.
1962. "Preface of the Editor" to *Logico-Philosophical Studies* (Dordrecht-Holland: D. Reidel), pp. VII-IX.

MERRELL, Floyd.
1975. "Structuralism and Beyond: A Critique of Presuppositions," *Diogenes* 92: 67-103.

MIGNE, J. P., ed.
1844-1855. *Patrologiae Cursus Completus, Series Latina* (P.L., customarily), (Paris), 217 volumes.
p.1844. *Manlii Severini Boetii opera omnia, non solum liberalium disciplinarum, sed etiam majorum facultatum studiosis utilissima, mo et sine quibus Aristoteles in praecipuis locis intelligi non potest,* etc. (Bibliothecae Cleri universae), P.L. 64 (being the second of two volumes comprising hopefully the *versiones Boethii* extant to our time: see entry for Boethius above).

MILL, John Stuart.
1843. *System of Logic* (London).

MOODY, Ernest A.
1935. *The Logic of William of Ockham* (New York: Russell and Russell).
1967. The section, "Medieval Logic," pp. 528-534, in the several-authored general entry, "Logic, History of," pp. 513-571 in *The Encyclopedia of Philosophy*, ed. Paul Edwards (New York: Macmillan), Vol. 4.

MORRIS, Charles.
1946. *Signs, Language and Behavior* (Englewood Cliffs, N.J.: Prentice-Hall; reprinted 1955 by George Braziller, New York. Page references in the present work are to the 1955 reprint).
1971. *Writings on the General Theory of Signs* (The Hague: Mouton).

MUELLER, Ian.
1978. "An Introduction to Stoic Logic," in *The Stoics*, ed. John M. Rist (Berkeley: University of California Press), pp. 1-26.

NICOLE, Pierre: see entry for ARNAULD, Antoine.

NYS, D.
1942. *Cosmology. The Philosophical Study of the Inorganic World*, translation and adaptation by Sidney A. Raemers (Milwaukee: Bruce), in 2 vols.

OCKHAM, William of.
i.1317-1328. *Summa Logicae.* Partial ed. by Philotheus Boehner (New York: St. Bonaventure, 1951-1954).

OESTERLE, Jean.
  1962. Translation with Introduction (pp. 1-15), *Aristotle: On Interpretation. Commentary by St. Thomas and Cajetan* (Milwaukee: Marquette University Press).

OESTERLE, John A.
  1944. "Another Approach to the Problem of Meaning," *The Thomist*, VII, 233-263. A valuable analysis of key distinctions in Poinsot, which does not however penetrate to the level of his semiotic proper (see Part I, Section 5, note 9 above), concluding with a point-by-point comparison between Poinsot and Ogden and Richards, *The Meaning of Meaning* (New York: Harcourt, Brace, and Co., 1923).

OSGOOD, Charles E.
  1953. *Method and Theory in Experimental Psychology* (New York: Oxford University Press).

PARKER, F. H., and VEATCH, Henry.
  1959. *Logic as a Human Instrument* (New York: Harper).

PAULUS VENETUS ("Paul of Venice," c. 1369-1429).
  p.1393(?). *Logica Magna, Prima Pars (tractatus de terminis)*, microfilm of a Vatican Library early edition and the bi-lingual presentation by Norman Kretzmann 1979 (q.v.) were consulted but not cited in preparing this essay. Also consulted was the *Tractatus de Suppositionibus* from the first part of the *Logica Magna*, in the edition and translation of Alan R. Perreiah (St. Bonaventure, New York: Franciscan Institute Publications, Text Series No. 15, 1971).

PEANO, G.
  1889. *Arithmetices principia, novo methodo exposita* (Turin: Augustae Taurinorum).

PEIRCE, Charles Sanders.
  1871. Review of Fraser's Edition of the Works of George Berkeley, in *The North American Review*, 113 (October), 449-472, as reproduced in *Collected Papers*, Vol. VIII, pp. 9-38. References above are to the CP reprint.
  1902. *Minute Logic*, draft for a book complete consecutively only to Ch. 4. Published in the *Collected Papers* in extracts scattered over six of the eight volumes: details in Burks' "Bibliography of the Works of Charles Sanders Peirce" at the end of Vol. 8, pp. 293-294.

PELC, Jerzy.
  1977. "On the Prospects of Research in the History of Semiotics," *Semiotic Scene* 1/3 (September), 1-12.
  1979. "Semiotics and Logic," in Chatman, Eco, and Klinkenberg 1979 (q.v.): 41-51.

PERRON, Paul, ed.
  1981. *The Neurological Basis of Signs in Communication Processes*, Proceedings of a Symposium held in June, 1980, as part of the first Interna-

tional Summer Institute for Semiotic and Structural Studies, revised for publication (Victoria University: Toronto Semiotic Circle).

PETER OF SPAIN (Petrus Hispanus).

c.1245. *Summulae Logicales*, ed. I. M. Bochenski (Rome: Marietti, 1947).

PETERS, James.

1978. "Semiotics as a Paradigm for Critical Inquiry: A Report on the First NEH Summer Seminar in Semiotics," *Semiotic Scene*, Vol. II, No. 4 (November), 155-159.

POINSOT, John (cfr. Deely 1983).

1631. *Textus Summularum* seu *Artis Logicae Prima Pars* (Alcalá, Spain). The Reiser edition of this work (Volume I; Turin: Marietti, 1930: pp. 1-247), was used in preparing the present book.

1632. *Tractatus de Signis*, embedded within the *Artis Logicae Secunda Pars* (Alcalá, Spain), as explained in Deely 1983, q.v. The Reiser edition of this work (Volume I; Turin: Marietti, 1930: pp. 249-839) was used in preparing this essay.

1631-1635. *Cursus Philosophicus*, available in the modern edition of B. Reiser (Turin: Marietti, 1930-1938: in 3 volumes), comprising:

 1631. *Artis Logicae Prima Pars* (Alcalá, Spain).

 1632. *Artis Logicae Secunda Pars* (Alcalá, Spain).

 1633. *Naturalis Philosophiae De Ente Mobili in Communi* (Madrid, Spain).

 1634. *Naturalis Philosophiae De Ente Mobili Corruptibili* (Alcalá, Spain).

 1635. *Naturalis Philosophiae De Ente Mobili Animato* (Alcalá, Spain).

1637-1667. *Cursus Theologicus* (in modern ed. of Ludovicus Vivès, Paris: 1883-1886; tomes 1-4 in 5 vols. of Solesmes critical ed., 1932-1953), from which we have had occasion in this work to refer specifically to:

 1637. *Tomus Primus* (explanation of the *Sentences* of Peter Lombard, general Isagoge to the *Summa theologiae* and specific commentary on I. qq. 1-14; Alcalá, Spain). Being Vols. I and II to p. 529 of the Solesmes ed. Paris: Desclée, 1931 and 1934.

 1667. *Tomus Octavus* (*De Sacramentis*; ed. P. Combefis; Paris, France). Being Vol. IX of the Vivès ed. (Paris: 1885).

PORPHYRY.

c.271. *Porphyrii Isagoge et in Aristotelis Categorias Commentarium* (Greek text), ed. A. Busse (Berlin, 1887). English trans. by Edward W. Warren, *Porphyry the Phoenician: Isagoge* (Toronto: Pontifical Institute of Mediaeval Studies, 1975).

PORT-ROYAL LOGIC: see ARNAULD, Antoine, and NICOLE, Pierre.

POWELL, Ralph A.

1982(?). *Freely Chosen Reality* (Washington, D.C.: University Press of America). A remarkable essay tracing an entire history of philosophy through the primary sources in Greek, Latin, and national language traditions up to the present by the Ariadne's thread of real relations, which the author shows is in some sense a common doctrine across the schools as concerns the origin of human experience. Centrally inspired by the *doctrina signorum* or semiotic in the strictest "inward turning, all but subterranean" sense characterized by Sebeok ("Foreword" above), this book yet never so much as mentions the term. One can only hope its author will complete the 4-volume project of which this is the first, establishing, as was said, the basic thesis that real relations are the origin of experience and, being themselves free realities (indifferent to their subjective ground, as explained in note 9 to Section 5 above), become within the context of culture and under certain circumstances the objects of free choice. From this, the second volume, *Totally Empirical Ethics*, now completed about halfway, argues further that the origin of morality lies precisely in those real relations which come to be freely chosen. A third volume proposes to account for the path understanding can take from the experience of real relations to a critically controlled grasp of the intrinsic nature of things, while the final fourth volume proposes to deal with the ultimate overall coherence of the universe through real relations, that is, the question of God as it arises precisely from experience.

PREZIOSI, Donald.
   1979.   *The Semiotics of the Built Environment* (Bloomington: Indiana University Press).

PRICE, H. H.
   1950.   *Perception* (2nd ed., rev.; Methuen & Co. Ltd.).

QUINE, W. V. O.
   1952.   "Preface" to Joseph T. Clark's *Conventional Logic and Modern Logic, A Prelude to Transition* (Woodstock, Maryland: Woodstock College Press), pp. V-VII.
   1960.   *Word and Object* (Cambridge, Mass.: M.I.T. Press).

RAMUS, Petrus.
   1555.   *Dialectique*. (The first work on logic written in French.)

RANDALL, Jr., John Herman.
   1962.   *The Career of Philosophy*, Volume I, *From the Middle Ages to the Enlightenment* (New York: Columbia).

RANSDELL, Joseph.
   1966.   *Charles Peirce: The Idea of Representation* (New York: Columbia University, unpublished doctoral dissertation).
   1980.   "Semiotic and Linguistics," in *The Signifying Animal*, ed. Irmengard Rauch and Gerald F. Carr (Bloomington: Indiana University Press), pp. 135-185.

RASMUSSEN, Douglas B.
   1980. "Deely, Wittgenstein, and Mental Events," *The New Scholasticism*, LIV (Winter), 60-67.

RAUCH, Irmengard.
   1980. "Between Linguistics and Semiotics: Paralanguage," in *The Signifying Animal*, ed. Irmengard Rauch and Gerald F. Carr (Bloomington: Indiana University Press), pp. 284-289.

RAUCH, Irmengard, and CARR, Gerald F., eds.
   1980. *The Signifying Animal* (Bloomington: Indiana University Press).

de RIJK, Lambertus M.
   1962. *Logica Modernorum. A Contribution to the History of Early Terminist Logic* (Assen, Netherlands: Koninlijke Van Gorcum & Comp.); Vol. I, "On the Twelfth Century Theories of Fallacy"; Vols. II & III, "The Origin and Early Development of the Theory of Supposition."

RISSE, Wilhelm.
   1965. *Bibliographia Logica. Verzeichnis der Druckschriften zur Logik mit Angabe ihrer Fundorte* (Hildesheim: Gg. Olms), Vol. I, 1472-1800.

ROCHBERG-HALTON, Eugene, and McMURTREY, Kevin.
   1981. "An Outline of the Foundations of Modern Semiotic," in *Semiotics 1981* (Proceedings of the Semiotic Society of America), ed. John N. Deely and Margot D. Lenhart (New York: Plenum, in press). The remarks these authors make on the role of "authorities" in the Latin scholastic philosophies is completely imaginary, but they well serve to illustrate how general prejudices of the sort noted at the opening of Section 5 in Part I of this book, once established, survive like vampires.

ROLLIN, Bernard E.
   1976. *Natural and Conventional Meaning: An Examination of the Distinction* (The Hague: Mouton).

ROMEO, Luigi.
   1976. "Heraclitus and the Foundations of Semiotics," *Versus* 15 (dicembre), 73-90.
   1977a. "The Derivation of 'Semiotics' through the History of the Discipline," in *Semiosis* 6, ed M. Bense, G. Deledalle, and E. Walther, Heft 2, pp. 37-49.
   1977b. "In Margin to Sebeok's 'Marginalia,' " *Historiographia Linguistica* IV/3: 413-420.
   1979. "Pedro da Fonseca in Renaissance Semiotics: A Segmental History of Footnotes," *Ars Semeiotica* II: 2, 187-204.

ROSSI-LANDI, Ferruccio.
   1978. "On Some Post-Morrisian Problems," *Ars Semeiotica* 3: 3-32.

RUSSELL, Anthony F.
   1981. "The Logic of History as a Semiotic Process of Question and

Answer in the Thought of R. G. Collingwood,'' in *Semiotics 1981* (Proceedings of the Semiotic Society of America), ed. John N. Deely and Margot D. Lenhart (New York: Plenum, in press).

RUSSELL, Bertrand.
1905.   "On Denoting," *Mind*, XIV: 479-493. See gloss on entry for 1919.
1910.   "Incomplete Symbols," third introductory chapter to Whitehead-Russell 1910-1913 (q.v.): 66-84. See gloss on entry for 1919.
1919.   *Introduction to Mathematical Philosophy* (London: George Allen and Unwin Ltd.). Russell's so-called "Theory of Descriptions" first appeared in 1905 (q.v.). The most technical and "logically simple" exposition of the theory is perhaps the version incorporated into the third introductory chapter of the *Principia Mathematica* under the title "Incomplete Symbols." See entry for 1910. But insofar as philosophy is more concerned with underlying assumptions and principles than with the resolution of problems into definite conclusions, the most philosophically important exposition of the theory is probably that found in Chapters 15-17 of this 1919 book. Discussion in Deely 1975b: 262 ff.

RUSSMAN, Thomas A.
1981.   "Two Paradigms of Reality and Objectivity," *The New Scholasticism* LV (Winter): 1-15.

de SAUSSURE, Ferdinand.
1916.   *Cours de Linguistique Générale*, publié par Charles Bally et Albert Sechehaye avec la collaboration de Albert Riedlinger, édition critique preparée par Tullio de Mauro (Paris: Payot, 1972).

SAVONAROLA, G. (S. Hieronymus).
1516.   *Compendium Logicae* (Leipzig).

SCHRÖDER, E.
1877.   *Der Operationskreis des Logikkalkuls* (Leipzig).
1890-1905. *Vorlesungen über die Algebra der Logik* (Leipzig: I, 1890; II/1, 1891; III, 1895; II/2, 1905).

SCRUTON, Roger.
1980.   "Possible Worlds and Premature Sciences," in *The London Review of Books*, 7 February 1980, reviewing Preziosi 1979 and Eco 1976, without much good to report, but without much depth, either.

SEBEOK, Thomas A. (See also Umiker-Sebeok.)
1972.   *Perspectives in Zoosemiotics* (The Hague: Mouton).
1974.   "Semiotics: A Survey of the State of the Art," in *Linguistics and Adjacent Arts and Sciences*, Vol. 12 of the *Current Trends in Linguistics* series, ed. by Sebeok (The Hague: Mouton), pp. 211-264. Reprinted in Sebeok 1976 (q.v.), 1-45: page references in the present book are to this 1976 reprint.
1975a. "The Semiotic Web: A Chronicle of Prejudices," *Bulletin of Literary Semiotics*, 2 (1975), 1-63, as reprinted with essential corrections and additions in Sebeok 1976 (q.v.): 149-188.

1975b. "Zoosemiotics: At the Intersection of Nature and Culture," in *The Tell-Tale Sign*, ed. T. A. Sebeok (Lisse, The Netherlands: Peter de Ridder Press), pp. 85-95.

1976. *Contributions to the Doctrine of Signs* (Bloomington: Indiana University RCLSS Publications, and Lisse, The Netherlands: Peter de Ridder Press).

1977. "Zoosemiotic Components of Human Communication," in *How Animals Communicate*, ed. Thomas A. Sebeok (Bloomington: Indiana University Press), Chap. 38, pp. 1055-1077.

1978. " 'Talking' with Animals: Zoosemiotics Explained," *Animals*, 111:6 (December), pp. 20ff.

1979a. "The Vocabulary of Gestures: Nonverbal Communication in Foreign Languages," *Research and Creative Activity*, III, 1 (September): 6-11.

1979b. "Looking in the Destination for What Should Have Been Sought in the Source," in *The Sign & Its Masters* (Austin: University of Texas Press), Chapter 5, pp. 84-106.

1979c. "Neglected Figures in the History of Semiotic Inquiry: Jakob von Uexküll," in *The Sign & Its Masters*, Chap. 10 (Austin: University of Texas Press), pp. 187-207.

1979d. "Teaching semiotics: report on a pilot program," Appendix III to *The Sign & Its Masters* (Austin: University of Texas Press), pp. 272-279.

1981a. "Naming in Animals, with reference to playing: a hypothesis," *Recherches Sémiotiques/Semiotic Inquiry*, Vol. 1, No. 2: 121-135.

1981b. "The Ultimate Enigma of 'Clever Hans': The Union of Nature and Culture," in Sebeok and Rosenthal, eds. (q.v.), 199-205.

1981c. "Karl Bühler: A Neglected Figure in the History of Semiotic Inquiry," in *The Play of Musement*, Chap. 5 (Bloomington: Indiana University Press), pp. 91-108.

1981d. "On Hard Facts and Misleading Data," *Reviews in Anthropology*, Vol. 8, no. 1 (Winter), 9-15.

SEBEOK, Thomas A., HAYES, Alfred S., and BATESON, Mary Catherine, eds.

1964. *Approaches to Semiotics*. Transactions of the 1962 Indiana University Conference on Paralinguistics and Kinesics (1972 second printing; The Hague: Mouton).

SEBEOK, Thomas A., and ROSENTHAL, Robert, eds.

1981. *The Clever Hans Phenomenon: Communication with Horses, Whales, Apes, and People* (New York: The New York Academy of Sciences). An entertaining account of this conference can be found in *The New Yorker*'s "Talk of the Town" for May 26, 1980.

SEBEOK, Thomas A., and UMIKER-SEBEOK, Jean, eds.

1980. *Speaking of Apes. A Critical Anthology of Two-Way Communication with Man* (New York: Plenum). This anthology is a landmark in the study of man-animal communication, bringing to bear, as it does, a state of the art critical consciousness that has so far been conspicuously lacking in this area of research. Further under Umiker-Sebeok.

SHUKMAN, Ann.
  1977. *Literature and Semiotics: A Study of the Writings of Yu. M. Lotman* (Amsterdam: North Holland).

SIMON, Yves R.
  1955. "Foreword" to *The Material Logic of John of St. Thomas*, selections made and trans. from the Latin of Poinsot 1632 by Yves R. Simon, John J. Glanville, and G. Donald Hollenhorst (Chicago: The University of Chicago Press), pp. ix-xxiii. This work is unusable as a guide to Poinsot's semiotic: details in Deely 1983: EA note 13, which I quote: "Nonetheless, in view of the scarcity of works in this area and the difficulty of the problems involved in their mastery, this pioneering effort of Simon and his collaborators is an indispensable mine of scholastic lore in Simon's 'Notes' and 'Foreword' to the text. Simon's vignettes of reflection on the distinction between formal and material logic in the scholastic context (pp. ix-xviii) bear particular mention in this regard."
  1961. "To Be and To Know," *Chicago Review* 15, no. 4 (Spring), 83-100.
  1970. *The Great Dialogue of Nature and Space* (posthumous), ed. Gerard J. Dalcourt (New York: Magi Books).
  1971. "An Essay on the Classification of Action and the Understanding of Act" (posthumous), ed. J. N. Deely, *Revue de l'Université d'Ottawa*, 41, no. 4 (octobre-décembre), 518-541.

SIMPSON, George Gaylord.
  1963. "The Nonprevalence of Humanoids" (based on lectures entitled "Life on Other Worlds"), in *This View of Life* (New York: Harbinger), pp. 253-271.

SLUGA, Hans.
  1980. *Gottlob Frege* (Boston: Routledge & Kegan Paul).

SMART, Benjamin Humphrey.
  1842. *Beginnings of a New Metaphysics*. Three essays in one volume: (1) *Outline of Sematology* (1831); (2) *Sequel to Sematology* (1837); (3) *An Appendix* (1839) (London: Longman, Brown, Green and Longmans). From review by Baer 1980, q.v.

SOTO, Dominic (1494-1560).
  1529. *Summulae* (Salamanca, Spain).
  1544. *In dialecticam Aristotelis Commentarii* (Salamanca, Spain).

SPIAZZI, Raymundus.
  1955. "Introductio Editoris" to his edition of Aquinas, c. 1269-1274 (q.v.), pp. v-xvii.

STATUTS de la Société de Linguistique de Paris.
  1868. *Memoires de la Société de Linguistique de Paris* (Paris: Librairie A. Franck), Vol. I, p. 3.

STRASSER, Stephen.
    1963.   *Phenomenology and the Human Sciences. A Contribution to a New Scientific Ideal* (Pittsburgh: Duquesne University Press).

STRAWSON, P. F.
    1952.   *Introduction to Logical Theory* (London: Methuen).

SUAREZ, Francis.
    1605.   *De Sacramentis* (Venice: Apud Societatem Minimam). Vol. XX of the "Opera Omnia editio nova, a Carolo Berton" (Paris: Vivès, 1860), was used in preparing the present work.

SULLIVAN, John Edward.
    1963.   *The Image of God: The Doctrine of St. Augustine and Its Influence* (Dubuque, Iowa: The Priory Press).

SWIFT, Jonathan.
    1726.   *Gulliver's Travels*, critical edition by Robert A. Greenberg (2nd redaction; New York: W. W. Norton, 1970).

TERRACE, H. S.
    1981.   "A Report to an Academy, 1980," in Sebeok and Rosenthal, eds. (q.v.), 94-114.

THOMAS, Ivo.
    1967.   "Logic, History of," in *The New Catholic Encyclopedia* (New York: McGraw-Hill), Vol. 8, pp. 958-962.

von UEXKÜLL, Jakob.
    1926.   *Theoretical Biology*, trans. D. L. Mackinnon (New York: Harcourt, Brace & Co.).

UMIKER-SEBEOK, Jean, and SEBEOK, Thomas A. (The four articles comprising this entry constitute a single, jointly produced, ongoing critique, substantially expanded and continually updated in each stage or version, that probably marks a turning point in the discussion of animal "language." The order of the names in this particular case does not uniformly represent priority of authorship for the component entries, as this seems to have shifted, e.g., between the 1980 and 1981b versions.)
    1979.   "Performing Animals: Secrets of the Trade," *Psychology Today*, Vol. 13, no. 6, 78-91.
    1980.   "Questioning Apes," in *Speaking of Apes*, ed. Thomas A. Sebeok and Jean Umiker-Sebeok (New York: Plenum), pp. 1-59.
    1981a.   "Clever Hans and Smart Simians: The Self-Fulfilling Prophecy and Kindred Methodological Pitfalls," *Anthropos* 76 (1-2): 89-165.
    1981b.   "Smart Simians: The Self-Fulfilling Prophecy and Kindred Methodological Pitfalls," in *The Play of Musement*, by Thomas A. Sebeok (Bloomington: Indiana University Press), Chapter 8, pp. 134-209.

VALLA, Lorenzo.
    c.1440.   *Dialecticae Disputationes contra Aristotelicos*.

VEATCH, Henry B.
    1951.　"Formalism and/or Intentionality in Logic," *Philosophy and Phenom-enological Research* 11, pp. 348-364. Debate with Copi 1951.
    1952.　*Intentional Logic* (New Haven: Yale University Press).

VON FRISCH, Karl.
    1950.　*Bees, Their Vision, Chemical Senses, and Language* (Ithaca, New York: Cornell University Press).

WALLACE, William A.
    1980.　"Albertus Magnus on Suppositional Necessity in the Natural Sciences," in *Albertus Magnus and the Sciences. Commemorative Essays 1980*, ed. James A. Weisheipl (Toronto: Pontifical Institute of Mediaeval Studies), pp. 103-128. Wallace documents a remarkable discussion in Albert's *De Praedicabilibus*, tract. 7, ch. 2, and tract. 8, ch. 10 (in Vol. I of the *Opera Omnia*, Borgnet ed., pp. 122a-b and 140a, respectively) of the conditions of egg-formation under which a crow that was not black would be produced.

WARREN, Edward W.
    1975.　"Introduction" to his translation of *Porphyry the Phoenician: Isagoge* (Toronto: Pontifical Institute of Mediaeval Studies, 1975), pp. 9-25.

WAUGH, Linda R.
    1976.　*Roman Jakobson's Science of Language* (Lisse, Netherlands: The Peter de Ridder Press).

WEISHEIPL, James A.
    1965.　"Classification of the Sciences in Mediaeval Thought," *Mediaeval Studies*, XXVII, 54-90.
    1980a,b. "Life and Works of Albert the Great," and "Appendix I. Albert's Work on Natural Science (*libri naturales*) in Probable Chronological Order," in *Albertus Magnus and the Sciences. Commemorative Essays 1980*, ed. James A. Weisheipl (Toronto: Pontifical Institute of Mediaeval Studies), pp. 13-51 and 565-577.

WHEWELL, William.
    1837.　*History of the Inductive Sciences, From the Earliest to the Present Time* (London), in 3 volumes.
    1840.　*Philosophy of the Inductive Sciences* (London).

WHITEHEAD, Alfred North, and RUSSELL, Bertrand.
    1910-1913. *Principia Mathematica* (Cambridge), 3 vols.

WILD, John.
    1947.　"An Introduction to the Phenomenology of Signs," *Philosophy and Phenomenological Research*, VIII (December), 217-244.
    1956.　Review of *The Material Logic of John of St. Thomas* (see entry for Simon 1955, above), in *Philosophy and Phenomenological Research*, XVII (June), 556-559.

WILDEN, Tony.
    1981. "Semiotics as praxis: strategy and tactics," *Recherches Sémiotiques/ Semiotic Inquiry*, Vol. 1, No. 1: 1-34.

WILLIAMS, Brooke.
    1981. "The Feminist Revolution in Ultramodern Perspective," *Cross Currents*, Vol. XXXI, no. 3 (Winter), 307-318.

WILSON, Thomas.
    1551. *The Rule of Reason, containing the arte of logique.* (One of the first attempts to present logic in English.)

ZIGLIARA, Thomas M.
    1882. Synopses and Annotations to the Tomus Primus of the leonine *Opera omnia sancti Thomae Aquinatis*, containing St. Thomas' uncompleted commentary *In Aristotelis libros perihermenias expositio*, composed c.1269-1274.

INDEX OF CONCEPTS AND TERMS

INDEX OF PERSONS, PLACES, AND WORKS

This index includes only those works mentioned by name in the text and notes, excepting note 16 pp. 188ff. It does not include titles of works mentioned by author only. Complete information on most works in any way mentioned, of course, is found in the References.

A

Abelard, Peter: 160
Ackrill, J. F.: 158 n. 4, 208
Adler, M. J.: 173, 174, 208
Aegidius Columna: 191-192
Agricola, R.: 160, 208
Albertus Magnus: 69, 191, 208, 232
Alcalá, University of: viii, 31, 34, 35, 36, 49, 52, 151 n. 3
Alcuin of York: 150
Aldrich, H.: 161 n. 9, 208
Aldus Pius Manutius: 189
Alexander of Aphrodisias: 147 n. 5, 190, 191
Alston, William P.: 132, 208
Ammonius Saccas: 189
Anderson, Fulton H. (trans. and ed.): 210
Andronicus of Rhodes: 13
Anshen, Ruth Nanda (ed.): 222
Apel, Karl-Otto: 164 n. 1
Aquinas, St. Thomas: 15, 22, 49, 59, 72, 127, 151 n. 3, 154, 155 n. 1, 157 n. 2, 158 n. 3, 159 n. 4, 159 n. 5, 162 n. 2, 163, 170, 182 n. 5., 189, 190, 191, 192, 193 n. 16, 208, 209, 222, 230, 233
In Aristotelis libros perihermenias expositio (Aquinas-Cajetan): 59, 208-209
Aristotle: viii, 2, 10, 11, 12, 13, 14, 15, 16, 18, 19, 20, 21, 22, 24, 26, 28, 30, 32, 34, 36, 37, 38, 39, 40, 43, 50, 51, 56, 59, 63, 64, 68, 69, 78, 97, 128, 146 n. 5, 147 n. 5, 147 n. 6, 147 n. 1, 152 n. 6, 152 n. 7, 154, 157 n. 3, 158 n. 3, 159 n. 4, 159 n. 5, 160, 161 n. 6, 161 n. 8, 162 n. 2, 166 n. 3, 169, 171, 180 n. 3, 181 n. 3, 181 n. 5, 182 n. 5, 188 n. 15, 190, 191, 209

Arnauld, Antoine: 68, 161 n. 6, 209, 223, 225
Ars Logica (Poinsot): 67
Artis logicae compendium (Aldrich): 161 n. 9, 208
Ashley, Benedict: 39, 155 n. 1, 169, 209
Ashworth, E. J.: 31, 161 n. 7, 209
Aspasias: 190
Athens: 19
Augustine of Hippo, St.: v, 8, 9, 12, 17, 18, 21, 54, 55, 56, 57, 60, 148, 149, 209
Averroes: 45, 210
Ayer, A. J.: 132, 210

B

Bacchus: 166
Bacon, Francis: 69, 70, 180 n. 3, 182 n. 6, 210
Baer, Eugen: 7, 146 n. 4, 210, 230
Bally, Charles (ed.): 228
Balnibarbi: 138
Bañez, Domingo: 31, 210
Barthes, Roland: 195, 210
Bartholomaeus Sylvanius: 189
The Basic Works of Aristotle (McKeon, ed.): 162 n. 2, 209
Bateson, Mary Catherine: 199 n. 1, 229
Begriffsschrift (Frege): 188 n. 15
Belgium: 161 n. 7
Belove, P. Lawrence: 174
Benjamins, Claire: v
Benjamins, John: v
Bense, M. (ed.): 227
Berkeley, George (Bishop): 176, 210, 224
Berton, Carolo (ed.): 231
Bibliographia Logica (Risse): 161 n. 7, 227
Binsse, H. L. (trans.): 222